The Abolitionist Decade,
1829–1838

The Abolitionist Decade, 1829–1838

A Year-by-Year History of Early Events in the Antislavery Movement

KEVIN C. JULIUS

McFarland & Company, Inc., Publishers
Jefferson, North Carolina, and London

LIBRARY OF CONGRESS CATALOGUING-IN-PUBLICATION DATA

Julius, Kevin C.
   The abolitionist decade, 1829–1838 / a year-by-year history of early events in the antislavery movement / Kevin C. Julius.
      p.   cm.
   Includes bibliographical references and index.

   ISBN 0-7864-1946-6 (softcover : 50# alkaline paper)

   1. Antislavery movements—United States—History—19th century—Chronology. 2. Slavery—Southern States—History—19th century—Chronology. I. Title.
E449.J93   2004
326'.8'097309034—dc22   2004022347

British Library cataloguing data are available

©2004 Kevin C. Julius. All rights reserved

No part of this book may be reproduced or transmitted in any form or by any means, electronic or mechanical, including photocopying or recording, or by any information storage and retrieval system, without permission in writing from the publisher.

Manufactured in the United States of America

On the cover: ball and chain image ©2004 Creatas;
Susan B. Anthony letter courtesy Library of Congress

McFarland & Company, Inc., Publishers
   Box 611, Jefferson, North Carolina 28640
      www.mcfarlandpub.com

Dedicated, with love:

to my wife, Gina,
who saw me through this;

to my children, Elizabeth, Sarah, and Kyle,
who saw less of me because of this;

and to my parents, Neal and Kaye,
who never got to see it.

Table of Contents

Preface ix

One • 1776–1828   1
Two • 1829   39
Three • 1830   55
Four • 1831   69
Five • 1832   86
Six • 1833   104
Seven • 1834   126
Eight • 1835   133
Nine • 1836   167
Ten • 1837   201
Eleven • 1838   224

Epilogue   239

Appendix 1: Influence of Slaveholding States on the Federal Government   241
Appendix 2: Emily West: The Yellow Rose of Texas   255
Select Bibliography   257
Index   261

Preface

It was while attending Mercyhurst College in the early 1980s that I developed an interest in American history, for which I heartily thank professors Dr. Barry Grossman and Dr. William Garvey. The primary scope of those courses was the period of the founding fathers. I found myself fascinated by Washington, Hamilton, Adams, Jefferson and Madison. After completing my studies, I continued to pursue my reading, and soon dropped colonial history in favor of the Civil War.

It must have been in the mid–1990s that some friends and I started attending the once-monthly meetings of the Erie Civil War Roundtable. These military enthusiasts seemed to know every battle, every troop movement, every minute detail. There seemed to be nothing about this war they didn't know.

And then it hit me: Maybe there was one thing. Somewhere along the way, perhaps the human aspect was missing. What was the motivation that drove countless thousands of Americans to battle, sometimes against their own family members? This led me to the ultimate question, which this fine group of military scholars seemed unable to answer: When, where and why did the Civil War begin?

Was it the firing upon Fort Sumter? Or John Brown's raid? Or did it, as I am now convinced, go back much further than those two events?

I began to focus my energies on the period between the two historical watersheds of the American Revolution and the Civil War that I already felt I knew. I even naively offered to do a presentation to the roundtable on the events that led up to the American Civil War.

That was five years and four presentations ago, and although I have barely scratched the surface, the research I have done has led me into a rich and fascinating period of American history and then to the writing of this book.

There is very little of what could be called original material within these pages. (One should not expect any revisionist revelations.) I do feel, however, that this work presents a much more thorough presentation of the era covered than is available in any other single source, and makes a long-needed contribution to the reader's understanding of the antebullum era.

There is a lot here for the casual reader or the interested amateur as well. I wish I had had this book to refer to when I was preparing my lectures.

Of course, it would be impossible to cover the entire pre–Civil War history of the United States in a single volume. I have decided therefore to focus instead on what I call "The Abolitionist Decade"—specifically, the years 1829–1838. Familiarity with these years has, at least for me, brought a fuller understanding of what precipitated the "Great Conflict."

There are three basic themes running through this work.

First is the inescapable issue of slavery. I have, however, made no attempt to describe the debasement and abuse of the American slaves. Instead, I have attempted to show how the existence of a servile race in the South dramatically impacted the lives of white Americans, both North and South. This is not meant to ignore the plight of the unfortunate bondsmen. But since it was the white race that was running the country—and deciding the fate of the black race—I have tried to show how the lives of whites were profoundly affected by the existence of slavery.

Most whites in the 1830s cared little for blacks, and probably even less for the abolitionists. Yet the social awareness of an entire generation seems to have been dramatically altered by a handful of visionaries. So much so that when war came, many whites would be willing to make the ultimate sacrifice without really knowing or understanding why they were fighting.

Second, I have tried to interject a flavor of other events of the times. While the struggles of the abolitionists represent the main theme of this book, it has been my intention to provide an indication of what the country was like during this period. What I hope I have ended up with is a picture of both the big issue of slavery as well as an overall sense of American society at the time. To this end, I have concluded each chapter with some brief remarks about other things that were going on during the years in question.

And third, I have tried to present a portrait of the men and women who fought for the rights of the oppressed race. The abolitionists were one of the most maligned and misunderstood groups in all of American history. Reviled, threatened, and abused throughout their lifetimes, they have not yet been rewarded with a fair reputation in the U.S. national consciousness. Fighting generations of entrenched bigotry, they often stood alone against both North and South as the only friend of the hapless slave.

Even when the abolitionists have been noticed with sympathy, they have not often been given their due. Many modern writers still feel obligated to overstate the role of religion in the abolitionist movement. For example: Paul Goodman, in his 1998 book *Of One Blood: Abolitionism and the Origins of Racial Equality,* spends a great amount of space discussing the revivalist antecedents of many of the early abolitionists. He seems to pay homage to the traditional (Southern) portrayal of the abolitionists as overly-zealous and wild-eyed—as if to excuse their revolutionary doctrines as the products of fanaticism. Certainly there were many different impulses motivating those involved in the antislavery movement and undoubtedly strong religious beliefs were among them. But one does not need religion to believe that slavery is wrong.

Many things can be said about the "American character," and not all of them are positive. Americans have a not entirely undeserved reputation for being greedy and self-serving, often ready to better themselves through the exploitation of others. They also have a tendency to be apathetic towards problems that do not directly concern them, which at least partially explains (though by no means justifies) the Northern reluctance for so many generations to directly address the issue of slavery.

Americans also have, however, many redeeming characteristics. Chief among these may be a sense of justice and fair play. They hate to see someone being taken advantage of; they tend to cheer for the underdog. It is this very tendency that makes many people so sympathetic to the myth of the Confederacy. The pro–Southern argument leads many into thinking that the South was unfairly insulted and attacked by the larger, more powerful northern states. The North is depicted as the uncaring, interfering "big government," while the proud, independent Southerner seems to represent liberty and justice. The problem with this picture is that it ignores the oppressive nature of the South toward the slaves.

Throughout my research over the years, I continually came across instances of injustice towards the poor bondsmen and their beleaguered advocates, the abolitionists, that gave rise within me to feelings of sadness and anger. If a modern researcher can have these emotions across the span of more than a century and a half, it should not be difficult that similar misgivings stirred the souls of those who were directly experiencing these events.

That many individuals at the time did, in fact, feel a comparable disquietude is demonstrated in the lives of such as John Quincy Adams and William Leggett. Neither of these men was ever strongly identified with the anti-slavery movement, but both of them became champions of its cause, defending the rights of the abolitionists to think and say what they believed. I contend that many of those who ultimately joined the ranks of the abolitionists did so at least in part in reaction to the repeated insults and injuries heaped upon them.

The sincerity of those who made the decision to take part in this struggle should be acknowledged and less effort, should be expended to explain away their role as simply the result of enthusiastic evangelism. It is almost as if Americans are still reluctant to challenge the Southern scheme of things or to be associated with the unpopular position of the abolitionists. The work of the abolitionists is often relegated to a few passing remarks or casual footnotes in so many histories of the era. Rather than trying to apologize for their atypical and "antisocial" behavior, historians should be celebrating their strengths and accomplishments.

Some critics will say the abolitionists made matters worse with their constant agitation—but the abolitionists' relentless verbal assault on the otherwise apathetic populace ultimately forced the country to deal with a problem that would never have gone away on its own.

The Civil War was both frightening and fascinating. It appeals to modern sensibilities like no other period in U.S. history because it had such an enormous impact on every element of society. This was not a war between feuding principalities nor one fought by hired mercenaries for someone else's gain. It was everyman's war. But to know the Civil War without knowing the years before it could be likened to walking into a play just as the final act opens. One may still be witness to all the drama and spectacle but have missed the point of the production. One watches the actors perform yet fails to understand what motivates them.

The purpose of this volume, therefore, is to show the reader what might have been missed. My humble hope is that after reading the book one can revisit the final act, and find it richer than it had previously seemed.

ONE

1776–1828

The struggle against slavery in the United States is much older than the country itself. The first slaves were introduced into North America through the Virginia colony. According to the records of the Virginia Company, a "Dutch man of Warr" carrying "20 and odd Negroes" arrived at Point Comfort in 1619. This was the modest beginning of the transatlantic American slave trade. It is doubtful that anyone at the time could have guessed how much the future of the country would be affected by that small shipload of human cargo.

By the eve of the Revolution, slavery was thoroughly entrenched in the American consciousness. If we date the formation of the new country from the Declaration of Independence, then we would have to begin our discussion of slavery with the events leading up to that document.

In 1776, slavery was already on the decline throughout most of the North. Yet it was still sanctioned by law in all thirteen colonies. (It was a year later practically to the day—July 2, 1777—before Vermont would enter the Union as the first state to never have had slavery within its borders.) The total population of the country at that time was approximately two and a half million. One-fifth of these inhabitants were black, with 90 percent of them living in what would become known as the "slave states." The overwhelming majority of these half a million souls were slaves. It was only natural that this oppressed portion of the population would receive some notice by the political leaders striving to carve a new nation out of the British possessions.

Most people know that it was Thomas Jefferson who penned the original draft of the Declaration of Independence. Many are probably aware as well that in his original document, there was a harangue against slavery. Common folklore tells us that if Jefferson had had his way, the slavery issue could have been settled right then. If only South Carolina hadn't insisted on removal of said clause, then the status of the blacks would have been forever altered long before the constitutional delegates had to deal with it.

Unfortunately, such an interpretation does not ring true. If we examine the omitted phrase (as provided for posterity by Jefferson himself), we read:

> [King George] has waged cruel war against human nature itself, violating its most sacred rights of life and liberty in the persons of a distant people who never offended him, captivating & carrying them into slavery in another hemisphere, or to incur miserable death in their transportation thither. This piratical warfare, the opprobrium of INFIDEL powers, is the warfare of the CHRISTIAN king of Great Britain. Determined to keep open a market where MEN should be bought and sold, he has prostituted his negative for suppressing every legislative attempt to prohibit or to restrain this execrable commerce.

Many people over the intervening years have interpreted this as an effort on the part of the humanitarian Jefferson to strike a blow at slavery. But if you reread this passage, you will note that he is not criticizing slavery per se, but merely the African slave trade. It may interest the reader to know that from about 1750 on, the colony (later state) of Virginia had a surplus of slaves. Slaves were, therefore, a potential valuable export commodity for Virginians. During the same period, most of the rest of the South, particularly South Carolina, had an acute shortage of slaves. The choice for such states was to purchase the surplus from their neighbors or acquire fresh stock cheaply from the tropics.

Up to one-third of all Africans entering the country died within their first year, but they were still cheaper than buying from a neighboring colony (or state). Those slaves born in America, or already acclimated to it, were much more expensive. Also, many slaves were "used up" in the unhealthy Southern climate, and it just didn't make sense to buy a few choice slaves at a high price when a much larger number of affordably disposable stock could be acquired from abroad. (If this discussion sounds crassly impersonal, welcome to the realities of the slave culture.)

So when a Virginian such as Jefferson (or later Mason) pushes for a termination of the slave trade, you have to wonder: Whose interests were they really considering? The slaves, or their own?

We would like to think of our great men as being somehow superhuman, able to rise above the petty beliefs and limitations of their own times and situations. Unfortunately, when it came to his slaves, Jefferson was just as bigoted as any typical white slaveowner. But to make matters worse, Jefferson put his feelings into print, where they would serve to soothe many a slaveowner's troubled breast over the next few decades.

In the early 1780s, Jefferson published his *Notes on the State of Virginia*. Many of his "observations" on the colored race contained in this volume read like a primer for later-day Ku Klux Klansmen. For example:

> [I]t appears to me, that in memory they are equal to the whites; in reason much inferior, as I think one could scarcely be found capable of tracing and comprehending the investigations of Euclid.... [N]ever yet could I find a black that had uttered a thought above the level of plain narration; never see even an elementary trait of painting or sculpture.... They seem to require less sleep.... They are at least as brave, and more adventuresome. But this may perhaps proceed from a want of forethought, which prevents their seeing a danger till it be present.... Their griefs are transient. Those numberless afflictions ... are less felt, and sooner forgotten....
>
> The improvement of the blacks in body and mind, in the first instance of their mixture with the whites, [that is, when the two races mingle sexually] has been observed by every one, and proves that their inferiority is not the effect merely of their condition of life.... Add to [this...] their own judgment in favour of the whites, declared by their preference of them, as uniformly as is the preference of the Oranootan for the black woman over those of his own species....
>
> I advance it therefore as a suspicion only, that the blacks, whether originally a distinct race, or made distinct by time and circumstances, are inferior to the whites in the endowments both of body and mind.... This unfortunate difference of colour, and perhaps of faculty, is a powerful obstacle to the emancipation of these people. Many of their advocates, while they wish to vindicate the liberty of human nature, are anxious also to preserve its dignity and beauty.... What further is to be done with them?

Not surprisingly, the enlightened Jefferson had an answer to his own question. Recognizing slavery as an evil, he conceded that all blacks should be emancipated. Yet he recognized the (to him) self-evident danger of doing so. If the slaves were to be emancipated

> ... they should [then] be colonized to such place as the circumstances of the time should render most proper.... It will probably be asked, Why not retain and incorporate the blacks into the state, and thus save the expence of supplying ... the vacancies they leave? Deep rooted prejudices entertained by the whites; ten thousand recollections, by the blacks, of the injuries they have sustained; new provocations; the real distinctions which nature has made, and many other circumstances, will divide us into parties, and produce convulsions which will probably never end but in the extermination of the one or the other race.

Jefferson is, of course, but echoing what every good Southerner already knew: That there was no way that whites and blacks could live peaceably together except in the roles of master and subservient. We will hear this theme repeated again and again before the guns are fired upon Fort Sumter.

After successfully gaining their independence, the colonies for a short time were governed under the generally inefficient Articles of Confederation. During this period there was one piece of significant legislation passed that had an impact upon the slavery issue. Properly called the Ordinance of 1787, it is more commonly referred to as the Northwest Ordinance. This measure determined the manner in which new states could be organized out of the territory between the Ohio and Mississippi rivers. In the course of doing so, it specifically prohibited the introduction of slavery into the wilderness region. This interesting clause was made at the suggestion of the representative from Virginia, Thomas Jefferson.

The Northwest Ordinance represented the first attempt on the part of those in the emerging new country who were opposed to slavery to legislate against it. It would, however, be their last clear success in doing so. Perhaps frightened by the boldness of this measure, the delegates from the pro-slavery states arrived in Philadelphia that same year determined not to yield in their demands. The document that ultimately emerged would be seriously flawed due to their tenacity of purpose.

If you take the time to read the debates of the Continental Convention of 1787, it becomes clear that one of the hardest problems those dedicated men faced during that hot summer in Pennsylvania was what to do about "those people in bondage." In fact it seems as if they spent much of their time trying to avoid the issue entirely, even though they all must have realized it was something that had to be addressed. During the third week of August, the issue at last became unavoidable, as they had to determine what status the Negro slaves would receive in the final document they were creating. Were the slaves "men," and therefore, entitled to the vote? (Never really a serious consideration, it seems, by any of the delegates.) Were they property, and, therefore, eligible to be taxed as such? Or were they somewhere in between? The question quickly became confounded with another, equally perplexing issue: Should the proposed federal government be authorized to ban the importation of slaves from Africa altogether? Or should such trade be considered solely a state's own affair?

It was during this time that some of the strongest arguments against slavery were voiced, particularly by Virginian George Mason. In words that echoed Jefferson's complaints against the slave trade from eleven years earlier, Mason began by criticizing "this infernal traffic [which] originated in the avarice of British merchants. The British Government constantly checked the attempts of Virginia to put a stop to it.... He lamented that some of out Eastern brethren had from a lust of gain embarked in this nefarious traffic." History seemed to be repeating itself, as a distinguished Virginian blamed England for allowing the slave trade and New England for profiting by it, but seemed reluctant to attach any fault to the South for perpetuating it.

To Mason's credit, he did offer some genuine criticism of the institution:

> Slavery discourages arts & manufactures. The poor despise labor when performed by slaves. They prevent the immigration of Whites, who really enrich & strengthen a Country. They produce the most pernicious effect on manners. Every master of slaves is born a petty tyrant. They bring the judgment of heaven on a Country. As nations can not be rewarded or punished in the next world they must be in this. By an inevitable chain of causes & effects providence punishes national sins, by national calamities.

All of which would be grand and noble-sounding, except for its blatant hypocrisy, since Mason himself owned 200 slaves. Once again one wonders whether a Virginian's criticism is being directed at slavery itself or simply the African slave trade? Regardless, one cannot but agree with the accuracy of his ultimate forecast for the nation's future.

At least Charles Pinckney of South Carolina was honest in his response to Mason:

> South Carolina & Georgia cannot do without slaves. *As to Virginia she will gain by stopping the importations. Her slaves will rise in value, & she has more than she wants.* [Emphasis added.] It would be unequal to require South Carolina & Georgia to confederate on such unequal terms.... He contended that the importation of slaves would be for the interest of the whole Union. The more slaves, the more produce to employ the carrying trade; The more consumption also, and the more of this, the more of revenue for the common treasury.

Apparently such economic arguments carried some weight that summer, for the unfortunate non-answer of the delegates was to count the slaves as not wholly property, but also not wholly as men. Instead, they skirted the issue altogether by counting them as "precisely 3/5 men." It was a compromise that completely pleased no one and left future generations arguing over what the precise intention of the founding fathers actually was.

It's uncertain that any other group of men faced with a similar problem under similar circumstances could have reached a better solution. But as soon as this compromise was accepted by all parties involved, the Civil War was likely inevitable. For instead of solving the issue of slavery, the framers of the United States of America made it infinitely worse.

No longer was the presence of the slave merely an economic or sociological issue. Now it became a political one as well, a tool to augment the very power of those most reluctant to see the end of the "peculiar situation." If the only rights involved had been those of the slaves, then well-meaning Southerners would undoubtedly have been able to work out a viable solution in time. With the ratification of the Constitution and the acceptance of the three-fifths clause, the rights of the slaves became inexorably linked with the rights of the whites. (As well as with those of the then nonexistent entities called "the states.") A difficult problem thus became impossible.

Between 1787 and 1861, many men would argue whether the Constitution was pro- or anti-slavery. The truth is that it was a pragmatic document that was written to bring the states together, not to push them further apart. Slavery was already on the decline in the North, and those who were opposed to it assumed, foolishly, that the problem would go away of its own if left alone. Therefore, they were willing to compromise to get the job at hand accomplished, confident that in time slavery would disappear even if they had to temporarily accept its presence.

In retrospect, it is hard to imagine how they could have been so naive. If indeed, as they imagined, slavery was dying out, then why were the Southern representatives so steadfastly unwilling to yield on the issue? The Northerners may have deluded themselves into thinking that slavery was on its way out. The Southerners knew otherwise. It was too fully ingrained in their culture, their economy, and their way of life for them to ever consider letting it go unless absolutely compelled to do so.

There was another, more mundane reason why the North was willing to give this advantage to the South. Edward Everett—remembered best by Civil War enthusiasts as the man who spoke for two hours at Gettysburg before Lincoln's Address—explained the situation quite clearly to his listeners during an address in New York on July 4, 1861. As Everett expressed it, the Constitutional compromise that gave birth to the three fifths clause also provided that

> ... direct Taxes should be apportioned among the States on the same basis of population, ascertained by adding to the whole number of free persons three-fifths of the slaves. It was expected at this time that the Federal Treasury would be mainly supplied by direct taxation. While, therefore, the rule adopted gave to the South a number of representatives out of proportion to the number of her citizens, she would be restrained from exercising this power to the prejudice of the North, by the fact that any increase of the public burdens would fall in the same increased proportion on herself. For the additional weight which the South gained ... the North received no compensation.

In other words, it was expected that the South would pay for its increased share of representation by assuming a proportionately larger share of the financial burden of running the federal government. As the nation developed, this financial burden turned out to be a mere chimera, though in 1789 there was no way of foreseeing that this would be the case.

Many Southern sympathizers, both at the time and more recently, have used this concept of direct taxation as an argument to justify, or rationalize, the South's long-running political control of the federal government. But as things actually transpired, what might have been a financial burden for the South turned out to be a pretty good deal after all. As Everett continued in his previously-quoted speech:

> But now mark the practical operation of the compromise. Direct taxation, instead of being the chief resource of the Treasury, has been resorted to but four times since the foundation of the Government, and then for small amounts; in 1798 two millions of dollars, in 1813 three millions, in 1815 six millions, in 1816 three millions again, in all fourteen millions, the sum total raised by direct taxation[.]

When one considers that the government's total revenue receipts during this period of 1789 through 1816 was well over $310 million dollars, the $14 million dollars that the South paid for 70 years of inflated representation in the House sounds like a bargain.

So what we ended up with was a document that accepted slavery without ever acknowledging it. There are only four passages in the Constitution concerning the slaves, but they are not given that name in any of them. It is as if the writers of the document were embarrassed and didn't want posterity to know what they had done.

Article I, Section 2 has the first mention: "Representatives and direct Taxes ... shall be determined by adding to the whole Number of free Persons, including those bound to Service for a Term of Years, and excluding Indians not taxed, three fifths of *all other Persons*." This is the infamous "3/5" rule which has already been mentioned.

In Article I, Section 9 we find: "The Migration or Importation of *such Persons* as any of the States now existing shall think proper to admit, shall not be prohibited by the Congress prior to the year one thousand eight hundred and eight...." This is a curious clause whose meaning may not initially seem clear. In effect, it was a promise to South Carolina and the other slave-importing states that the federal government would not touch the African slave trade for at least twenty more years, during which time those states that wanted to could continue the "execrable commerce" that Jefferson had so lamented eleven years previously.

Perhaps the most significant passage comes in Article IV, Section 2, which states, "No *person held to Service or Labour* in one State, under the

Laws thereof, escaping into another, shall, in Consequence of any Law or Regulation therein, be discharged from such Service or Labour, but shall be delivered up on Claim of the Party to whom such Service or Labour may be due." Another slightly confusing statement that means in effect that if a slave escapes from a slave state into a free state, he is still to be considered a slave, and the authorities of the free state are by duty required to return him upon demand to his owners. These words will be responsible for much contention between the North and the South in the next 74 years. It would be this clause, in particular, that would bolster the South's often repeated claim that the Constitution was a pro-slavery document and guaranteed them the right to own other human beings.

And, finally, the least obvious but, in many ways most interesting point came in Article V within the description of the Amendment process. After detailing the procedure that would allow for Constitutional amendments, there is added the note: "Provided that no Amendment which may be made prior to the Year One thousand eight hundred and eight shall in any Manner affect the first.... Clause in the Ninth Section of the first Article...." This, of course, refers to the clause guaranteeing not to tamper with the African slave trade. Or, to paraphrase the Southern view of what this meant as: "now that the "bargain" has been made and you've agreed to give us 20 more years to import our laborers, there's no trying to weasel out of the deal."

The Southern states would not take long to demonstrate to the North just how fully they were dedicated to the preservation of their "peculiar institution." Their first test of wills came in the Second Session of the very first Congress. A petition was presented in February 1790 from the Pennsylvania [Quaker] Abolition Society, calling upon Congress to deal with the issue of slavery. It concluded by saying:

> From a persuasion that equal liberty was originally, and still is, the birthright of all men, and influenced by the strong ties of humanity and the principles of their institutions, your memorialists conceive themselves bound to use all justifiable endeavors to loosen the bonds of slavery, and to promote the general enjoyment of the blessings of freedom. Under these impressions they earnestly entreat your attention to the subject of slavery; that you will be pleased to countenance the restoration to liberty of those unhappy men who, alone, in this land of freemen, are groaning in servile subjection; that you will devise means for removing this inconsistency of character from the American people; that you will promote mercy and justice towards this distressed race; and that you will step to the very verge of the power vested in you for discouraging every species of traffic in the persons of our fellowmen.

The petition was signed by the president of the society, Benjamin Franklin.

The memorial was referred to a select committee, which made its report early in March.

James Jackson of Georgia immediately jumped to the defensive. He feared that even a discussion of the petition "would produce infinite mischiefs in the Southern States; it would excite tumults, seditions, and insurrection." Michael Jenifer Stone of Maryland "thought that persons who were not interested ought not to interfere; such interferences savored very strongly of an intolerant spirit, and he could not suppose that any one of the States had a right to interfere in the internal regulations of another. States were not accountable to each other for their moral conduct."

The debate continued throughout the month of March. Alexander White of Virginia "was fully of the opinion that Congress has no right to interfere in the business." Thomas Hartley of Pennsylvania "was not a little surprised to hear the cause of slavery advocated in that House."

John Brown of Virginia "enlarged on the pernicious consequences that may be expected to flow from the interference of Congress; ... and if Congress should adopt the report as it stands, the consequences would be pernicious in the highest degree. The negro property will be annihilated." One can only imagine Mr. Brown's indignation as he spoke. He concluded by stating that "he was fully of [the] opinion that Congress has no right to interfere in the business...."

Edanus Burke of South Carolina "entered into a very extensive consideration of the subject. He gave an account of the humane treatment which slaves of the Southern States received, ... [and] then showed that their emancipation would tend to make them wretched in the highest degree." He finished with "a few more observations on the injustice of the measure of interference, as it respected the property of the Southern States."

William Smith of South Carolina spoke at greatest length against the proceedings.

> [H]e lamented much that this subject had been brought before the House; that he had deprecated it from the beginning, because he foresaw that it would produce a very unpleasant discussion; that it was a subject of a nature to excite the alarms of the Southern members, who could not view, without anxiety, any interference in it on the part of Congress. ... The memorials ... contained, in his opinion, a very indecent attack on the character of those States which possess slaves. It reprobates slavery as bringing down reproach on the Southern States.... He could not but consider it as calculated to fix a stigma of the blackest nature on the State he had the honor to represent, and to hold its citizens up to public view as men divested of every principle of honor and humanity. Considering it in that light, he felt it incumbent on him not only to refute these atrocious calumnies, but to resent the improper language made use

of by the memorialists.... [H]e could not ascribe their conduct to any other cause but to an intolerant spirit of persecution. This application came with the worst grace possible....

He then showed that the State Governments clearly retained all the rights of sovereignty which they had before the establishment of the Constitution....

He applied these principles to the case in question; and asked, whether the Constitution had, in express terms, vested the Congress with the power of manumission? Or whether it restrained the States from exercising that power...? [He declared that] Congress had not an exclusive right to manumission.... But [even] admitting that Congress had authority ... and were disposed to exercise it, would the Southern States acquiesce in such a measure without a struggle? Would the citizens of that country tamely suffer their property to be torn from them? Would even the citizens of the other States ... desire to have all the slaves let loose upon them? Would not such a step be injurious even to the slaves themselves? It was well known that they were an indolent people, improvident, averse to labor: when emancipated, they would either starve or plunder.

He continued by pointing out that, even if freed, the blacks would never be able to blend in with the whites:

It is known, from experience, that the whites had such an idea of their superiority over the blacks, that they never even associated with them...; [He] then read some extracts from Mr. Jefferson's NOTES ON VIRGINIA, proving that negroes were by nature an inferior race of beings; and that the whites would always feel a repugnance at mixing their blood with that of the blacks.... If the blacks did not intermarry with the whites, they would remain black to the end of time...; if they would intermarry with the whites, then the white race would be extinct, and the American people would be all of the mulatto breed. In whatever light, therefore, the subject was viewed, the folly of emancipation was manifest.

Smith was particularly angered by the petitioner's claim

... that the public opinion was against slavery. How did that appear? Were there any petitions on the subject excepting that from the Pennsylvania Society[?] ... There were no petitions against slavery from the Southern states, and they were the only proper judges of what was for their interest. The toleration of slavery in the several States was a matter of internal regulation and policy, in which each State had a right to do as she pleased, and no other State had any right to intermeddle with her policy or laws.... [These Quakers] were interfering in the concerns of others, and doing everything in their power to excite the slaves in the Southern States to insurrections...;

The Northern States knew that the Southern States had slaves before they confederated with them. If they had such an abhorrence for slavery, why, said Mr. S., did they not cast us off and reject our alliance...? [T]he Northern States adopted us with our slaves, and we adopted them with their Quakers.... But what have the citizens of the other States to do with our slaves? Have you any right to interfere with our internal policy?

Smith continued his argument by describing how awful emancipation would be for the slaves, since they "would not benefit by it; free negroes never improve in talents, never grow rich, and continue to associate with the people of their own color.... The author already quoted has proved that they are an inferior race...."

And what about the Southern States?

> [W]ill the abolition of slavery strengthen South Carolina? It can only be cultivated by slaves; the climate, the nature of the soil, ancient habits, forbid the whites from performing the labor.... If the slaves are emancipated, they will not remain in that country—... What, then becomes of its strength? Instead of increasing the population of the whites, there will be no whites at all. If the low country is deserted, where will be the commerce, the valuable exports of that country[?] ... If you depopulate the rich low country of South Carolina and Georgia, you will give us a blow which will immediately recoil on yourselves.... Without the rice swamps of Carolina, Charleston would decay, so would the commerce of that city: this would injure the back country. If you injure the Southern States, the injury would reach our Northern and Eastern brethren; for the States are links of one chain: if we break one, the whole must fall to pieces."

And, of course, no Southerner could defend himself without reminding the Northern states that they had "found slavery ingrafted in the very policy of the country when we were born, and we are persuaded of the impolicy of removing it...."

These speeches from the Congressional records not only show how strongly the slave owners fought to protect slavery, but also how deeply ingrained their bigotry was even at this early period in our nation's history. They had dehumanized the slaves so much that they were literally unable to concede that blacks deserved any consideration whatsoever.

It is also important to remember when these speeches occurred—full seventy years before Fort Sumter—and note that already their arguments are well-established. The clarion call of "State's Rights" sounds as loudly here as it will during the Nullification Crises.

They also illustrate three of the most powerful tools in their arsenal of arguments: That slavery really wasn't their fault, they'd been born to it. That, after all, the Northern whites certainly didn't want all these black moving North. And, of course, the concept of mutual dependency in that what might ruin the South could also ruin the North.

Like it or not, if you accepted their logic, the North stood as much to lose as did the South. So, as would usually happen, the anti-slavery arguers backed down. The resolutions that ultimately came out of that Congress made the situation, if anything, worse than before the petition had been discussed: "Resolved, That Congress have no authority to interfere in the emancipation of slaves, or in the treatment of them in any of the States; it remaining with the several States alone to provide rules and regulations therein which humanity and true policy may require."

Any fleeting hopes that slavery might disappear on its own in the South were soon dashed by, of all people, a New Englander. In 1793, a 28-year-old Massachusetts inventor named Eli Whitney invented a cheap, simple device called the cotton gin. It was so easy to construct that they started popping up on plantations in the South even before Whitney could get his patent established. The cotton gin—a device that which separated the seeds from the fibers of the cotton plant—over-night made the cultivation of cotton profitable. In 1791, before Whitney's gin, the entire cotton production of all the Southern states was 189,500 pounds. By 1801, the amount had risen to 41 million pounds. The demand for slaves skyrocketed.

During the same time period, another crucial argument was added to the pro-slavery repertoire. The immediate situation being addressed was the passing of the highly unpopular (and constitutionally questionable) Alien and Sedition Acts. Thomas Jefferson's response was the Kentucky Resolutions of November 16, 1798. (Though presented anonymously at the time, Jefferson's identity as the author was common knowledge by the early 1820s.) While the ideas presented here seem to make sense, it would have been political suicide for any government to follow them through to their natural consequences. In the Kentucky Resolutions, Jefferson argued:

> [T]he several States composing, the United States of America; are not united on the principle of unlimited submission to their general government; but ... by a compact ... reserving, each State to itself, the ... right to their own self-government; and that whensoever the General Government assumes undelegated powers, its acts are unauthoritative, void, and of no force ... [and] each party has an equal right to judge for itself, as well of infractions as of the mode and measure of redress.
>
> [T]o take from the States all the powers of self-government and transfer them to a general and consolidated government, without regard to the special delegations and reservations solemnly agreed to in that compact, is not for the peace, happiness or prosperity of these States; and that therefore this commonwealth is determined ... to submit to undelegated, and consequently unlimited powers in no man, or body of men on earth.... [W]here powers are assumed which have not been delegated, a nullification of the act is the rightful remedy: that every State has a natural right in cases not within the compact ... to nullify of their own authority all assumptions of power by others within their limits.... Congress being not a party, but merely the creature of the compact.

As Rousseauan philosophy this sounds alluringly attractive. In the harsh reality of political science the result would be chaos and anarchy, if each party to any compact could pick and choose for itself which rules it wanted to follow and which rules it would simply ignore. Yet for the "fiercely independent" Southerners, Jefferson's words would become the foundation upon which to build both nullification and secession.

Meanwhile, events were transpiring in the West Indies that would profoundly affect the Southern slave mentality. On the island of Hispaniola, the site of Christopher Columbus's original landfall in the new world, the eastern two-thirds of the island was under Spanish rule and called Santo Domingo. The western portion was a French colony called Saint-Domingue. (Contemporary references use all three names interchangeably, as well as St. Domingo.)

The French colony of Saint-Domingue was the jewel in that country's colonial crown, primarily due to its thriving sugar plantations. At the beginning of the nineteenth century, the population consisted of three main classes. At the top, and controlling all the power and influence, were the approximately 30,000 whites, who were mostly French. A smaller group of mulattos, mostly freedmen, numbered about 27,000. This group could ostensibly own property, but in reality had very few rights and little influence on the colony's business due to restrictive racial laws imposed by the whites. The largest group in the colony consisted of approximately 465,000 black slaves whose position was analogous to those in the United States.

Social unrest had long existed upon the island, primarily within the disenfranchised mulattos, who were generally better educated than the larger group of black slaves, and whose position enabled them to communicate with each other to a degree not afforded to the plantation slaves. Saint-Domingue was a powder keg waiting for a spark, and the spark came from, of all places, the mother country.

The French document called the "Declaration of the Rights of Man" was passed on August 26, 1789. It stated: "In the eyes of the law all citizens are equal.... The aim of all political associations is the preservation of the natural rights of liberty, property, security, and resistance to oppression." This was, of course, the last message that white colonists wanted spread about on an island where they were outnumbered by the blacks sixteen-to-one, and they did everything in their power to suppress it.

To their dismay, the message was brought to the island anyway, in part through the intervention of a group of French abolitionists, the first of its kind in the world, calling themselves the "Société des amis des noirs," or the "Society of the Friends of the Blacks." The deputies representing the (white) National Assembly on the island were appalled by the society's interference, claiming that its members "take hold of the Declaration of the Rights of Man," and stating that this work was "beneficial to enlightened men, but inapplicable," "and therefore dangerous to our regulations" apparently because it posed a threat to their control of the blacks.

"The journals in [The Society's] pay or under [their] influence, give the declaration vent in the midst of our gangs. The writings of the Amis des Noirs, openly announce, that the freedom of the Negroes is proclaimed by the Declaration of Rights."

Nor were they the only ones. It was reported that arriving French soldiers, flush with the heady excitement of liberty and fraternity, "on landing at Port-au-Prince, had given the fraternal embrace to all Mulattoes and all Negroes, telling them that the Assembly in France had declared all men free and equal." Naturally, the white authorities in the colony did everything within their power to suppress the message, but it was too late.

By 1791, the blacks were in armed resistance. The first full-scale slave revolt in the Western hemisphere was underway. It would last a dozen years, during which time horrid reports of violence and atrocities made their way into the Southern states. The colony was devastated by fighting, with prosperous plantations pillaged and burned. Ultimately, tens of thousands of lives were cut short by the violence. The white presence on the island was virtually annihilated. Finally, on January 1, 1804, the independent black state of Haiti was proclaimed, the culmination of the only successful slave revolt in history.

The specter of Haiti would haunt Southern slaveowners for generations. If it could happen there, what would prevent it from happening in America? As abolitionists loudly proclaimed that "All Men are Created Equal" echoes of armed slave insurrections and racial genocide sounded in Southern ears. Much of their resentment towards the abolitionists can be seen as a reaction to the events in Haiti.

How unfortunate it was that the South learned the wrong lesson from Haiti. The violence on the island, while admittedly deplorable, was a result of the white minority trying to keep down the black majority. However, in the eyes of the South, it seemed the blacks were unable to manage or govern themselves. To the Southern slaveowning mentality, the terror that was unleashed on Saint-Dominque was attributable to the blacks wreaking vengeance upon the whites after gaining their freedom. Thus was intensified the myth, hinted at in Jefferson's notes on Virginia, that if you freed the slaves, there would be racial wars.

Again and again, the abolitionists tried to warn the slaveholders: You have nothing to fear from the emancipated black. It is the enslaved black who is your enemy. Yet their words fell upon deaf ears.

In view of the significant Southern slaveowning presence in the federal government, it should not be surprising that newly established Haiti was not immediately recognized by the United States. To recognize it would have validated the slaves' revolution against their masters, a contingency unthinkable for those who were masters of slaves themselves. Also, to grant recognition would have meant accepting blacks as being politically equal to whites, which to many Americans in both the North and the South was at least as unthinkable.

In fact, the United States would not extend diplomatic recognition to Haiti until 1862 when the pro-slavery representation had removed itself from the government ranks.

On March 4, 1801, Thomas Jefferson gave his inaugural address, thus becoming the third man (and the second slaveowner) to serve as President of the United States. Exhorting the citizens of the young country to cooperate for the common good, he pointed out, "All, too, will bear in mind this sacred principle, that though the will of the majority is in all cases to prevail," "that will to be rightful must be reasonable; that the minority possess their equal rights, which equal law must protect, and to violate would be oppression."

This is an especially interesting idea coming from the man who barely more than two years earlier was suggesting that each state could ignore the will of the majority if it so chose. Here Jefferson is referring to the Northerners as the majority, and is suggesting that they are trying to violate the rights of the Southern minority. This was the typical Southern attitude, which reflected its transparent hypocrisy. They viewed themselves as the unfortunate minority, downtrodden and abused by their Northern oppressors. Quick to point out even the slightest unfairness on the part of their Northern brothers towards them, they never seemed to be aware that any injuries they had received (or imagined themselves to have received) paled in comparison to those they inflicted upon the unfortunate black minority within their own borders.

Even now, many Civil War enthusiasts and historians seem to be sympathetic to the Southern cause. Many people want to see in the "plight" of the Southerner the classic struggle of the fierce, independent underdog who wants nothing more than to be left alone to manage his own affairs. This would be acceptable if those affairs had not consisted of the systematic exploitation of other human beings.

There was just something about the Southern personality that could drive their Northern contemporaries to utter distraction. The almost pathological persecution complex developed within the slave owners—and, by extension, the Southern culture as a whole—contributed to a societal paranoia that led to seeing insults and affronts even when none was intended.

It appears the typical white Northerner, regardless of his feelings or attitudes towards the black race, finally got "fed up" with the Southern bantering and posturing. The abolitionists contributed significantly to this change in Northern sensibilities. While this certainly exacerbated the already strained relations between the two regions, it may ultimately have been the essential catalyst that forced the country to come to grips with the issues and solve the slavery problem. Though the cost of the solution was tremendous, the price of allowing slavery to continue longer than it did might have been even greater.

On December 20, 1803, the United States government purchased the Louisiana Territory from Napoleon for $15 million. Initially, Congress attempted to restrict the importation of slaves into the new territories, but its efforts soon proved futile. The land and the climate were perfect for growing the wonderful cash crop, cotton. Bowing to the pressures of Southern slave owners, who seemed intent to carry their chattel to the territories with or without the blessing of the Federal government, resistance finally caved in. As of March 2, 1805, all restrictions upon the slave trade in the territories were officially swept away.

According to the official report of Senator O'Brien Smith of South Carolina, between January 1, 1804, and December 31, 1807, the number of African slaves entering the country through the port of Charleston numbered 39,075. And most of these, it appeared, were headed to Louisiana. (One can only speculate that the actual number entering the country during this period was probably even higher than the official records indicated.)

There were two main reasons why the numbers were so high for these years. Obviously, one was the almost insatiable demand for labor in the territories. The other was that the anti-slavery members of Congress had finally passed the legislation that had been constitutionally forbidden for twenty years. In March 1807, there was passed "An act to prohibit the importation of Slaves into any port or place within the jurisdiction of the United States, from and after the first day of January, in the year of our Lord one thousand eight hundred and eight."

While well-intentioned, this statute had, unfortunately, three fatal flaws. First, by announcing the date nearly a year in advance, the South was able to legally import slaves at a hectic pace before the law went into effect, which contributed significantly to the high number of slaves introduced during this period.

Second, the law was not designed or intended to impact the interstate slave trade at all, thereby allowing the number of slaves being carried westward to continue at an alarming rate past the cut-off date stipulated for the foreign trade. Therefore, the law had absolutely no effect on the burgeoning numbers of slaves entering the rapidly developing territories.

And third, but most pathetically, the law provided for no means of enforcement or regulation. Capitulating to the previously established congressional resolution that slavery was a "local" issue upon which the states should be allowed to run their own affairs, the statute left it to the discretion of each individual state to decide how best to deal with any transgressions of the law.

Over the course of the next few decades, each state would set its own laws and regulations concerning disposition of illegally imported slaves. Typical of these laws was one from the Alabama and Mississippi Territory, dated December 8, 1815, which stated that any slaves brought illegally into the territory were "to be sold at auction, and the proceeds to be divided between the territorial treasury and the collector or informer." Or the North Carolina Act of November 18, 1816, which stated that "Every slave illegally imported after 1808 shall be sold for the use of the state." You will notice that neither act provided for the release of the unfortunate blacks.

And since most of the Southern states were starving for more labor, they were reluctant to severely punish those caught importing slaves illegally; since, after all, these people were actually doing the state a service. No records were found of any severe punishment for illegal trading ever being meted out during the antebellum period. (In fact, the only man ever hung as a consequence of illegally importing slaves into the United States was Captain Nathaniel Gordon, whose his death occurred on February 21, 1862.)

In the absence of the likelihood of any severe punishment, the business was so profitable that any fines that were levied, or threats of fines if caught, were not significant enough to deter those who were determined to profit on the trade of human cargo.

It also seems reasonable to conclude that very few Southern states were conscientiously dedicated to stamping out the trade. Indeed, there was no need to be since it was easy for the traders to get around the letter of the law. All they had to do was stop in a port such as Havana, Cuba, and transfer their human cargo to another vessel. The Act of 1807 only prevented the import of slaves from Africa. Slaves coming from another slave country, such as Cuba, could be freely entered into the country without violating the federal statute.

In reality, it is unlikely that the 1807 law had much of an effect on the slave trade. As evidence of this assumption, the state of Massachusetts would formally complain in the year 1820 that "...Should slavery be further permitted, an immense new market for slaves would be opened. It is well known that ... thousands are now annually imported from Africa."

Of course, by 1820 the state of Massachusetts had every reason to be concerned—both politically and for humanitarian reasons—about the further extension of slavery since in the previous year the citizens of Missouri had asked to be admitted into the union. Missouri would be the first new state to be carved out of the vast Louisiana Territory, and Missouri was pro-slavery.

However, before examining that story, it is necessary to look at one attempt that was made to solve the "Negro Problem." In 1816, Reverend Robert Finley, a Presbyterian minister from New Jersey, and Virginia congressman Charles Fenton Mercer co-developed a scheme that seemed to offer help to the slaves. They met that year in Washington with a group of exclusively white upper-middleclass men to work out the details of the program. Among them were Bushrod Washington (the nephew of George, who would be elected president of the group), James Monroe, Francis Scott Key, Henry Clay and Daniel Webster. This group formed the nucleus of what would come to be called the American Colonization Society, or ACS.

When noticed at all in the history books, the ACS is generally described as a well-intentioned organization, that viewed its work as potentially beneficial to the black race. However, one wonders at their sincerity when it is noted that the original name was the "American Society for Colonizing the Free People of Color in the United States." Their goal was not originally, nor did it ever become, one of freeing slaves. Their task was to assist in the voluntary removal of free blacks from the American continent.

Accepting the Southern rhetoric that blacks could not remain safely in the proximity of their former masters, there must have been some members of the ACS who thought that they would actually be doing some good. Perhaps they even deluded themselves into thinking that Southern slaveowners would free their bondsmen if they knew that the ACS was pledged to remove them from our shores. The Northern members were particularly heartened to see how willingly the South responded to their proposals—fooling themselves into thinking that the Southerners' intentions were the same as theirs. They were not.

To the Southerners, slaves could be controlled. The freemen were a bigger problem. Give a black freedom, and he starts getting ideas, the thinking went. Keep him in contact with his enslaved brothers, and they start getting ideas. It would be best if the freed slave could be somehow "removed" from Southern society.

In the 1820s, there was still a sizable free black population in the South, in some states approaching ten percent of the total black population. As the years went by, the repressive behavior of the whites made it harder and harder for blacks to become, or remain, free. By the time of the Civil War, it was illegal in most states for anyone to emancipate their slaves. Those that were free were required to carry "free papers" upon their persons at all times, and were subject to every indignity from casual harassment to imprisonment to re-enslavement to physical violence and even death at the hands of the whites.

Since it seemed to offer a means to reduce the undesirable free black population, most Southerners wholeheartedly embraced the aims of the ACS, as long as they didn't try to interfere with their slaves. The exceptions were South Carolinians such as John C. Calhoun, who resented even well-meaning and beneficent interference in their affairs. To them, the ACS was just another clever subterfuge of the abolitionists to deprive them of their laborers.

To most Northerners, the goals of the ACS seemed humanitarian and charitable. The ACS doctrine served the double purpose of seeming to help the poor black man, and, at the same time, keeping them out of the Northern states where they weren't really wanted (which to most Northerners was at least as big an issue as opposing slavery).

The ACS did accomplish something. Its program was responsible for establishing the colony of Liberia in Africa in the early 1820s It has been estimated that the ACS sponsored the emigration of between 12,000 and 20,000 African Americans during the nineteenth century. But as far as addressing the issue of slavery, it would remain for the abolitionists to demonstrate to the nation that the ACS way was not the way to go.

Within the "History of Congress," one will find the occasional passage demonstrating that there were times when the opponents of slavery tried to take a stand. For example, in December 1818, John Linn of New Jersey offered the following as a remedy to one of the shortcomings of the Act of 1807:

> Resolved, That [a] committee ... be instructed to inquire into the expediency of passing a law prohibiting the ... transportation of slaves or servants of color from any State to any other part of the United States....
>
> Mr. Linn said, in introducing his resolution, that it related to a subject of much interest in his part of the country, and, as the resolution only proposed an inquiry, he hoped it would not be objected to.
>
> Mr. [George] Poindexter, of Mississippi, objected to it. Any man, he said, had a right to remove his property from one State to another, and slaves as well as any other property....

Though stymied this time, it would not be long before the opponents of slavery would have their voices heard in the halls of Congress.

In the great American political battle between North and South, free and slave, there stand two landmark compromises marking times in our history when it seemed that the two sides had somehow worked out their differences to "save the union." The first of these was, of course, the Missouri Compromise of 1820. As was also the case of the second celebrated compromise which would come 30 years later, any "saving" that was done was more imagined than real. Nothing was actually settled in 1820, though the illusion of agreement seemed to quiet the situation for a few years.

It was indeed unfortunate that things turned out the way they did. If the North had not acceded to the South's demands, perhaps some less nebulous solution might have been reached. But, of course, it's futile to second-guess history. It can only be assumed that those who played their parts achieved the best that they thought they could at the time. Unfortunately, their best was not good enough.

In February of 1819, the residents of what would become the state of Missouri petitioned the federal government to accept them into the union. The subject had barely been introduced when Representative James Tallmadge of New York proposed "that the further introduction of slavery ... be prohibited, ... and that all children within the State, after the admission thereof into the Union, shall be free at the age of twenty-five."

He suggested that this be considered a necessary requirement for admission into the union that would guarantee there should be no slavery in the state. Missouri, which had been largely settled by people from the South, was already decidedly pro-slavery. Its citizens had no more intention of accepting such a proposal than the other Southern states had of allowing them to. Representative Tallmadge and his supporters must have known this even as he introduced the idea. So why did he?

Was the Civil War fought over slavery? The literature associated with the antebellum period provides the impression that many people do not accept it as the reason. Many other theories political, sociological or economic—have been advanced over the years, and all of them have some merit. However, if one takes the time to read the words that were spoken, it appears that many people were genuinely opposed to slavery.

John W. Taylor of New York spoke first as a supporter of the Tallmadge Amendment. He felt certain that "those whom we shall authorize to set in motion the machine of free government beyond the Mississippi, will, in many respects, decide the destinies of millions.... Our votes this day will determine whether the high destinies of this region, and of these generations, shall be fulfilled, or whether we shall defeat them by permitting slavery, with all its baleful consequences, to inherit the land."

He further pointed out that according to the Constitution,

> New States may be admitted by the Congress into the Union. This grant of power is evidently alternative; its exercise is committed to the

sound discretion of Congress.... [And] if Congress has the power of altogether refusing to admit new States, much more has it the power of prescribing such conditions as may be judged reasonable....

Gentlemen have said the amendment ... impairs the property of a master in his slave. Is it then pretended, that ... one individual can have a vested property not only in the flesh and blood of his fellow man, but also in generations not yet called into existence...?

Can it ... be maintained that ... we have no right to provide against the further increase of slavery within [the Territory of Missouri]...? [That] we cannot provide for the gradual abolition of slavery within its limits, nor establish those civil regulations which naturally flow from self-evident truth?

Having proved, at least to his own satisfaction, that Congress had the right to make such a demand of Missouri, he proceeded to place the Southerners on the spot:

[H]ere I might rest satisfied with reminding my opponents of their own declarations on the subject of slavery. How often, and how eloquently, have they deplored its existence among them? What willingness, nay, what solicitude have they not manifested to be relieved from this burden? How have they wept over the unfortunate policy that first introduced slaves into this country! How have they disclaimed the guilt and shame of that original sin, and thrown it back upon their ancestors? I have with pleasure heard these avowals of regret and confided in their sincerity; I have hoped to see its effects in the advancement of the cause of humanity. Gentlemen have now an opportunity of putting their principles into practice; if they have tried slavery and found it a curse; if they desire to dissipate the gloom with which it covers their land; I call upon them to exclude it from the Territory in question; plant not its seeds in the uncorrupt soil; let not our children, looking back to the proceedings of this day, say of them, as they have been constrained to speak of their fathers: "we wish their decision had been different; we regret the existence of this unfortunate population among us; but we found them here: we know not what to do with them: it is our misfortune, we must bear it with patience."

History will record the decision of this day as exerting its influence for centuries to come over the population of half our continent. If we reject the amendment and suffer this evil, now easily eradicated, to strike its roots so deep in the soil that it can never be removed, shall we not furnish some apology for doubting our sincerity, when we deplore its existence[?]

He continued by alluding to some previous words of Henry Clay of Kentucky who had

... pressed into his service the cause of humanity. He has pathetically urged us to withdraw our amendment and suffer this unfortunate population to be dispersed over the country. He says they will be better fed, clothed, and sheltered, and their whole condition will be greatly improved. Sir, true humanity disowns his invocation. The humanity to which he appeals is base coin; it is counterfeit, ... Sir, my heart responds to the call of humanity; I will zealously unite in any practicable means of bettering the condition of this oppressed people. I am ready to appropriate a territory to their use, and to aid them in settling it—but I am not willing, I never will consent to declare the whole country west of the Mississippi a market overt for human flesh. In vain will you enact severe laws against the importation of slaves, if you create for them an additional demand, by opening the western world to their employment. While a negro man is bought in Africa for a few gewgaws or a bottle of whiskey, and sold at New Orleans for twelve or fifteen hundred dollars, avarice will stimulate to the violation of your laws.... [T]he slave trade continues—a vigilant execution of the laws may diminish it, but, while you increase the demand and offer so great temptation to the cupidity of unprincipled men, they will encounter every peril in the prosecution of this unhallowed traffic....

To the objection that this amendment will, if adopted, diminish the value of a species of property in one portion of the Union, and thereby operate unequally, I reply: that if, by depriving slaveholders of the Missouri market, the business of raising slaves should become less profitable, it would be an effect incidentally produced, but is not the object of the measure.... It is further objected, that the amendment is calculated to disfranchise our brethren of the South, by discouraging their emigration to the country west of the Mississippi.... [B]ut, when we place all on an equal footing, denying to all what we deny to one, I am unable to discover the injustice or inequality.... If slavery shall be tolerated, the country will be settled by rich planters, with their slaves; if it shall be rejected, the emigrants will chiefly consist of the poorer and more laborious classes of society.... If the rejection of slavery will tend to discourage emigration from the South, will not its admission have the same effect in relation to the North and East.... Do you believe that these people will settle in a country where they must take rank with negro slaves? Having neither the ability nor will to hold slaves themselves, they labor cheerfully while labor is honorable; make it disgraceful, they will despise it. You cannot degrade it more effectually than by establishing a system whereby it shall be performed principally by slaves.

Taylor also talked about the Southern slaveowners' disdain of physical labor.

[W]hat ideas do you suppose are entertained of laboring men by the majority of slaveholders? A gentleman from Virginia (Mr. Barbour) replies, ... their rights are respected.... But in a country like this, where the people are sovereign ... the mere exemption from flagrant wrong is no great privilege.... But whom of [the laboring] class have [the slaveholders] ever called to fill stations of any considerable responsibility? When have we seen a Representative on this floor, from that section of our Union, who was not a slaveholder? Who but slaveholders are elected to their State Legislatures? Who but they are appointed to fill their executive and judicial offices...?

He doubted the Southern claim that the introduction of slavery into the territories would increase the value of the land. But even if it might, he asked if they were willing "to barter the present happiness and future safety of unborn millions ... for a few cents on an acre of land.... I entreat gentlemen to pause and solemnly consider how deeply are involved the destinies of future generations in the decision now to be made."

While admitting that the Constitution guaranteed the citizens of each state "all the privileges ... of citizens of the several States," he felt that "[t]o keep slaves—to make one portion of the population the property of another, hardly deserves to be called a privilege, since what is gained by the masters must be lost by the slaves."

Taylor ended the moral section of his argument with what now appears to have been an uncanny prediction. "The expediency of this measure is very apparent. The opening of an extensive slave market will tempt the cupidity of those who otherwise perhaps might gradually emancipate their slaves.... Instead of emancipation of the slaves, it is much to be feared that unprincipled wretches will be found kidnapping those who are already free, and transporting and selling the hapless victims into hopeless bondage."

Taylor was not the only, or the most important, anti-slavery speaker during the deliberations surrounding the admission of Missouri. But he was one of the earliest, and his words are representative of many of their later arguments. Southern contemporaries (and many historians since then) have accused the Northern politicians of manipulating the situation for their own political gains. While there were certainly political stakes involved, it is difficult to read his arguments and not believe that they display at least some level of genuine concern for the enslaved population. It is also clear that the speaker, and, presumably, many of his counterparts were already tiring of much of the Southern rhetoric.

The Southern rejoinders, of course, included many of the old arguments already heard. They also introduced a new scheme that is often referred to as "Diffusionism." The basic idea behind this theory is that emancipation would be more likely to occur in the South if "we spread them [the slaves] over a much larger surface by permitting them to be carried beyond the river."

"The greatest kindness you can do a slave," claimed another, "is to tempt his master to remove with him to the Western countries."

Louis McLane, of Delaware, expressed this idea quite well. According to him, if the slaves

> ... were permitted to be carried by the children of the Southern planter, when emigrating to the Western country in pursuit of the riches which that fruitful territory holds ... they would by this means become dispersed over a wider field; their condition would necessarily be improved, (for they always thrive and do better when held in small numbers;) and the chances of emancipation would certainly be multiplied in both coun-

tries; the number would be less in the South and West; they would be less formidable to the white population; and in the course of time gradually acquire ease and freedom.

This disingenuous idea had just enough of a kernel of truth about it to make it sound plausible. If one looked at the history of the states in which slavery had already been abolished, it was true that the act was preceded by a period in which the slave population declined. The conclusion that the Southerners wanted to imply was that if you reduced the slave population of an area by removing some of its slaves to a new territory or state, then you increased the likelihood of emancipation in the depleted section. This may indeed have worked in practice if the rate of depletion significantly exceeded the rate of increase due to (illegally) imported new slaves and natural increase (i.e. reproduction). However, at no time was this to be the case in any of the slave states.

One wonders whether any Southerner sincerely believed in this theory. One thing is certain. Despite all their tirades against slavery, they felt, wrongly or rightly, that they were too dependent upon it to give it up even if they could have seen a way to accomplish this. They were so dedicated to maintaining their system of slavery that they would never have risked putting it in jeopardy.

If they really thought that diffusionism would eliminate slavery in their states, then they would have fought to prevent the movement of slaves into the new States or territories even more strongly than did the Northerners.

Diffusionism, like so many other Southern claims, seemed just another way to rationalize the perpetuation of slavery.

One can't help questioning the sincerity of a speaker like Philip Barbour of Virginia, who would claim that

> ... although they [the slaves] were held as property, yet they were considered and treated as the most valuable, as the most favored property; their masters remembered that they were men, and ... we felt for them those sympathies which bind one man to another, ... [S]uch were the feelings of the Southern people towards their slaves, that nothing scarcely but the necessity of the master, or the crime of the slave, would induce him to sell his slave.

If Barbour thought his vision of the kindly, paternalistic slave owner would fool his listeners, he was soon dissuaded of his illusion.

> Slavery in America [stated Arthur Livermore of New Hampshire] is the condition of man subjected to the will of a master, who can make any disposition of him short of taking away his life.... The bodies of slaves may, with impunity, be prostituted to any purpose, and deformed in any manner by their owners. The sympathies of nature in slaves are disregarded; mothers and children are sold separated....

> Let us no longer tell idle tales about the gradual abolition of slavery; away with colonization societies, if their design is only to rid us of free blacks and turbulent slaves....

One particularly curious aspect of the whole controversy is that the Southerners faulted the Northerners for causing all the trouble. The problem did not lie with slavery, they claimed, but with the Northern agitation of the slavery issue. The Southerners, in general, felt that slavery was a "delicate subject" that ought not to be discussed in a public forum. In fact, they did not want to have it discussed. "Let us not make the Mississippi another great natural boundary, for the purpose of ... dividing our country," said Barbour.

> To such gentlemen [said Taylor] it may be "a delicate subject;" but to me I confess it is not. In my estimation ... the delicacy of the subject is lost, and ought to be forgotten in its immense importance. "A delicate subject!" In which is involved the security and happiness of unborn millions; a subject too delicate for discussion!—because our debate may be overheard by a negro in the gallery. Sir, it is a subject vastly important to my children, and the children of my constituents, who shall hereafter emigrate [to the slave territories.]

Hugh Nelson of Virginia "has expressed an opinion," said Taylor,

> ... that if our ancestors had maintained the doctrine embraced in the [Tallmadge] amendment, the Federal Constitution would never have been formed, and he has thought proper to warn us that, if it be persisted in, the confederation will be dissolved. Has it then come to this? Is the preservation of our Union made to depend on the admission of slavery into a territory not belonging to the States when the Constitution was adopted?

At one point, Henry Clay went so far as to warn

> ... the advocates of this measure against the certain effects which it must produce. Effects destructive of the peace and harmony of the Union. He believed that they were kindling a fire which all the waters of the ocean could not extinguish. It could be extinguished only in blood!

As the years rolled on, the Southern speakers and their precise words might change, but the attitudes would remain the same.

The debate on the Missouri issue runs to hundreds of pages in the annals of Congress. It does demonstrate that at least some Northerners were more than just politically minded in their attacks upon slavery. And that many Northerners were getting fed-up with Southern bantering. Many Southerners seemed to be completely unable to recognize any justice in the Northern claims. Both sides, unfortunately, had reached the point that they no longer heard what the other was saying.

As the bickering continued and intensified, the advocates of Missouri's claims managed to combine their issue with the pleas of the citizens of Northwestern Massachusetts who wanted to become the state of Maine. One of the most macabre statements of the entire debate came at this time from Edward Lloyd of Maryland who emphatically stated, "Unless we can obtain the admission of Missouri into the Union, on the same terms and *as free and unshackled* [emphasis added] as Maine, I am decidedly of opinion we ought to admit neither." The use of slave terminology in Southern rhetoric dates back to the colonial era, but whenever I come across it, it strikes me as particularly appalling. Their ability to claim that slavery was good for the blacks, yet was the height of infamy and oppression when applied to their own situations, never ceases to amaze me.

One noteworthy example of this Southern tendency was Patrick Henry's famous speech given at St. John's Church in Richmond, Virginia, on March 23, 1775. Most people are familiar with the stirring conclusion, but in less than three typed pages he uses slave imagery numerous times. In the opening paragraph, he refers to the upcoming times as "nothing less than a question of freedom or slavery." Later he calls the actions of the British crown "the implements of ... subjugation," intended to "force us to submission." He speaks of British navies and armies that are bound for America "to bind and rivet upon us those chains which the British ministry have been so long forging."

He cautions his listeners not to be complacent "until our enemies have bound us hand and foot." In his eyes, the battle has already started, and there will be "no retreat but in submission and slavery! Our chains are forged! Their clanking may be heard on the plains of Boston!"

At the dramatic end of his discourse, he asks: "Is life so dear, or peace so sweet, as to be purchased at the price of chains and slavery? Forbid it, Almighty God! I know not what course others may take; but as for me, give me liberty or give me death!"

These are noble sentiments indeed coming from a man who owned slaves himself, from the same man who just a few years prior (on January 18, 1773) had written about slavery in a letter to Robert Pleasants:

> It is not a little surprising that Christianity, whose chief excellence consists in softening human heart ... should encourage a Practice so totally repugnant.... What adds to the wonder is that this Abominable Practice has been introduced in the most enlightened Ages....
> Every thinking honest Man rejects it in Speculation, how few in Practice from conscientious Motives...?
> Would any one believe that I am Master of Slaves of my own purchase!

I am drawn along by the general inconvenience of living without them, I will not, I cannot justify it.

I suspect that the final honest sentiment in this passage—rarely voiced aloud by Southerners—was not unique to Mr. Henry.

In March 1820 came the Missouri Compromise that, like most halfway measures, totally pleased no one. With this compromise, it was agreed that both Maine and Missouri would be brought into the United States. This established the Noah-like precedent of bringing states in two-by-two, one slave and one free, thereby maintaining the delicate balance.

It was further stipulated that within the part of the Louisiana Territory "which lies north of 36 degrees 30 minutes North latitude, not included within the limits of the state [of Missouri], slavery ... is hereby, forever prohibited."

As on so many other occasions, one wonders why the anti-slavery members of Congress were willing to agree to such a compromise. They had yielded a vast Southern territory to slavery in exchange for a guarantee that it would not be permitted into the Northern section. One wonders what could have made them think that Southern promises in 1820 would be kept any more sacrosanct than those that had been made in 1787 concerning the Northwest Territory? It was as if slavery was determined to go wherever it pleased, regardless of promises or protests to the contrary.

While the Missouri controversy was going on, John Quincy Adams was the Secretary of State. He was also the son of the only non-slaveholder who had ever been president in the country's 32-year history. At one time he had the opportunity to talk the issues over with his fellow cabinet member, Secretary of War John C. Calhoun of South Carolina. Adams, who never considered himself an abolitionist, recorded in his diary his impressions of what Calhoun had said:

> ... in the Southern country ... domestic labor was confined to the blacks; and such was the prejudice that if he, who was the most popular man in his district, were to keep a white servant in his house, his character and reputation would be irretrievably ruined.
> I [Adams] said that this confounding of the ideas of servitude and labor was one of the bad effects of slavery; but he thought it attended with many excellent consequences. It did not apply to all kinds of labor—not, for example, to farming. He himself had often held the plough; so had his father. Manufacturing and mechanical labor was not degrading. It was only manual labor—the proper work of slaves. No white man could descend to that. And it was the best guarantee to equality among the whites. It produced an unvarying level among them. It not only did not excite but did not even admit of inequalities, by which one white man could domineer

over another. I told Calhoun I could not see things in the same light. It is, in truth, all perverted sentiment—mistaking labor for slavery, and dominion for freedom. The discussion of this Missouri question has betrayed the secret of their souls. In the abstract they admit that slavery is an evil, they disclaim all participation in the introduction of it, and cast it all upon the shoulders of our old Grandam Britain. But when probed to the quick upon it, they show at the bottom of their souls pride and vainglory in their condition of masterdom. They fancy themselves more generous and noblehearted than the plain freemen who labor for subsistence. They look down upon the simplicity of a Yankee's manners, because he has no habits of overbearing like theirs and cannot treat Negroes like dogs.

It is among the evils of slavery that it taints the very sources of moral principle. It establishes false estimates of virtue and vice; for what can be more false and heartless than this doctrine which makes the first and holiest rights of humanity to depend upon the color of the skin? It perverts human reason, and reduces man endowed with logical powers to maintain that slavery is sanctioned by the Christian religion, that slaves are happy and contented in their condition, that between master and slave there are ties of mutual attachment and affection, that the virtues of the master are refined and exalted by the degradation of the slave; while at the same time they vent execrations upon the slave trade, curse Britain for having given them slaves, burn at the stakes Negroes convicted of crimes for the terror of the example, and writhe in agonies of fear at the very mention of human rights as applicable to men of color. The impression produced upon my mind by the progress of this discussion is that the bargain between freedom and slavery contained in the Constitution of the United States is morally and politically vicious, inconsistent with the principles upon which alone our Revolution can be justified; cruel and oppressive, by riveting the chains of slavery, by pledging the faith of freedom to maintain and perpetuate the tyranny of the master; and grossly unequal and impolitic, by admitting that slaves are at once enemies to be kept in subjection, property to be secured or restored to their owners, and persons not to be represented, but for whom their masters are privileged with nearly a double share of representation. The consequence has been that this slave representation has governed the Union....

I have favored the Missouri Compromise, believing it to be all that could be effected under the present Constitution, and from extreme unwillingness to put the Union at hazard. But perhaps it would have been a wiser as well as a bolder course to have persisted in the restriction [of slavery] upon Missouri, till it should have terminated in a convention of the states to revise and amend the Constitution. This would have produced a new Union of thirteen or fourteen States, unpolluted with slavery, with a great and glorious object to effect; namely, that of rallying to their standard the other states by the universal emancipation of their slaves. If the Union must be dissolved, slavery is precisely the question upon which it ought to break. For the present, however, this contest is laid asleep.

There is little doubt that many other Northerners had feelings very similar to those expressed by Adams. Be that as it may, what were the effects of the Missouri Compromise? Had it "saved" the Union?

Not really. It seemed instead to have established a general feeling of guarded distrust between the two sections.

The Northerners had begun to understand just how deeply entrenched slavery was in the South, and to realize that it would take more effort than they had so far been able to expend to change it. Part of the trouble came from within their own region. There were many Northerners who begrudgingly conceded some validity to the Southerners' claims to constitutional protection, and, therefore, were not willing to take a stand against them. Likewise, there were others who feared the disruption to the union that seemed certain to follow any concentrated efforts to eradicate slavery. As such, there was not, at least at this time, a strong united front in the North dedicated to carrying on the fight.

Conversely, the South was always united on the major issue of keeping its bondsmen. A vote on any issue impacting the institution found the South unanimously (or nearly so) in agreement, with just enough vacillating Northerners siding with them to carry the issue in their favor. In time, many Southerners came to believe that the North would always back down in the face of enough threats or bluffs. For the next 40 years, it seemed like they were correct in their assessment.

On June 29, 1820, the slave ship *Antelope* was intercepted off the coast of St. Augustine, Florida, by the United States revenue cutter *Dallas*. At the time the ship was flying the American flag, and it had on board 281 chained Africans; obviously bound for sale in America.

To complicate matters, 93 of these Africans had been abducted from a Spanish ship and another 130 from a Portuguese vessel. Since neither of those countries had outlawed the slave trade, those countries could claim their share of the Africans as "rightful" property. It was up to the courts to sort things out. The case would eventually reach the Supreme Court, but not for another five years.

Since his retirement from active politics in 1808, Thomas Jefferson, the "Sage of Monticello," had been dispensing his own brand of political wisdom while living the life of a "gentleman farmer" (which, South of the Mason-Dixon line, of course meant "slaveowner"). In a highly quoted letter to William Short dated August 4, 1820, Jefferson had his say about the Missouri Compromise. "[T]his momentous question, like a fire bell in the night, awakened and filled me with terror," he wrote. "I considered it at once as the knell of the Union."

Make no mistake about Jefferson's meaning in this sentence. The question that terrified him was not whether slavery should or should not be abolished; it was whether Congress had a right to so legislate. And, of course, Jefferson felt that it did not have such a right.

In Jefferson's mind, just as it was for the pro-slavery congressmen previously quoted, the problem was not with slavery. The problem was with Northerners trying to legislate slavery when they clearly had no right to do so. As Jefferson continued his letter to Short, he sounds less like a wise, venerable old philosopher, and more like a typical Southern bigot.

> The cession of that kind of property ... would not cost me a second thought, if, in that way, a general emancipation and *expatriation* could be effected; and gradually, and with due sacrifices, I think it might be. But as it is, we have the wolf by the ears, and we can neither hold him, nor safely let him go. Justice is in one scale, and self-preservation in the other. Of one thing I am certain, that as the passage of slaves from one State to another, would not make a slave of a single human being who would not be so without it, so their diffusion over a greater surface would make them individually happier, and proportionally facilitate the accomplishment of their emancipation, by dividing the burthen on a greater number of coadjutors. An abstinence too, from this act of power, would remove the jealousy excited by the undertaking of Congress to regulate the condition of the different descriptions of men composing a State. This certainly is the exclusive right of every State, which nothing in the constitution has taken from them and given to the General Government.

In late May 1822, a slave named George Wilson, living in South Carolina, revealed to his master a plan for a slave insurrection that was scheduled for July of that year. In the course of the subsequent excitement, authorities uncovered what may have been the most extensive and carefully planned slave conspiracy in American history. The leader and organizer, Denmark Vesey, was a free black and a leader of the recently suppressed African (Methodist) Church of Charleston.

Accounts of the foiled uprising claim that the slaves involved numbered anywhere from 6,600 to 9,000. Reportedly, 131 were arrested, and 37, among them Vesey himself, were ultimately hanged. In August of that year, the city council of Charleston authorized publication of the official report of the incident, avowing that it should be a "lesson, among a certain portion of our population, that there is nothing they are bad enough to do, that we are not powerful enough to punish."

The Vesey conspiracy may have been extraordinary in its scope, but the potential of slave insurrection in the South was a constant threat. Herbert Aptheker undertook a study of antebellum slave unrest and concluded there were 250 separate slave insurrections between the Colonial Period and the Civil War. To classify as an "insurrection" in his study, the occurrence must have involved ten or more slaves. By this criteria, isolated events of individual or small-group resistance, of which there were undoubtedly many, were not considered. (Another historian, John Hope Franklin, claims that "nearly every year, in virtually every state in the South, slaves were indicted for killing their owners.")

Also to be considered in Aptheker's report, the incident must have been reported in the local press. One can only assume there were additional insurrections of which he was unable to find any report, either because the records no longer exist or because contemporaries of the event intentionally suppressed it. Therefore, his number should be viewed as a lower limit, not as a fair estimate of the total. Under such conditions, to say that Southerners lived with the constant threat of violence at the hands of their "happy" slaves does not seem to be an overstatement.

Of course, Southern vanity never allowed the slaveowner to admit any fear of slave violence. To do so would be to admit a weakness that they were unwilling to acknowledge. And yet, they were constantly criticizing the abolitionists for trying to incite insurrections. If their slaves were indeed as contented as claimed and if their control was as absolute as they bragged, why did they consider the words of the abolitionist so dangerous to their wellbeing?

On January 3, 1823, Stephen Austin was granted the right to enter and colonize the Mexican territory of Texas with American citizens. Most of the Americans that followed him were from the South, and many of them brought their slaves with them. This simple grant by a foreign government would have a significant affect on the future of the United States.

In January 1824, the Ohio State legislature advocated a plan to terminate slavery. Referring to the practice as a "national" evil, they called upon the other states to join them in "the duties and burdens of removing it." Eight Northern states endorsed their idea.

Governor John Wilson of South Carolina responded by urging upon the representatives of his state "a firm determination to resist, at the threshold, every invasion." In response, the state senate passed a resolution against "any claim of right, of the United States, to interfere in any manner."

In March 1825, the Supreme Court finally made its ruling in the case of the *Antelope*. The decision was written by Chief Justice John Marshall of Virginia who felt that the slave trade was "contrary to the laws of nature," but conceded that "the usages, the national acts, and the general assent" of many nations "claimed all the sanction which could be derived from long usage and general acquiescence." Or to paraphrase: "We may not do it here in our country, but we can't stop other countries from doing it if they so desire."

As no Portuguese claimant had stepped forward since the ship was seized, that country's claim was thrown out. The United States, however, could not legally deprive the nation of Spain of its property.

Sadly, almost half of the captured Africans had died in prison while awaiting the court's decision. Through some sort of judicial mathematics, it was "determined" that Spain's share of the original 281 had been therefore reduced to 36. Since there was no way to determine which slaves belonged to Spain, 36 (some sources say 39) individuals were chosen by lottery and delivered to Spanish authorities residing in Florida.

The remaining illegally imported slaves, numbering approximately 120, were ultimately transported to Liberia through the aid of the American Colonization Society, though it took until 1827 to do so. Since that year also marked the twentieth anniversary of the closing of the African slave trade, it might be appropriate to ask: How effective had this legislation been?

It is patently impossible to say, because those involved in illegal smuggling seldom kept records. There is, however, one interesting account from that year in the autobiography *Twenty Years of an African Slaver*, by Captain Theodore Canot.

By way of demonstrating the immense profits of such a voyage, which "the readers may scarcely credit," he included "an account of the fitting of a slave vessel from Havana in 1827, and the liquidations of her voyage in Cuba." In a very business-like manner he listed all costs associated with the venture, including the original building and fitting out of the schooner *La Fortuna*, provisions and wages for the crew and officers, "200,000 cigars and 500 doubloons, cargo," "clearance and hush-money," and all expenditures for the voyage to and from Africa. "Total of expenses out and home: $27,162.46," he reported.

His expenses in Havana included "government officers, at $8 per head" (apparently bribes paid on the 217 Negroes successfully brought to port), his "commission," and all other expenses, which when added to those already cited, brought the "total of all expenses" to $39,970.46.

The boat was apparently sold "at auction" for $3,950. This was not such an unusual practice, as slave ships were so fouled after even just a few voyages that they were no longer usable. The "Proceeds of 217 slaves" came to $77,469.00, bringing the net return on the venture to $81,419. Simple arithmetic will show that the net profit of $41,448.54 exceeded the total expenses. Not a bad business, financially, for those willing to participate in it.

And there would always be those so willing. Canot claimed that by 1835, a clipper with an average round trip cost of $20,000 would yield earnings of over $100,000.

It will never be known how many Africans were illegally brought into the United States between the years of 1807 and 1860, though estimates range from a low of 250,000 to a high of 1,000,000 or more. So much for Jefferson's defense of diffusionism.

In the same year that *La Fortuna* was delivering its human cargo,

U.S. Senator Robert Y. Hayne of South Carolina warned Congress not to interfere with the rights of the states in their property. He received the full support of his state legislature which resolved that it was united "with a firm determination not to submit" to any federal interference.

Slavery was not the only bone of contention between the regions. In 1828, Congress passed a special tariff that was designed to benefit industry and manufacturing. Since most of this took place in the North, the tariff was viewed, not without some justification, as being unfair to the South.

It is beyond the scope and intent of this work to argue the merits or faults of the 1828 Tariff Act. However, it is worth noting that once again South Carolina would issue a resolution challenging the federal authorities.

It was a well-known secret that the author of the South Carolina Exposition and Protest of 1828 was John C. Calhoun, though the theory sounded decidedly Jeffersonian. The Exposition said in part that "a single State might suspend a federal law which it regarded as unconstitutional until three quarters of the States had justified the law through the amending power." Or, in other words, South Carolina did not consider itself bound to adhere to the tariff.

In the protest, it was pointed out that

> South Carolina, from her climate, situation, and peculiar institutions, is and must ever continue to be wholly dependent upon agriculture and commerce, not only for her prosperity but for her very existence as a state; because the valuable products of her soil ... are among the few that can be cultivated with any profit by slave labor; and if, by the loss of her foreign commerce, these products should be confined to an inadequate market, the fate of this fertile state would be poverty and utter desolation.

While specifically arguing against the tariff, this passage makes it clear that South Carolina considered its prosperity irreversibly tied to slavery.

The election of 1828 was celebrated by many as the "return of democracy" as slaveowner Andrew Jackson, the hero of The Battle of New Orleans, gained the presidency. This was only the second time in the 40 year history of the young republic that an incumbent had not been reelected. The first time had been John Adams; this time it was his son, John Quincy Adams. Between them, their eight years of office represented the only years to date that the chief executive officer wasn't a slaveowner.

In the judiciary, justices from the slave states had outnumbered those from the free states at all times since 1790. John Marshall of Virginia had been Chief Justice since 1801. The two Adams between them had been responsible for appointing just four out of the 23 justices who had ever sat on the bench. The other 19 had all been appointed by slave holding presidents.

In the legislature, the President Pro Tempore of the Senate had been from a slave state for 27 of the last 31 years, while the number of slave/free senators had maintained an exact equality since 1814 and would continue to do so until the eve of the Civil War. Only in the House of Representatives would the free states ever be in the majority, though this was misleading, as the three-fifths rule had inflated the number of Southern members beyond what it should have been.

According to the 1820 census, the population of the free states totaled 5,624,384, as opposed to just 2,933,897 in the slave states. Or, in other words, the population of the free states represented just over 65 percent of the country's free population of 8,558,281. Had representation in the House been based solely upon free population, the Northern states would have held claim to 123 seats, while the Southern states would have had just 66, nearly a two-to-one advantage for the North.

However, since the three fifths rule inflated the numbers in the South by counting every five slaves as three free citizens, the South's "adjusted" population soared to 3,969,197. As there were still some slaves living in the Northern states, their numbers were also augmented by the three fifths rule, but not as significantly. The North's "adjusted" population rose slightly to just 5,635,879. The North's represented majority shrunk to 59 percent of the total. While the number of Northern representatives remained unaffected at 123, the actual number of Southern representatives for that year was 90, an increase of 24 actual House seats in recognition of the over 1,720,000 unrepresented slaves in the South.

It may not be inappropriate to point out that most of the measures in the House that were lost by the anti-slavery members were lost on very close votes. Without those additional 24 "slave" representatives, the Tallmadge Amendment would probably have been passed easily, and there would never have been a Missouri Compromise.

It might also be pointed out that, despite the North's majority of members, the Speaker of the House had been a representative of a slave state for 22 of the last 30 years.

It would do well to consider these statistics when, in the years before the Civil War, Northerners would refer to the "slavocracy" that had dominated the history of the United States.

It would also be interesting to know just what portion of the Southern population actually composed the so-called "slavocracy." Unfortunately, the official United States census did not include "slaveholder" as a data category until 1860, and it is probably very risky to try to extrapolate backwards to arrive at figures for the population 30 years earlier. However, since the numbers for that year will be of interest to the Civil War enthusiast, I will include them here.

The census showed 12,240,293 of the country's total 1860 population of 31,183,582 lived in slaveholding states. The total number of actual slaveholders was only 393,967. This represents just 3.2 percent of the total Southern population and just 1.26 percent of the nation's population. (It's interesting to note that at 476,748 there were actually more Free Blacks in the country than there were slaveholders.)

Even in South Carolina, which had the largest percentage of slave-owners per population of any state in 1860, less than 10 percent of the free population owned slaves on the eve of the war.

Even more telling is that of the nation's slaveowners, less than half owned more than five slaves. (One in five slaveowners possessed just a single slave.) Therefore, it is patently obvious that most Southerners at the outbreak of the Civil War were not slaveowners. But could the same be said of 30 years earlier?

The biggest change in the slaveowning population during the years 1830–1860 was probably the concentration of slaves in the possession of property-rich, large plantations. Therefore, if one were to guess how the figures were different at the beginning of the "Abolitionist Decade," one might assume that an even larger percentage of the slaveholders in 1830 owned five or fewer slaves. Therefore, the total number of slaveowners may have been bigger in the earlier period, but it seems doubtful that the number of free citizens who owned slaves was ever the majority of the population.

However, to conclude that slaveholders were a minority of the South's population should not be misconstrued as proof that the majority did not condone—or support—slavery. In a racially bigoted society that valued the presence of a servile race within its midst, it was not necessary to be a slaveowner yourself in order to desire to perpetuate the institution. There were many reasons why non-slaveholders might wish the arrangement to be maintained. William C. Cooper, Jr., in his book *Liberty and Slavery* (1983) stresses the notion that "racial identity [was] a powerful force for white unity." Cooper quotes Congressman Peter Early of Georgia as proclaiming that most Southerners "do not believe it immoral to hold human flesh in bondage...." According to Early, "A large majority of people in the Southern states do not consider slavery as an evil."

"In fact," adds Cooper from a modern perspective, "no evidence suggests that a majority of white Southerners ever thought slavery an evil."

John Quincy Adams, beaten and embittered, retired to his home in Massachusetts. His presidency, marred by his fierce independence and reluctance (or inability) to be politically accommodating, would be remembered as one of the least effectual in the nation's history. His future, however, would hold a few unexpected surprises.

Jackson's ascendancy seemed to vindicate the Southern position. It can be assumed that even the South Carolinians were pleased to once again see one of their own kind holding the reins of power. However, Jackson's future career would also include a few surprises; not all of which would be appreciated by the State of South Carolina.

Important Figures Living in the Abolitionist Decade

Any student of the Civil War should be familiar with the following names. What's significant to bear in mind is that many of these people lived their formative years during the "Abolitionist Decade." Most of them reached adulthood without ever seeing a period without sectional controversy. Few of these individuals will have any impact on the present story, yet its impact upon each of them was no doubt great.

A 34-year-old slave named Sam is living in Virginia with his master, Peter Blow. When his master dies, he will be sold to an Army surgeon named Dr. John Emerson. Over the course of this decade he will travel with his master often into states or territories where slavery is not recognized. Eventually Sam will marry and change his name to Dred Scott.

A 32-year-old slave named Isabella is living in New York with her son, Peter. Though slavery has been abolished in the state, it does not apply to those such as Isabella who were born before 1799. However, she has quietly "freed" herself by walking off. In 1843, she will change her name to Sojourner Truth.

John Brown is 29 and is operating a tannery in northwestern Pennsylvania. His abolitionist days are long ahead of him.

William Henry Seward is 28 and living in Auburn, New York. In 1830, he will be elected to his first public position in the New York state senate.

Gideon Welles is 27 and is a member of the legislature of the state of Connecticut.

Robert E. Lee is 22 years old. He will graduate second in his class from West Point in 1829.

Salmon Chase is 21. He has just been admitted to the bar in Washington D.C., but meager job prospects in that city will motivate him to relocate to Cincinnati, Ohio. He is one of the few players in this list who will have a role in the story of the next 10 years.

Jefferson Davis is 21 and graduated in 1828 from West Point. His class rank was twenty-third in a class of 32, and he finished the academy with 327 demerits. He has been assigned to frontier duty in the Wisconsin-Illinois area.

Andrew Johnson is also 21. He is working as a tailor in Greenville, Tennessee. In 1829, he will be elected to serve on the town council, the first in a series of political positions which will culminate in the White House.

Abraham Lincoln is 20 years old and is still living in Indiana with his father and stepmother.

Charles Sumner is 18 and is an undergraduate student at Harvard.

Harriett Beecher is 18. She is living in Hartford, Connecticut. She is attending her sister Catherine's Female Seminary, where she will soon be teaching.

Alexander Stephens is 17 and will enter Franklin College in Georgia in 1829.

Stephen A. Douglas is 16 and living in Vermont.

George Meade is 14 and living in Pennsylvania.

Tecumseh Sherman is 9 years old, and living in Lancaster, Ohio. In 1829, his father will die unexpectedly. With his mother unable to care for the family, he will be taken in by friends of hers named Thomas and Maria Ewing. Later in the year, when they attempt to have the young boy baptized, the officiating priest will insist upon a Christian name and "William" will be added.

A slave named Araminta Ross is 8 or 9 years-old, one of 11 children of a slave family in Dorchester, Maryland. In 1844, she will marry and change her name to Harriett Tubman. She will escape to freedom in Philadelphia in 1849.

Nathan Bedford Forrest is 8 and living in Tennessee.

Clara Barton is also 8 and living in Massachusetts.

Hiram Ulysses Grant is 7 and living in Georgetown, Ohio. It will be another ten years before he'll set off for West Point, dropping the "Hiram" at that time and adding his mother's maiden name of "Simpson" due to a government clerical error.

Matthew Brady is 6 and living in Saratoga Springs, New York.

Thomas Jonathan Jackson is 5 and living in Clarksburg Virginia. His father has been dead for three years, and, in two more years, his mother will die. He will be raised after that by a bachelor uncle.

George Pickett is 4 and living in Huntsville, Alabama.

Stephen Foster is 3 and living east of Pittsburgh, Pennsylvania, in Lawrenceville. Many of the songs he will write ("Oh Susanna," "Old

Folks at Home," "Massa's in de Cold Cold Ground," and "My Old Kentucky Home") will become standards of the pre-war period.

George B. McClellan is 3 years old, and living in Philadelphia, Pennsylvania.

On September 8, 1828, Joshua Chamberlain, immortalized in the film *Gettysburg* for his valiant defense of Little Round Top during that battle, was born in Brewer, Maine.

Two

1829

The "Abolitionist Decade" can be said to have officially started on July 4th, 1829. This date not only has obvious symbolic significance, but it represents the beginning of the abolitionist career of the individual whose name has been most often and most strongly associated with the movement. On this day, in front of the Park Street Church in Boston, Massachusetts, 24-year-old William Lloyd Garrison made his first public address against slavery.

To many Southerners, Garrison would come to represent all that was vile and detestable in the North. He was castigated during his lifetime as an incendiary, inciting slaves to slaughter their masters. Likewise, he was ridiculed as a religious fanatic, so obsessed with his own sense of morality that he was inflexible and intolerant of anything or anyone that seemed to disagree with him.

Much of this image has followed him even to the current day. Indeed, it's difficult to find a work that paints a sympathetic picture of him. But, in fairness, many of his modern-day detractors seem to be seeing him as a reflection of his Southern image. When one actually takes the time to read his words, it's hard to disagree with many of his points. He never minced words, and was sometimes less than sensitive with his denouncements; making it easy to understand why slave owners would be offended by many of his remarks.

It didn't take Garrison very long on that summer day to warm up to his subject:

> I stand up here in a ... solemn court, ... to obtain the liberation of 2 million of wretched, degraded beings, who are pining in hopeless bondage, over whose sufferings scarcely an eye weeps or a heart melts or

a tongue pleads either to God or man.... I assume as distinct and defensible propositions:

1. That the slaves of this country, whether we consider their moral, intellectual, or social condition, are preeminently entitled to the prayers and sympathies and charities of the American people; and their claims for redress are as strong as those of any Americans could be in a similar condition.

2. That as the free states, by which I mean nonslaveholding states, are constitutionally involved in the guilt of slavery by adhering to a national compact that sanctions it, and in the danger by liability to be called upon for aid in case of insurrection, they have the right to remonstrate against its continuance and it is their duty to assist in its overthrow.

3. That no justificative plea for the perpetuity of slavery can be found in the condition of its victims, and no barrier against our righteous interference in the laws which authorize the buying, selling, and possessing of slaves, nor in the hazard of a collision with slaveholders.

4. That education and freedom will elevate our colored population to a rank with the whites, making them useful, intelligent, and peaceable citizens.

In the first place, ... it is the duty of every nation primarily to administer relief to its own necessities[.]...

The condition of the slaves, ... , is deplorable, entitling them to a higher consideration, on our part, than any other race....

And here let me ask—what has Christianity done, by direct effort, for our slave population...? [S]he can gaze without emotion on a multitude of miserable beings at home, large enough to constitute a nation of freemen, whom tyranny has heathenized by law. In her public services they are seldom remembered, and in her private donations they are forgotten....

[A] very large proportion of our colored population were born on our soil and are therefore entitled to all the privileges of American citizens. This is their country by birth, not by adoption. Their children possess the same inherent and inalienable rights as ours; and it is a crime of the blackest dye to load them with fetters.

Every Fourth of July, our Declaration of Independence is produced, with a sublime indignation, to set forth the tyranny of the mother country and to challenge the admiration of the world. But what a pitiful detail of grievances does this document produce in comparison with the wrongs which our slaves endure...!

I am sick of unmeaning declamation in praise of liberty and equality; of our hypocritical cant about the inalienable rights of man.

While it's easy to understand that many of his listeners at the time may have taken offense with the harshness of his comments, it's difficult to disagree with the sentiments. Perhaps his biggest fault was in his timing. People just weren't ready to hear the message. But to those who criticize Garrison for speaking his mind so clearly and so boldly, one can suggest that the country needed to hear the plain truth. By forcing people to consider the realities of slavery, Garrison was instrumental in preparing the path that would ultimately lead to emancipation.

Garrison continued that day with an argument against the often-repeated claims of the South that slavery was no one else's business.

> I come to my second proposition, the right of the free states to remonstrate against the continuance and to assist in the overthrow of slavery.
>
> This, I am aware, is a delicate subject, surrounded with many formidable difficulties. But if delay only adds to its intricacy, wherefore shun an immediate investigation? I know that we of the North affectedly believe that we have no local interest in the removal of this great evil; that the slave states can take care of themselves, and that any proffered assistance on our part would be rejected as impertinent, dictatorial, or meddlesome; and that we have no right to lift up even a note of remonstrance. But I believe that these opinions are crude, preposterous, dishonorable, unjust. Sirs, this is a business in which, as members of one great family, we have a common interest; but we take no responsibility, either individually or collectively. Our hearts are cold, our blood stagnates in our veins, We act, in relation to the slaves, as if they were something lower than the brutes that perish.
>
> ... I assert the right of the free states to demand a gradual abolition of slavery, because, by its continuance, they participate in the guilt thereof and are threatened with ultimate destruction; because they are bound to watch over the interests of the whole country without reference to territorial boundaries; because their white population is nearly double that of the slave states, and the voice of the overwhelming majority should be potential; because they are now deprived of their just influence in the councils of the nation; because it is absurd and anti-republican to suffer property to be represented as men and vice verse; because it gives the South an unjust ascendancy over other portions of territory, and a power that may be perverted on every occasion....
>
> Now I say that, on the broad system of equal rights, this monstrous inequality should no longer be tolerated. If it cannot be speedily put down, *not by force but by fair persuasion* [emphasis added]; if we are always to remain shackled by unjust constitutional provisions when the emergency that imposed them has long since passed away; if we must share in the guilt and danger of destroying the bodies and souls of men *as the price of our Union*; if the slave states will haughtily spurn our assistance and refuse to consult in the general welfare, then the fault is not ours if a separation eventually takes place....

While Garrison's language in a passage such as this seems harsh, his words seem tame compared to many of the comments from Southern legislators at the time of the Missouri Compromise. He was still, at this point, willing to admit that the Southern states had the legal right to control their own destinies. Yet he hoped that they would allow the North to influence them into making the right decision.

> ... I grant that we have not the right, and I trust not the disposition, to use coercive measures. But do these laws [of the States which condone slavery] hinder our prayers or obstruct the flow of our sympathies? Cannot our charities alleviate the condition of the slave, and perhaps break his fetters...?
>
> Suppose that, by a miracle, the slaves should suddenly become white. Would you shut your eyes upon their sufferings and calmly talk of constitutional limitations? No, your voice would peal in the ears of the taskmasters like deep thunder; you would carry the Constitution by force if it could not be taken by treaty...; You would say: It is enough that they are white and in bondage, and they ought immediately to be set free....
>
> But the plea is prevalent that any interference by the free states, however benevolent or cautious it might be, would only irritate and inflame the jealousies of the South and retard the cause of emancipation.
>
> If any man believes that slavery can be abolished without a struggle with the worst passions of human nature, quietly, harmoniously, he cherishes a delusion. It can never be done unless the age of miracles returns....

Garrison himself had not yet reached the point where he demanded immediate emancipation. He was still willing to accept the Southern argument that the task of freeing the slaves was fraught with danger:

> [I admit that] the emancipation of all the slaves of this generation is most assuredly out of the question. The fabric which now towers above the Alps must be taken away brick by brick and foot by foot, till it is reduced so low that it may be over-turned without burying the nation in its ruins. Years may elapse before the completion of the achievement; generations of blacks may go down to the grave, manacled and lacerated, without a hope for their children; the philanthropists who are now pleading in behalf of the oppressed may not live to witness the dawn which will precede the glorious day of universal emancipation; but the work will go on, laborers in the cause will multiply, new resources will be discovered, the victory will be obtained, worth the desperate struggle of a thousand years. Or, if defeat follow, woe to the safety of the people! The nation will be shaken as if by a mighty earthquake.... The terrible judgments of an incensed God will complete the catastrophe of republican America.

It's certain many Southerners misinterpreted Garrison's warnings of upheaval as threats of violence. Yet, in view of the eventual consequences of the South's unyielding position on maintaining slavery, one can hardly deny the accuracy of his prophecy:

> I will say, finally, that I despair of the republic while slavery exists therein.... If we had any regard for our safety and happiness, we should strive to crush the vampire which is feeding upon our lifeblood. All the selfishness of our nature cries aloud for a better security. Our own vices are too strong for us and keep us in perpetual alarm. How, in addition to

Two • 1829

these, shall we be able to contend successfully with millions of armed and desperate men, as we must eventually if slavery does not cease?

While this was certainly a dire warning, it hardly justifies being called an incitement to slave revolution. Garrison is not calling upon the slaves to rebel; he is warning the Southern slaveholders that such will eventually be their fate if they do not attempt to deal fairly with the black population.

While Garrison would soon be leading the abolitionists, his words were not the only ones calling out against slavery. Just two months after this Boston speech, a free black by the name of David Walker would publish a pamphlet entitled *"David Walker's Appeal, in Four Articles: Together With A Preamble To The Coloured Citizens Of The World, But In Particular, And Very Expressly, To Those Of The United States Of America."* More commonly referred to simply as "David Walker's Appeal." it is not much mentioned anymore, but seems to have made quite a stir in its day. It is often referenced in other abolitionist works as a piece that apparently was well-known in its day. It is still interesting reading today, particularly as it represents one of the few early anti-slavery documents written by a black man. Like Garrison, Walker would be denounced vehemently in the South. Walker begins by stating his opinion "that we, (coloured people of these United States,) are the most degraded, wretched, and abject set of beings that ever lived since the world began." So much for Southern claims that the slaves were "happy" and "contented.

He continues with a heartrending call to the tormentors of his people.

> ...I call upon the professing Christians, I call upon the philanthropist, I call upon the very tyrant himself, to show me a page of history, either sacred or profane, on which a verse can be found, which maintains, that the Egyptians heaped the *insupportable insult* upon the children of Israel, by telling them that they were not of the *human family*.... Have they not, after having reduced us to the deplorable condition of slaves under their feet, held us up as descending originally from the tribes of *Monkeys* or *Orang-Outangs*? O! my God! I appeal to every man of feeling—is not this insupportable? Is it not heaping the most gross insult upon our miseries, because they have got us under their feet and we cannot help ourselves? Oh! pity us we pray thee, Lord Jesus, Master.—Has Mr. Jefferson declared to the world, that we are inferior to the whites, both in the endowments of our bodies and our minds? It is indeed surprising, that a man of such great learning, combined with such excellent natural parts, should speak so of a set of men in chains. I do not know what to compare it to, unless, like putting one wild deer in an iron cage, where it will be secured, and hold another by the side of the same, then let it go, and expect the one in the cage to run as fast as the one at liberty.

Walker referred to the classical Roman custom, cited by Jefferson, that "when a master was murdered, all his slaves in the same house, or within hearing, were condemned to death," and argued

> ... had I not rather die, or be put to death, than to be a slave to any tyrant, who takes not only my own, but my wife and children's lives by the inches? Yea, would I meet death with avidity far! far!! in preference to such *servile submission* to the murderous hands of tyrants. Mr. Jefferson's very severe remarks on us have been so extensively argued upon by men whose attainments in literature, I shall never be able to reach, that I would not have meddled with it, were it not to solicit each of my brethren, who has the spirit of a man, to buy a copy of Mr. Jefferson's "Notes on Virginia," and put it in the hand of his son. But let us review Mr. Jefferson's remarks respecting us some further.
> Comparing our miserable fathers, with the learned philosophers of Greece, he says: "Yet notwithstanding these and other discouraging circumstances among the Romans, their slaves were often their rarest artists. They excelled, too, in science, ... but they were of the race of whites. It is not their *condition*, then," [concludes Jefferson], "but *nature*, which has produced the distinction." See this, my brethren!! Do you believe that this assertion is swallowed by millions of whites? Do you know that Mr. Jefferson was one of as great characters as ever lived among the whites? See his writings for the world, and public labours for the United States of America. Do you believe that the assertions of such a man, will pass away into oblivion unobserved by this people and the world? If you do you are much mistaken—See how the American people treat us—have we souls in our bodies? Are we men who have spirits at all?

Walker continued by calling upon the black population, observing

> ... that unless we try to refute Mr. Jefferson's arguments respecting us, we will only establish them....
> I must observe to my brethren that at the close of the first Revolution in this country, with Great Britain, there were but thirteen States in the Union, now there are twenty-four, most of which are slave-holding States, and the whites are dragging us around in chains and in handcuffs, to their new States and Territories to work their mines and farms, to enrich them and their children—and millions of them believing firmly that we being a little darker than they, were made by our Creator to be an inheritance to them and their children for ever—the same as a parcel of *brutes*.
> Are we MEN!!—I ask you, O my brethren—are we MEN?
> Did our Creator make us to be slaves to dust and ashes like ourselves? Are they not dying worms as we are? Have they not to make their appearance before the tribunal of Heaven, to answer for the deeds done in the body, as well as we? Have we any other Master but Jesus Christ alone? Is He not their Master as well as ours?—What right then, have we to obey and call any other Master, but Himself? How we could be so *submissive* to a gang of men..., I never could conceive.... The whites have always been an unjust, jealous, unmerciful, avaricious, and blood-thirsty set of beings, always seeking after power and authority....

> [T]o my no ordinary astonishment, [a] Reverend gentleman got up and told us (coloured people) that slaves must be obedient to their masters—must do their duty to their masters or be whipped—the whip was made for the backs of fools, etc. Here I pause for a moment, to give the world time to consider what was my surprise, to hear such preaching from a minister of my Master, whose very gospel is that of peace and not of blood and whips[.]... American preachers... have newspapers and monthly periodicals, ... on the pages of which, you will scarcely ever find a paragraph respecting slavery, which is ten thousand times more injurious to this country than all the other evils put together; and which will be the final overthrow of its government, unless something is very speedily done; for their cup is nearly full.—Perhaps they will laugh at or make light of this; but I tell you Americans! that unless you speedily alter your course, *you* and *your Country are gone!!!*
>
> ...The Americans say, that we are ungrateful—but I ask them for heaven's sake, what should we be grateful to them for—for murdering our fathers and mothers?—Or do they wish us to return thanks to them for chaining and handcuffing us, branding us, cramming fire down our throats, or for keeping us in slavery, and beating us nearly or quite to death to make us work in ignorance and miseries, to support them and their families. They certainly think that we are a gang of fools.... [D]o slave-holders think that we thank them for keeping us in miseries, and taking our lives by the inches?
>
> Let no man of us budge one step, and let slave-holders come to beat us from our country. America is more our country, than it is the whites—we have enriched it with our *blood and tears*. The greatest riches in all America have arisen from our blood and tears:—and will they drive us from our property and homes, which we have earned with our *blood*? They must look sharp or this very thing will bring swift destruction upon them. The Americans have got so fat on our blood and groans, that they have almost forgotten the God of armies.
>
> Do the colonizationists think to send us off without first being reconciled to us... for the cruelties with which they have afflicted our fathers and us? Do they think to drive us from our country and homes, after having enriched it with our blood and tears, and keep back millions of our dear brethren, sunk in the most barbarous wretchedness, to dig up gold and silver for them and their children? Surely, the Americans must think that we are brutes, as some of them have represented us to be. They think that we do not feel for our brethren, whom they are murdering by the inches, but they are dreadfully deceived.
>
> ...Americans, I do declare to you, while you keep us and our children in bondage, and treat us like brutes, to make us support you and your families, we cannot be your friends....
>
> Treat us like men, and we will be your friends.

These are not the words of a man trying to incite racial hatred. This is a plea for mercy, compassion and simple justice. It's too bad that Southerners were unable to understand Walker's message. Somehow they twisted the words around, convincing themselves—or at least claiming to believe—that if they freed the blacks, they would be endangering their own lives. The blacks were not out for vengeance against the slaveholders, though who could actually have blamed them if they had been? Nowhere in this work does Walker suggest that the whites would be in danger if they emancipated the slaves. To the contrary, he makes it very clear that the danger to the whites lies in perpetuating slavery, not in ending it.

> ... But remember, Americans, that as miserable, wretched, degraded and abject as you have made us in preceding, and in this generation, to support you and your families, that some of you, (whites) on the continent of America, will yet curse the day that you ever were born. You want slaves, and you want us for slaves!!! My colour will yet, root some of you out of the very face of the earth!!!!!! You may doubt it if you please. I know that thousands will doubt—they think they have us so well secured in wretchedness, to them and their children, that it is impossible for such things to occur.
>
> See your Declaration Americans!!! Do you understand your own language? Hear your language, proclaimed to the world, July 4th, 1776—"We hold these truths to be self evident—that ALL MEN ARE CREATED EQUAL!! that they *are endowed by their Creator with certain unalienable rights*; that among these are life, *liberty*, and the pursuit of happiness!!" Compare your own language above, extracted from your Declaration of Independence, with your cruelties and murders inflicted by your cruel and unmerciful fathers and yourselves on our fathers and on us—men who have never given your fathers or you the least provocation!!!!!!

Needless to say, Walker's appeal did not achieve its desired goal of convincing the slaveholders of the legitimacy of the blacks' position.

Instead, Walker succeeded only in giving the Southerners more fuel for the fire. Four black men were arrested in New Orleans for possession of *The Appeal*. The town of Richmond was dismayed to find thirty copies of the work in the home of a black laborer, and dozens of copies were discovered being smuggled into the port of Savannah. The work did little to arouse the charity of the slaveowners, but much to arouse their ire.

The Southern whites, even those who did not own slaves, wanted to have a servile race among them. It freed them from the onus of manual labor. It provided them with a convenient scapegoat for any problems in their society. And by degrading the blacks, the whites elevated their own status.

Despite all their fine rhetoric, one can assume it was the rare Southerner who would have willingly lived without slavery even had an easy solution been available.

In the same month that Walker's appeal appeared, William Lloyd Garrison took over the position of editor for Benjamin Lundy's *Genius of Universal Emancipation,* a Baltimore publication that had been started the year before. While the two men did not always see eye-to-eye, Lundy allowed Garrison a great amount of freedom.

One of the paper's most provocative columns was the "Black List." which made a point of exposing accounts of cruelty to blacks. It was here that Garrison began to show his lack of mercy towards those involved in the slave "business." On November 13, the column carried a report about Austin Woolfolk, who the editor characterized as "the most notorious of the Baltimore Negro-buyers." According to the article, Woolfolk had arranged for a cargo of 75 slaves to be shipped from Baltimore to New Orleans on board the ship *Francis.*

The ship was owned by the merchant Francis Todd of Newburyport, who was not spared Garrison's wrath. "I recollect," he wrote "that it was always a mystery in Newburyport how Mr. Todd contrived to make profitable voyages" when all around him were unable to do so. But the cause now seemed clear. "Any man can gather up riches," continued Garrison, "if he does not care by what means they are obtained."

Having heard what an abolitionist and a black man were saying in 1829, it is interesting to contrast their words with those of a slaveowner and a colonizationist. And not an obscure individual, but none other than Henry Clay of Kentucky. Clay, although a slaveowner all of his life, is usually characterized as being "friendly" towards the blacks.

Clay had the honor of delivering an address to the Colonization Society of Kentucky. The place was Frankfort, and the date was December 17, 1829. No doubt Clay and many of his listeners thought that his words were quite liberal towards the blacks. Yet the speech he made that day is patronizing and bigoted.

He started with the obligatory Southern excuses. Of course, he had to do so to assure his Southern listeners that he and the Colonization Society had no ulterior designs on their property. He reminded his audience that:

> These African slaves... were brought to the colonies now constituting the United States, under the sanction, and by the authority of British laws[.]...
>
> The United States, as a nation, are not responsible for the original introduction, or the subsequent continuance of the slave trade.... Nor are the United States, as a sovereign power, responsible for the continuance of slavery within their limits, posterior to the establishment of their independence; because by neither the articles of confederation, nor by the present constitution, had they power to put an end to it by the adoption of any system of emancipation. But from that epoch the responsibility of the several states in which slavery was tolerated, commenced, and on them devolved the momentous duty of considering whether the evil of African slavery is incurable, or admits of a safe and practicable rem-

edy.... If the question were submitted, whether there should be either immediate or gradual emancipation of all the slaves in the United States, without their removal or colonization, painful as it is to express the opinion, I have no doubt that it would be unwise to do so. For I believe, that the aggregate of the evils which would be engendered in society, upon the supposition of such general emancipation, and of the liberated slaves, remaining promiscuously among us, would be greater than all the evils of slavery, great as they unquestionably are.

Clay took a moment to pay token respect to Southern "diffusionist" ideas of 10 years earlier, though now these ideas seemed to be given a new twist. "If the two descriptions of population [black and white] were equally spread and intermingled over the whole surface of the United States," he said, " their diffusion *might* diminish the danger of their action and corrupting influence upon each other. But... [t]he slaves of the United States are chiefly restricted to one quarter of the Union[.]... Within those limits all our slaves are concentrated, and, within a portion of them, *irresistible causes tend inevitably to their further concentration.*" [emphasis added.] This is an interesting comment coming from someone who had assured his Northern counterparts during the Missouri crisis that the removal of slaves to the new states and territories would hasten their emancipation in the old. Suddenly it was revealed that diffusionism wouldn't work as planned.

Clay took a few moments to placate the consciences of his slaveowning listeners by describing the fine treatment their slaves received at their hands. "The humanity of the slave states of the Union," he claimed, "has prompted them greatly to meliorate the condition of slaves. They are protected in all instances by just laws, from injury, extending to their lives, and in many, from cruelty applied to their persons."

Could Clay have actually believed his own words that the slaves were treated well? It seems highly unlikely. Many Northerners at the time probably knew much less about the actual conditions of slavery than we do today. But Clay was a slaveowner, and his closest associates were slaveowners. Certainly he must have been aware of how horribly many slaves were treated by their masters. Perhaps his inclusion of the conditional clause "in many" was an unconscious admission that things were not, in reality, the way he claimed they were. How else can one accept his further contention that the slaves "are treated with much kindness, and abundantly supplied with substantial food of meat and bread and vegetables, and comfortable clothing, whilst they are moderately tasked in labor."

Clay next proceeded to contrast the systems of free and slave labor. He suggested that with the passage of time, as the value of slaves diminished in comparison to the availability of free laborers, the owning of slaves would no longer be economically feasible. In fact, in his opinion, the only thing that had managed to "sustain the price of slaves in the United States has been, that very fact of the acquisition of Louisiana, but especially the increasing demand for cotton, and the consequent increase of its cultivation."

Clay was certainly correct as far as that went, but he demonstrated his lack of foresight when he predicted that "the multiplication of slaves, by natural causes, must soon be much greater than the increase of the demand for them, to say nothing of the progressive decline which has taken place, in that great Southern staple, within a few years, and which there is no reason to believe will be permanently arrested. Whenever the demand for the cultivation of sugar and cotton comes to be fully supplied, the price of slaves will begin to decline."

Perhaps things would have turned out this way if the demand for cotton had ever been satisfied. But the world's demand for "white gold" seemed to be insatiable. Remember the staggering 18 million pounds of cotton that the South produced in 1800? That number pales in comparison to the production 30 years later: Cotton exports for 1830 came to 300 million pounds, with a net value of over $30 million and accounted for an incredible 41 percent of the exports for the entire nation. It's unclear where Clay got the impression that the demand for cotton was on the decline, but he was grossly mistaken. (In 1860, cotton exports came to 1,700 million pounds, with a worth of $191 million and this single commodity comprised 57 percent of the nation's exports.)

Clay was so sure of his position that he confidently predicted that "adult slaves will, in process of time, sink in value below a hundred dollars each."

"Whenever the price of the adult shall be less than the cost of raising him from infancy," he asked, "what inducement will the proprietor of the parent have to incur that expense?"

Clay was momentarily more frank than the majority of Southerners when he observed that:

> ...it is impossible not to anticipate frequent insurrections among the blacks in the United States.... By the very condition of the relation which subsists between us, we are enemies of each other. They know well the wrongs which their ancestors suffered at the hands of our ancestors, *and the wrong which they believe they continue to endure*..." [Emphasis added. Was Clay suggesting that the blacks only imagined they were being mistreated?]
>
> Happily for us no such insurrection can ever be attended with permanent success, as long as our Union endures. It would be speedily suppressed by the all powerful means of the United States, and it would be the madness of despair in the blacks that should attempt it.... And, after it was put down, what other scenes of military rigor and bloody execu-

tions would not be indispensably necessary to punish the insurgents, and impress their whole race with the influence of a terrible example!

Remember that Clay is generally characterized as being "friendly" towards the blacks, which makes it difficult to contemplate what feelings were entertained by those who were "unfriendly" towards them.

At last he arrived at the purpose of his speech, in which he made very clear the motivations of the Colonization Societies.

> Of all... our population... the free people of color are by far, as a class, the most corrupt, depraved and abandoned.... But, if the reasoning which I have before employed be correct, this class is destined, by voluntary manumission or abandonment, to increase and ultimately perhaps to be more numerous in the United States, than their brethren in bondage, if there be no provision for their removal to another country.
>
> Is there no remedy, I again ask, for the evils of which I have sketched a faint and imperfect picture? Is our posterity doomed to endure forever, not only all the ills flowing from the state of slavery, but all which arise from incongruous elements of population, separated from each other by invincible prejudices, and by natural causes? Whatever may be the character of the remedy proposed, we may confidently pronounce it inadequate, unless it provides... for the total and absolute separation, by an extensive space of water or of land, at least, of the white portion, from that which is free of the colored.

So the truth clearly comes out: The Colonization Society has no desire to free any slaves, only to rid the nation of its unwanted free black population. The Society's "aim is to transport to the Western shores of Africa, from the United States, all such free persons of color as choose to voluntarily to go." Clay would emphatically point out that the group "has constantly disclaimed all intention whatever of interfering in the smallest degree, with the rights of property, or the object of emancipation, gradual or immediate." He again reassured his Southern listeners that the Society "knows that the subject of emancipation belongs exclusively to the several states, in which slavery is tolerated."

He pointed out with obvious pride that

> ...the Legislatures of more than half the States of this enlightened Union, among which I am happy to be able to mention my own, have been pleased to express their approbation of the scheme. It has conciliated the cordial support of the pious clergy of every denomination in the United States.... And the society enrolls amongst its members and patrons, some of the most distinguished men of our country, in its Legislative, Executive, and Judicial councils.
>
> ...All admit the utility of the separation of the free people of colour from the residue of the population of the United States, if it be practi-

cable. It is desirable for them, for the slaves of the United States and for the white race....

Why should such an unfortunate class desire to remain among us? Why should they not wish to go to the country of their forefathers...?

Why, indeed? Perhaps Clay should have read Walker's appeal?

As further proof that the free blacks would be better off leaving the country, Clay points out that the increased presence of them "in our great capitals has given rise to a new crime, perpetrated by unprincipled whites." He quoted from a New York paper:

> "Beware of kidnappers! It is well understood that there is at present in this city, a gang of kidnappers, busily engaged in their vocation of stealing colored children for the Southern market! It is believed that three or four have been stolen within as many days.... Let the public be on their guard." To which the editor... appends the following remarks: "It is still fresh in the memories of all, that a cargo or rather drove of negroes was made up from this city and Philadelphia, about the time that the emancipation of all the negroes in this state took place under our present constitution, and were taken through Virginia, the Carolinas, and Tennessee, and disposed of in the state of Mississippi. Some of those who were taken from Philadelphia were persons of intelligence, and after they had been driven through the country in chains, and disposed of by sale on the Mississippi, wrote back to their friends, and were rescued from bondage."

One should recall John Taylor's warnings at the time of the Missouri controversy: "[I]t is much to be feared that unprincipled wretches will be found kidnapping those who are already free, and transporting and selling the hapless victims into hopeless bondage."

Did Clay recollect these words of his former colleague as he related this news item to his listeners? Did it occur to him that his words and actions at that time were, to a large extent, responsible for the events that he was now reading about in the paper? Or did he find solace in his declaration that "the concurrence is unanimous as to the propriety of the separation of the free colored race, and their removal to some other country?" For how could he be at fault, when all the country was in agreement with him?

He praised the virtuous goals of the Society in the loftiest terms.

> Can a nobler service, in time of peace, be performed by the National flag, than that of transporting under its stars and stripes to the land of their ancestors, the sons of injured Africa, there to enjoy the blessings of our pure religion and a real liberty?...
> We may boldly challenge the annals of human nature for the record of any human plan... which promised more unmixed good, or more comprehensive benificence, than that of African Colonization[.]... Its Benevolent purpose... embraces two of the largest quarters of the earth, and

> the peace and happiness of both of the descriptions of their present inhabitants, with the countless millions of their posterity who are to succeed....
> If we were to invoke the greatest blessing on earth, which Heaven in its mercy, could now bestow on this nation, it would be the separation of the two most numerous races of its population and their comfortable establishment in distinct and distant countries.... [If we are unable to do so] who can contemplate the future without the most awful apprehensions?... The servile wars, the carnage and the crimes which will be its probable consequences, without shuddering with horror?

In Clay's mind, the noblest work that the white man could do in America was to remove the free blacks from its borders. Nowhere does he make it clear how doing so would improve the lot of those blacks left behind in slavery. To the contrary, he has plainly stated that "those" blacks are not his concern, nor that of the Society. The implication seems to be only that those blacks left in bondage would be less dissatisfied with their condition once the presence of free blacks was gone from the country.

It is doubtful that either Garrison or Walker would have agreed with Clay's appraisal of the situation.

He concluded with a few laudatory comments upon the Society and its goals.

> Gentlemen of the Colonization Society of Kentucky! not one word need be added, in conclusion, to animate your perseverance or to stimulate your labors, in the humane cause which you have deliberately espoused. We have reason to believe that we have been hitherto favored, and shall continue to be blessed with the smiles of Providence. Confiding in His approving judgment, and conscious of the benevolence and purity of our intentions, we may fearlessly advance in our great work. And, when we shall, as soon we must, be translated from this into another form of existence, ... we shall there behold the common Father of whites and of blacks, the great Ruler of the Universe, cast His All-seeing eye upon civilized and regenerated Africa, ... and... after dwelling with satisfaction upon the glorious spectacle, He will deign to look with approbation upon us, His humble instruments, who have contributed to produce it[.]

Many honest, well-meaning Americans would agree with Clay and the sentiments within his speech. However, it would not be long before a few brave individuals would be challenging the "lofty" goals of the colonizationists and exposing the racial prejudice that lay beneath their program of social manipulation.

Other events were going on during the year 1829 that also deserve mention. One particular hot spot was Cincinnati, Ohio. While situated in a free state, many of the city's most important commercial ties were across the Ohio River with the slave state of Kentucky. Also, it was common knowledge that many escaped slaves fleeing the South found their way through the Ohio city. In an effort to appease its Southern neighbors, the city began enforcing its 1802 Black Codes, which had been designed to limit the free movement of blacks in the city.

The increased pressure led to a three-day race riot, often referred to as the first such in any American city. As a direct consequence, 460 blacks left the area and traveled through Detroit to Canada. There they established the free black community of Wilberforce. Their presence in Canada would beckon to their enslaved fellows for the next 30 years.

Meanwhile, in Georgia, the Cherokee Indians were about to come under serious government attack. The relocation of the Cherokee to Georgia, which at the time was the "Western Frontier," had begun during Jefferson's administration. In the 20 years since, they had profoundly assimilated white culture; more so, in fact, than any other native American tribe. They dressed like white men, farmed like white men and lived in similar-style homes. In 1821, a Cherokee named Seqouyah had invented the Cherokee syllabary, which rapidly increased the tribe's literacy rate. The publication of the first native American newspaper, *The Cherokee Phoenix*, occurred in 1828.

The Cherokee seemed to be doing everything that the white man could have asked of them. However, there were two factors that were soon to profoundly affect their lives and over which they had no control. First was the rapid influx of white settlers into Georgia, the population of which had increased sixfold between 1790 and 1830. And secondly was the discovery of gold in Cherokee territory in 1828. The Cherokee nation would soon be struggling against the state of Georgia for its very existence.

An obscure, though financially successful, British scientist named James Smithson died in 1829, naming his unmarried nephew, Henry James Hungerford, as sole beneficiary of his estate. There is a stipulation in the will that if Hungerford dies heirless, the money will go to the United States, to be used for the establishment of a scientific institution.

Smithson had never visited America, and it is unclear why he chose to write this stipulation into his will.

October 5, 1829, saw the stage debut in London of 19-year-old Frances ("Fanny") Anne Kemble. The daughter and granddaughter of celebrated British actors, Fanny quickly became one of the darlings of the stage.

Also in 1829, England hosted the celebrated "Raintree" trials, a competition between builders of the newfangled iron horse. This event proved the feasibility of the steam locomotive. The winner was George Stephenson's "The Rockett." Civil War buffs may be interested to know that one of the losing competitors (there were only two others) was an engine called "The Novelty," built by a 26-year-old Swedish inventor named John Ericcson. He would later design the Union ironclad *The Monitor.*

A popular work published in 1829 was *The Frugal Housewife*, by Lydia Maria Child, a domestic advice book that will go through 33 editions in the United States alone. Child had been the publisher since 1826 of *The Juvenile Miscellany*, the nation's first successful children's magazine. This work established Child as one of the nation's most influential women.

The year 1829 saw the death of American jurist John Jay, who had been the first Chief Justice of the Supreme Court, serving from 1789–1795. After his retirement from the court, Jay had been the governor of the state of New York from 1795 until 1800. It was during his administration that the state established its act abolishing slavery that he, as governor, had signed into law.

And in the first clear victory against slavery in North America, Mexico became the first nation on the continent to abolish slavery, much, it must be assumed, to the chagrin of the relocated Americans who were already living in Texas with their property.

THREE

1830

The year's important events began with, of all things, a debate in Congress. A Northern attempt was made to restrict the sale of government lands in the territories, apparently in an effort to slow the migration of slaveowners and their property. The move was immediately assailed by Senator Robert Y. Hayne. His speech brought on a response by Massachusetts Senator Daniel Webster, and the result is referred to as the Hayne-Webster Debates.

Though the topic at hand was ostensibly federal land policy, the combatants would soon engage in the issue of slavery. Webster introduced the topic in his January 20 rejoinder to Hayne's initial criticism. Somehow he worked his way around to "the ordinance of '87.... It fixed forever, the character of the population in the vast regions north-west of the Ohio, by excluding from them involuntary servitude."

"It laid the interdict against personal servitude," he continued, "deeper ... than all local constitutions.... I look upon this original and reasonable provision, as a real good attained."

He spoke also of the advantages which a state such as Ohio had over a state like Kentucky due to the absence of slavery within its boundaries. "I should fear the rebuke of no intelligent gentleman of Kentucky," he suggested, "were I to ask whether if such an ordnance could have been applied to his own state ... he does not suppose it would have contributed to the ultimate greatness of that commonwealth?"

Apparently Webster's expectations were too sanguine, for the next day Hayne provided the rebuke. He seemed to consider Webster's words an affront to the state of Kentucky, to Southern manhood and somehow to his own state of South Carolina. It appears that in the typical Southern manner Hayne seemed to have taken more offense at the remarks than were justified.

> ... In contrasting the state of Ohio with Kentucky, for the purpose of pointing out *the superiority of the former*, and of attributing that superiority to *the existence of slavery* in the one state and its absence in the other, I thought I could discern the *very spirit of the Missouri question* intruded into this debate[.]... Did that gentleman, sir, when he formed the determination to cross the Southern border, in order to invade the state of South Carolina, deem it prudent[?]... Or was it supposed, sir, that, in a premeditated and unprovoked attack upon the South, it was advisable to begin by a gentle admonition of our *supposed weakness*, in order to prevent us from making that firm and manly resistance due to our own character and our dearest interests? Was the *significant hint* of the *weakness of slaveholding states*, when contrasted with *the superior strength of the free states*, like the glare of the weapon half drawn from its scabbard[?]... Mr. President [of the Senate], the impression which has gone abroad of the weakness of the South, as connected to the slave question, exposes us to such constant attacks, has done us so much injury, and is calculated to produce such infinite mischiefs, that I ... declare that we are ready to meet the question promptly and fearlessly....
>
> We are ready to make up the issue with the gentleman, as to the influence of slavery on individual or national character on the prosperity and greatness, either of the United States or of particular states.
>
> Sir, when arraigned before the bar of public opinion, on this charge of slavery, we can stand up with conscious rectitude, plead not guilty, and put ourselves upon God and our country.

What is perhaps most significant here is Hayne's divergence from the typical Southern apologies for slavery. He does not waste time saying what an evil it is and how much he'd like to see it obliterated. Instead, he defends the Southern slaveowner and their institutions. This attitude became more prevalent in Southern speakers in the next few years.

"If slavery, as it now exists in this country, be an evil, we of the present day found it readymade to our hands," he continued. "Finding our lot cast among a people whom God had manifestly committed to our care, we ... met it as a practical situation of *obligation and duty*."

In his view, it seems as though blacks were committed to the magnanimous care of the Southerners, almost as if by divine intervention. "We resolved to make the best of the situation in which Providence had placed us, and to fulfill the high trusts which had devolved upon us as the owners of slaves, in the only way in which such a trust could be fulfilled, without spreading misery and ruin throughout the land."

Apparently, then, slavery was the cross that the Southern states bore for the good of the rest of the union. This hardly explains, however, their constant efforts to spread the institution into new territories and states.

As a good South Carolinian, protective of his state's rights and intolerant of any outside interference, Hayne could not overlook the opportunity to criticize the abolitionists:

> What a commentary of the wisdom, justice, and humanity of the Southern slave owner is presented by the example of certain benevolent associations and charitable individuals *elsewhere*.... [T]hese "friends of humanity" set themselves to work to seduce the slaves of the South from their masters....
>
> And what has been the consequence?... Sir, there does not exist, on the face of the whole earth, a population so poor, so wretched, so vile, so loathsome, so utterly destitute of all the comforts, conveniences, and decencies of life, as the unfortunate blacks of Philadelphia, and New York and Boston. Liberty has been to them the greatest of calamities, the heaviest of curses. Sir, I have had some opportunities of making comparisons between the condition of the free negroes of the North and the slaves of the South, and the comparison has left not only an indelible impression of the superior advantages of the latter, but has gone far to reconcile me to slavery itself.

Hayne took some time to describe the various ways in which the nation had been strengthened and enriched at the expense of the South, emphasizing "how much slave labor has contributed to the wealth and prosperity of the United States, and how largely our Northern brethren have participated in the profits of that Labor." Both of his points were, of course, quite true. The nation had profited from the labors of the slaves, and the North had participated in the benefits. However, neither point should logically have been accepted as a rational for continuing or extending the country's dependence upon slavery.

In the view of the abolitionists, slavery was wrong regardless of who had started it or who was benefiting by it. However, Hayne represented a growing Southern perception of slavery not as a wrong, but as a right. Before long, his attitude would become ascendant in the slave states.

"The naked fact is," he continued, "that the demagogues in the Eastern States, not satisfied *with deriving all the benefit from the Southern section of the Union that they would from so many wealthy colonies* ... have uniformly treated it with outrage, insult, and injury."

Once more, though certainly not for the last time, a Southern speaker found himself "outraged, insulted, and injured," because a Northerner might try to limit the extent of slavery. Hayne warned his listeners that the Southern states had "been so long harassed with the complaints, the restlessness, the turbulence, and the ingratitude of the eastern states, that their patience has been tried almost beyond endurance."

The next point upon which he touched in his rambling discourse was the idea that the Northern (or eastern) states would be expected to rush to the aid of the beleaguered South in the event of a slave uprising.

I know it has been supposed by certain ill-informed persons, that the South exists only be the countenance and protection of the North. Sir, this is the idlest of all idle and ridiculous fancies that ever entered into the mind of man. In every, state of the Union, except one, the free white population actually preponderates; while in the British West India Islands, (where the average white population is less than ten per cent. of the whole,) the slaves are kept in entire subjection: *it is preposterous to suppose that the Southern States could ever find the smallest difficulty in this respect.* [Emphasis added.]

On this subject as in all others, we ask nothing of our Northern brethren but to "let us alone." Leave us to the undisturbed management of our domestic concerns, and the direction of our own industry, and we will ask no more. Sir, all our difficulties on this subject have arisen from interference from abroad[.]

This is a very fine piece of fallacious reasoning when one takes the time to examine it. First, it begins with an arrogant tone of bravado, emphatically declaring that the South would never have any difficulty in controlling its slaves. This is immediately followed by a plea to be left alone—obviously implying that if not left alone, trouble could arise. If the slaveowners were indeed as in control as they bragged, why did they fear outside interference so much? What was it about a small group of abolitionists that frightened them so much? The obvious conclusion is that Southerners such as Hayne knew that their so-called "control" was tenuous, at best, and it could be easily disrupted.

Another interesting point is that the speaker seems to have forgotten the cause of his speech. No motion had been suggested to "disturb" their domestic concerns. The idea being debated was a Northern attempt to discourage the spread of slavery, not to assault the institution in the states where it already existed. Why was every Northern attempt to control the spread of slavery viewed by the South as an attack upon the slave states themselves?

Hayne soon returned to his criticism of the abolitionists. "There is a spirit," he claimed, "which, like the father of evil, is constantly 'walking to and fro about the earth, seeking whom it may devour:' it is the spirit of FALSE PHILANTHROPY. The persons who it possesses ... are employed in lighting up the torches of discord throughout the community. Their first principle of action is to leave their own affairs ... [in order] to regulate the affairs and duties of others."

"It is a spirit which has long been busy with the slaves of the South," he argued. "It is this spirit which has filled the Land with thousands of wild and visionary projects, which can have no effect but to waste the energies and dissipate the resources of the country."

At last, he concluded his speech by quoting the British statesman Edmond Burke. According to Burke, the principles of devotion to liberty were most highly elevated in a slaveholding society. Hayne quoted from Burke's speech of March 22, 1775, in which he said the following:

> There is a circumstance attending the Southern colonies which makes the spirit of liberty still more high and haughty than in those to the northward. It is, that in Virginia and the Carolinas they have a vast multitude of slaves. Where this is the case, in any part of the world, those who are free are by far the most proud and jealous of their freedom. Freedom is to them not only an enjoyment, but a kind of rank and privilege.... [T]hese people of the Southern colonies are much more strongly ... attached to liberty than those to the northward.... [A]nd such will be all masters of slaves who are not slaves themselves. In such a people, the haughtiness of domination combines with the spirit of freedom, fortifies it, *and renders it invincible.*

What a sad commentary upon freedom and liberty to think that such ideals could only be fully realized through the enslavement of others. While certainly not the belief of all Southerners—and, one would hope, not even of most Southerners—it was becoming increasingly obvious that this was the belief of that portion of the Southern population that wielded the most control and influence.

Five days later, Webster gave his response. He began by readdressing the issue of the Northwest Ordinance:

> I spoke, Sir, of the Ordinance of 1787, which prohibits slavery, ... as a measure of great wisdom and foresight, and one which had been attended with highly beneficial and permanent consequences. I supposed that, on this point, no two gentlemen in the Senate could entertain different opinions. But the simple expression of this sentiment has led the gentleman, not only into a labored defence of slavery, in the abstract, and on principle, but also a warm accusation against me, as having attacked the system of domestic slavery now existing in the Southern States.... I did not utter a single word which any ingenuity could torture into an attack on the slavery of the South....
>
> And yet, ... [h]e represents me as making an onset on the whole South, and manifesting a spirit which would interfere with, and disturb, their domestic condition!
>
> ... I know full well, that it is, and has been, the settled policy of some persons in the South, for years, to represent the people of the North as disposed to interfere with them in their own exclusive and peculiar concerns. This is a delicate and sensitive point in Southern feeling[.]... This feeling ... is a lever of great power in our political machine.... There is not, and never has been, a disposition in the North to interfere with the interests of the South. Such interference has never been supposed to be within the power of government; nor has it in any way been attempted.... The gentleman, indeed, argues that slavery, in the abstract, is no evil. Most assuredly I need not say I differ with him, altogether and most widely, on that point. I regard domestic slavery as one of the greatest evils, both moral and political. But ... whether it be curable, and if so, by what

means;... I leave it to those whose right and duty it is to inquire and to decide. And this I believe, Sir, is, and uniformly has been, the sentiment of the North.

Webster took the time to retell the story of the Congressional debate of 1790, which ended with the resolutions that forbid the federal government from interfering with slavery. "From that day to this it has never been maintained or contended at the North, that Congress had any authority to regulate or interfere with the condition of slaves in the several States. No Northern gentleman, to my knowledge, has moved any such question in either House of Congress."

To fully appreciate the depth of these words, it is crucial to understand the difference between those like Webster who were anti-slavery and that small group of Northerners who were actually abolitionists. Webster's feelings on the subject were probably fairly typical of the majority of Northerners. He was personally appalled by the concept of slavery and found it extremely difficult to accept it in a republic that had been founded upon freedom and liberty. And yet, as a lawyer, he recognized the political justice of the South's position. Like Abraham Lincoln a generation later, Webster and others like him sincerely believed that they had no business interfering in the South's "domestic" affairs.

What was their business, however, was to try to prevent the spread of the contagion to other parts of the country. If they were able to keep the foul disease contained, it would be less of a blot on the national record. However, Webster, like Hayne, must have known that containing it would, indirectly, weaken it in those states where it already existed. Slavery needed new territories to expand into in order to thrive.

Unfortunately, the anti-slavery men found themselves in a very awkward position. While sincerely deploring the existence of slavery, they were unable, and politically unwilling, to attack the institution directly. They had to pretend to believe that they were not attacking it as they attempted to restrict it. Such ambiguity weakened their stand against slavery, and its obvious transparency infuriated the slaveholders of the South.

In the end, all of their arguments and political ploys became so many empty gestures. What they lacked was the courage to boldly declare that slavery needed to be dealt with.

It would be up to men like Garrison to recognize the fact that anti-slavery positions such as Webster's were ineffective. They would be the ones to boldly defy the slave interests. In doing so, they would initially earn the displeasure of not only the pro-slavery Southerners, but also that of many of the well-meaning anti-slavery men like Webster who should have been their allies. Their crusade to replace anti-slavery with abolitionism would not be an easy one, but it was a necessary, albeit painful, step for the country to take.

Webster followed up his remarks upon the 1790 Resolutions by observing that the "fears of the South ... were allayed and quieted ... till ... it became necessary, or was thought so, by some political persons, to find an unvarying ground for the exclusion of Northern men from confidence and from lead in the affairs of the republic." In other words, the South was using its defense of slavery as an excuse to retain its control of the country.

Webster was well aware of how much the South had dominated the national government in the young republic's history. Now it was the North's turn to take control of the ship of state. But the South was unwilling to relinquish the helm. "[T]he cry was raised," complained Webster, "that the influence of Northern men in the public counsels would undoubtedly endanger the relation of master and slave."

He was being less than candid when he declared "domestic slavery of the Southern States I leave where I find it,—in the hands of their own governments. It is their affair, not mine." If the free states had indeed wielded the proportionate amount of influence that their population warranted, slavery would be endangered.

But they did not wield their due influence. "Nor do I complain of the peculiar effect which the magnitude of that population has had in the distribution of power under this federal government," Webster said. "We know, Sir, that the representation of the States in the other house is not equal. We know that great advantage in that respect is enjoyed by the slaveholding States."

But Webster was in a mood to be conciliatory. "Nevertheless, I do not complain[.]... It is the original bargain, ... let it stand[.]... The Union itself is too full of benefit to be hazarded in propositions for changing its original basis. I go for the Constitution as it is, and for the Union as it is."

It would be unfair to Webster's reputation and dishonest to the historical record if the impression were left that the main theme of this speech was slavery. It was not. Webster's main goal was to discredit the South Carolina Exposition of 1828, and to focus the issue on the nature and interpretation of the union and the Constitution. That he did so admirably is recognized by most historians of the period. Though these issues are secondary to the focus of this volume, familiarity with them is essential to an understanding of the upcoming national conflict. For the benefit of his listeners, Webster offered:

> ... to inquire into the origin of this [National] government and the source of its power. Whose agent is it? Is it the creature of the State leg-

islatures, or the creature of the people? If the government of the United States be the agent of the State governments, then they may control it, provided they can agree in the manner of controlling it; if it be the agent of the people, then the people alone control it, restrain it, modify, or reform it. It is observable enough, that the doctrine for which the honorable gentleman contends leads him to the necessity of maintaining, not only that this general government is the creature of the States, but that it is the creature of each of the States severally, so that each may assert the power for itself of determining whether it acts within the limits of its authority. It is the servant of four-and-twenty masters, of different wills and different purposes, and yet bound to all. This absurdity (for it seems no less) arises from a misconception as to the origin of this government and its true character. It is, Sir, the people's Constitution, the people's government, made for the people, made by the people, and answerable to the people. The people of the United States have declared that the Constitution shall be the supreme law. We must either admit the proposition, or dispute their authority. The States are, unquestionably, sovereign, so far as their sovereignty is not affected by this supreme law. But the State legislatures, as political bodies, however sovereign, are yet not sovereign over the people.... We are all agents of the same supreme power, the people.

He discussed in brief the presumed rights of the states as derived from the Virginia Resolutions of 1798, and, by implication, those rights that the South Carolina Exposition and Protest seemed to grant to each state:)

I must now beg to ask, Sir, Whence is this supposed right of the States derived? Where do they find the power to interfere with the laws of the Union? Sir, the opinion which the honorable gentleman maintains is a notion founded in a total misapprehension, in my judgment, of the origin of this government, and of the foundation on which it stands. I hold it to be a popular government, erected by the people; those who administer it, responsible to the people; and itself capable of being amended and modified, just as the people may choose it should be.... It has its own powers; [the State governments] have theirs. There is no more authority with them to arrest the operation of a law of Congress, than with Congress to arrest the operation of their laws. We are here to administer a Constitution emanating immediately from the people, and trusted by them to our administration. It is not the creature of the State governments....

Sir, the very chief end, the main design, for which the whole Constitution was framed and adopted, was to establish a government that should not be obliged to act through State agency, or depend on State opinion and State discretion. The people had had quite enough of that kind of government under the Confederation.... Are we yet at the mercy of State discretion and State construction? Sir, if we are, then vain will be our attempt to maintain the Constitution under which we sit.

... The Constitution [established its own authority by] declaring, Sir, that *"the Constitution, and the laws of the United States made in pursuance*

> *thereof, shall be the supreme law of the land, any thing in the constitution or laws of any State to the contrary notwithstanding."*
> ... By this the supremacy of the Constitution and laws of the United States is declared.... No State law is to be valid which comes in conflict with the Constitution....
> For myself, Sir, I do not admit the competency of South Carolina, or any other State, to prescribe my constitutional duty; or to settle, between me and the people, the validity of laws of Congress, for which I have voted. I decline her umpirage. I have not sworn to support the Constitution according to her construction of its clauses.... And, Sir, if we look to the general nature of the case, could any thing have been more preposterous, than to make a government for the whole Union, and yet leave its powers subject, not to one interpretation, but to thirteen or twenty-four interpretations?... [S]hall constitutional questions be left to four-and-twenty popular bodies, each at liberty to decide for itself, and none bound to respect the decisions of the others[?]

Again and again, these ideas would echo across the country in the next 30 years. The concepts that Webster herein elaborated would become the underlying foundation for the political beliefs of an entire generation of men. These men would someday be willing to march off to war to defend the union that Webster had so eloquently described, and who would wholeheartedly agree with Webster's stirring closing sentiments:

> While the Union lasts, we have high, exciting, gratifying prospects spread out before us, for us and our children.... When my eyes shall be turned to behold for the last time the sun in the heaven, may I not see him shining on the broken and dishonored fragments of a once glorious Union; on States dissevered, discordant, belligerent; on a land rent with civil feuds, or drenched, it may be, in fraternal blood! Let their last feeble and lingering glance rather behold the gorgeous ensign of the republic, now known and honored throughout the earth, still full high advanced, its arms and trophies streaming in their original lustre, not a stripe erased or polluted, nor a single star obscured, bearing for its motto ... those ... words of delusion and folly, "Liberty first and Union afterwards"; but everywhere, spread all over in characters of living light, blazing on all its ample folds, as they float over the sea and over the land, and in every wind under the heavens, that other sentiment, dear to every true American heart,—*Liberty and Union, now and for ever, one and inseparable!*

The impact of Webster's words can not be overemphasized. It was probably the most widely read and most influential political statement of its time. Within three months, over 40,000 copies were published and distributed in pamphlet form, along with numerous other editions and reprintings in newspapers. It established Webster's identity as the spokesman of the nation.

But it did more than just that. It also cemented the concept of union in the minds of an entire generation. Prior to Webster's speech, the nation was referred to "these United States of America." It had now become, for the majority of the nation, the very singular "the United States of America."

Meanwhile, William Lloyd Garrison and his partner, Benjamin Lundy, were undecided as to how much attention they should devote to Walker's appeal. Lundy was hesitant to even dignify noticing it for fear of stirring up resentment. Garrison, it can only be assumed, was deeply moved by its message. "We have had this pamphlet on our table for some time past," he would write in the *Genius of Universal Emancipation*, "and are not surprised at its effect upon our sensitive Southern brethren. It is written by a colored Bostonian, and breathes the most impassioned and determined spirit. We deprecate its circulation, though we cannot but wonder at the bravery and intelligence of its author."

He would later write that the "circulation of [Walker's pamphlet] has proven one thing conclusively—that the boasted security of the slave States … is mere affectation, or something worse."

Garrison and Walker would both soon be under attack as a period of fierce persecution of those expressing abolitionist views soon commenced. Both the governor of Georgia and the mayor of Savannah had written to Harrison Gray Otis, the mayor of Boston, demanding that Walker and his pamphlet be suppressed after copies had made their way into the Southern city. Gray responded that Walker had broken no laws and that "the book had caused no excitement in Boston."

Excitement was high in the South. A reward was posted for the delivery of Walker to Savannah—dead or alive. Laws were passed making it illegal to distribute anti-slavery literature in many parts of the South.

Garrison came under attack in February when he and Lundy were indicted by a grand jury on the charge that they had published "a gross and malicious libel against Francis Todd" in relation to Garrison's "Black List" article of the previous year. Todd sought damages of $5,000.

The trial began in March. A young Baltimore lawyer named Charles Mitchell volunteered to handle their case pro bono. It should have been an easy one. Maryland's libel laws, dating back to 1804 and rarely used, recognized "the truth" of a statement as a "good" defense, thereby protecting the power of the press. All Mitchell should have needed to establish was that the facts, as reported in the *Genius*, were correct. However, things did not turn out quite that way.

Mitchell's first order of business was to show that Lundy had not even been in town when the offending article went to press. The court therefore agreed to continuing the charges against him indefinitely. They were never brought up again. For all intents and purposes, the trial was against Garrison alone.

And Garrison, through his editorials, had already managed to anger a number of prominent people in the state, including chief judge Nicholas Brice, who had assigned himself to the case. Garrison would always contend that the charges against him were politically motivated, and in view of the proceedings of the trial, it's difficult to question his assessment.

A few witnesses were called on the behalf of the prosecution. Their testimony did little but verify the accuracy of Garrison's claims. However, in a flagrant disregard of the specific charges, Judge Brice managed to turn the case into a general assault upon Garrison and his anti-slavery views. Over Mitchell's objections, Brice allowed Todd's lawyers to introduce passages from the *Genius* that had nothing to do with the libel charges at hand. The intention was to show how "fanatic and virulent" the publication was. The argument was made that the *Genius* (and, by implication, Garrison as well) should be placed under "wholesome restraint" as being a risk to the (slaveholding) community. When charging the jury to make their decision, Judge Brice welcomed them to "derive auxiliary aid" from the additional material that had been introduced.

It took the jury only fifteen minutes to return a guilty verdict.

The next few weeks were filled with fruitless appeals on Garrison's behalf. Ultimately he was sentenced to six month's jail time, or fines and court costs totaling $70. It is unlikely that Garrison would have paid the fines even had he been able to afford them. Therefore, on April 17, 1830, he entered the Baltimore jail becoming the first martyr to abolitionism. However, as the next few years would abundantly demonstrate, he would certainly not be the last.

While in jail, Garrison passed the time by writing a report of the trial, which, interestingly had not been covered in the local press. This report was published by Lundy in pamphlet form and widely circulated. Eventually it caught the attention of wealthy New York businessman and philanthropist Arthur Tappan, who wrote to Lundy:

> I have read the sketch of the trial of Mr. Garrison with that deep feeling of abhorrence of slavery and its abettors which every one must feel who [appreciates] the blessings of liberty. If one hundred dollars will give him his liberty, you are hereby authorized to draw on me for that sum, and I will gladly make a further donation of the same amount to aid you and Mr. G. in re-establishing the *Genius of Universal Emancipation* as published by you previous to its assuming the pamphlet form. Such a paper is much needed to hold up to American freemen, in all its naked deformity, the subject of slavery as it now exists in our country; and I earnestly hope you will find encouragement to resume it and to give it a wide circulation.

The introduction of Arthur Tappan into the abolitionist camp was a significant one. Tappan and his equally wealthy brother Lewis would soon be significant names in the abolitionist movement, often financing many of its endeavors. Their names will come up again and again over the next few years.

The manner in which Tappan's involvement was secured is also significant, as it would set a pattern repeated over and over again throughout the years ahead. Each time the supporters of slavery overplayed their hand by coming down heavily on the abolitionists, more people joined the ranks of the abolitionists. Over time, the persecution of the abolitionists came to be seen by the typical Northerner as attempts by the South to abridge or restrict Northern white rights, which had a fair degree of truth to it.

The backlash in the North against the South's "offended righteousness" probably did more to expose slavery and its ruthlessness than the abolitionists could ever have hoped to accomplish on their own. As the South attempted vainly to tighten its grip on the peculiar institution, the common Northerner came less to view the abolitionists as "the bad guys." Despite its much vaunted claims of freedom and liberty, the South came to be seen as a totalitarian state that would not allow any criticism of its domestic institutions.

Early in June, after having served just a month and a half of his sentence, Garrison's release was secured by Arthur Tappan's generous donation. However, the trial and its results spelled the death knell for the *Genius of Universal Emancipation*. Lundy was no longer interested in being involved in the kind of criticisms and unrest on which Garrison seemed to thrive.

The two parted company, and Garrison relocated to Boston where he went into partnership with Isaac Knapp. The periodical that these two would release the following year would set the country ablaze.

On June 28, 34-year-old David Walker died quite unexpectedly. Most modern sources state that the cause was a sudden illness. However, in her book *The Martyr Age of the United States*, published in 1839, British author Harriet Martineau claimed that Walker "was found murdered near his own door; but whether he had been assassinated for his book, or had been fatally wounded in a fray, is not known." Martineau, who traveled extensively in the United States in the years 1834 through 1836, had come to know many of the more prominent abolitionists personally. Presumably, she was acquainted with the details of Walker's death from those who were in a position to know.

Whatever the cause of his demise, it is generally acknowledged that many members of Boston's small free black community thought that his death was very suspicious. However, local authorities refused to investigate, and history will never know the truth. In any event, the words which he had published in his appeal would outlive him.

Though the results had not yet been tabulated by the end of the year, 1830 was a census year. The North's free population of 7,008,831 was barely effected by the 3,577 slaves still residing therein. Augmented by the Constitution's three-fifths rules, its "adjusted" population of 7,010,977 entitled the region to 142 seats in the House of Representatives.

The South's free population of 3,789,669—barely more than half of the North's—was swelled by the 1,983,862 slaves within its borders. That region's "adjusted" population came to 4,979,986, earning it 100 seats in the House. Twenty-four of those seats, a fourth of the total, represented the mute voice of the downtrodden slaves. If the South had been deprived of those additional 24 votes, it is unlikely it could have protected slavery from a concerted attack from the North.

The 1830 census demonstrated that America was still primarily an agricultural country since farmers outnumbered city dwellers by about ten to one. However, within the next decade, the urbanization of the population would take tremendous strides. By 1840, the ratio had been reduced to just five to one. And, by 1850, the population of towns of 8,000 or more had nearly doubled that of 1830.

There were, however, ominous signs that year of more problems yet to come. Americans were continuing to emigrate to Texas. Many of them came with their domestic property, despite the fact that the Mexican government had abolished slavery in the previous year. Alarmed by the increasing numbers of Americans and slaves within its borders, the Mexican government passed legislation in April forbidding further U.S. emigration into Texas. Thus was planted the first seeds of independence among Texans that would ultimately embroil the United States in conflict with its neighbor.

In the same month, at the Jefferson Day banquet in Washington D.C., president Andrew Jackson would pay homage to Webster's celebrated speech by toasting "Our Federal Union: It must be preserved." Vice President John C. Calhoun, who had not yet revealed his identity as the author of the South Carolina Exposition, responded by toasting to "The Union: Next to our Liberty the most dear; may we all remember that it can only be preserved by respecting the rights of the states."

In May 1830, bowing to the pressure of land- and gold-hungry Georgians, Congress approved the Indian Removal bill. (The bill was carried by a vote of 102 to 97. Needless to say, the close five-vote majority was decided by the South's extra 24 "slave" representatives.) This bill provided for the forced removal of the Cherokees from their homes. They would be relocated against their wishes west of the Mississippi River.

In September, former president John Quincy Adams was surprised when the residents of Plymouth, Massachusetts asked to be allowed to enter his name as a candidate for the House of Representatives. Adams was 63-years old and had never planned on returning to a public position. He reluctantly agreed to serve them if that was indeed their desire, but refused to campaign for the position.

Of the 2,565 votes cast in the 22-town district, he received 1,817. He agreed to the position on the terms that he would hold himself "accountable to no one party and to no one section." His only loyalty would be to his own conscience. The voters accepted him on his terms and continued to reelect him under the same conditions. He would serve as their representative for the next 18 years. During that time, he would fill the role of one of the great unsung heroes of freedom and the anti-slavery movement. His brightest moments were still ahead of him.

Twenty-two-year-old Angelina Grimké decided to leave her home in Charleston, South Carolina, and join her 38-year-old sister, Sarah, who had been living in Philadelphia since 1821. The Grimkes were the daughters of Judge John Faucheraud Grimké, who had died shortly before Sarah's move to the North. Their father had been an influential plantation owner, and both girls had grown up fully immersed in a pro-slavery atmosphere. Neither girl, however, had ever been comfortable with the South's "peculiar institution." Their failure to accept slavery was responsible both for their abandonment of their home in South Carolina and their independent decisions to become Quakers.

The less-oppressive atmosphere of Philadelphia allowed each woman to examine their anti-slavery tendencies more fully. They would be but patient observers of the abolition movement for a few years before committing themselves fully to the cause.

The first American built locomotive, Peter Cooper's "Tom Thumb," was built and tested. Its trial run was held on August 28 over a 13-mile course between Baltimore and Ellicott Mills. An impromptu race soon developed between the locomotive and a challenging horse-drawn railroad carriage. The horse won due to a mechanical breakdown of the locomotive. Despite this inauspicious beginning, America's love of the railroad was about to reach full steam.

The country had a scant 73 miles of railroad, with all but three of those in Pennsylvania. This contrasted with a canal system totaling 1,277 miles. New York led the nation with 546 of those miles. However, this was also the year that Robert L. Stevens would invent the "T-rail" and the iron tongue needed to connect them, both of which would become standard elements of railroad tracks. His humble innovations would be crucial to the development of a soon-to be burgeoning railroad industry.

Four

1831

Saturday, January 1 was the date of the first issue of William Lloyd Garrison's *The Liberator*. It would be published as a weekly newspaper, without interruption, for the next 35 years. It would not cease publication until December 1865, after the ratification of the Thirteenth Amendment that finally abolished slavery in the United States. It staggers the imagination to think of one man devoting such a long period of his life to such a single purpose.

There would be many changes in the abolitionist movement during that period, not all of which Garrison would agree with. Occasionally he would support other movements besides abolition, which often alienated his supporters. Yet never during that time did he waver in his determination that the slaves needed to be freed.

Much has been written about the religious fanaticism of the abolitionists; as if their singleminded devotion to their calling cannot be explained any other way. It is likely their strong religious convictions were often all that sustained them in their thankless and unpopular crusade.

But to attempt to suggest—as their Southern (and many modern-day) detractors often would—that their behavior was somehow aberrant or lunatic seems patently unfair to them.

To try to ascribe a single set of values or motivations to the abolitionists is as fruitless as it would be to try to describe all slaveowners as being identically molded. Each followed his own conscience and his own beliefs. Yet with no notable exceptions, it can be emphatically stated that the Abolitionists believed strongly and sincerely in what they were doing. They must have, to endure what they did in support of the poor slaves.

It is also important to remember that Garrison, like the majority of the abolitionists, was a pacifist. He believed in persuading the South to abandon slavery through arguments and logic, not through violence or terror. His words were never intended to incite servile insurrection, though the charge that he was responsible for much of the violence and unrest in the South has followed him even up to the present day.

He has even been accused of being the cause of problems that never occurred. One of the most pernicious of the pro-slavery arguments was the idea of "Negro Retribution." According to the argument, if the blacks were given their freedom as the abolitionists advocated, they would band together and scour the countryside, wreaking vengeance upon their former tormentors.

Historian Page Smith in *The Nation Comes of Age*, (1981) voices a common and oft-repeated theme when he insists that of all the fears of the South "the most terrible possibility of all, one that haunted the dreams of all Southerners and which *Garrison and other abolitionists did their best to cultivate* [emphasis added] [was] that the freed slaves would turn against their former masters and mistresses and murder them by the tens of thousands."

Though undoubtedly the Southern slaveowners would have agreed with these words of Dr. Smith, there appears to be no historical justification for placing the responsibility of this myth upon the shoulders of the abolitionists.

Where in their words is there a call for such vengeance? Not in Walker's *Appeal*. Certainly not from Garrison, the pacifist. Their words often painted a lurid picture of what would happen if the enslaved blacks were not given their freedom, but nowhere is evidence within their writings of any threat to former slaveowners from their emancipated charges. Nor is there any record of an emancipated black returning to "even the score" with his former master.

So why did the Southerners believe that the blacks would band against them if given an opportunity? If this fear was indeed as acute as Dr. Smith implies, what was its source, since it was not in the abolitionists? Ironically, its seeds seem to lie in the South itself. While it is difficult to trace directly, there are a few clues available.

One comes from Jefferson's *Notes on Virginia*. It was Jefferson who, with absolutely no corroborating evidence, emphatically pronounced that "ten thousand recollections, by the blacks, of the injuries they have sustained ... will divide us into parties, and produce convulsions which will probably never end but in the extermination of the one or the other race."

To a generation of Southern gentlemen who were weaned on the wisdom of the "Sage of Monticello," it was enough to know that Jefferson had said it was so, so it must be so.

Another comes from the record of previous slave insurrections, such as the aborted Denmark Vesey revolt of 1822. While the rebellion was ostensibly a "slave" uprising, the primary mover in the plan was a freedman. In the eyes of the slaveowners, it appeared that, having gained his release from thralldom, his intention now was to lead his enslaved fellows for revenge. Such a misconception of the facts says much about Southern paranoia. It would appear almost indisputable that Vesey's motivation was not revenge, but primarily, if not exclusively, an attempt to succor his less fortunate brethren. Had there been no slaves, there would have been no attempted uprisings.

The pro-slavery Southerners seemed to have missed the simple logic of this: that the only sure way to prevent slave uprisings was to eliminate slavery. Instead, the response was to try to eliminate the interfering freedmen (and abolitionists) who were trying to free the slaves. This is why black codes became more and more oppressive as the years passed. This is why the Colonization Societies were so popular in the South. And this is why the abolitionists and their messages were so vilified in the South.

Yet another clue seems to be in the record of Saint-Domingue. But again, the whites misinterpreted the information that was available to them, and failed to profit from the mistakes of others. While there is no denying that the death and destruction that resulted from the Haiti slave uprising was catastrophic, the South viewed this as the inevitable consequence of the slaves gaining their freedom.

But the whites had not freed their slaves; in fact, they had continued to repress the blacks even after revolutionary sentiments had been introduced into the island. The violence in Haiti was the struggle of revolutionaries fighting for their liberty. Had the controlling white colonists extended to the blacks those freedoms which they felt themselves entitled to, perhaps the violence would have been avoided.

The blacks on Haiti had slaughtered whites not because they had been given their freedom, but because it had been denied to them. This was the lesson which the South should have learned from Haiti.

Additionally, it would be hard to argue against the value of this "Negro Retribution" myth as a self-serving tool. What better excuse to deny granting freedom to the slaves than to convince others that there was danger in doing so? While it would be difficult to contend that slaveowners consciously fabricated the retribution hypothesis to further their control over blacks, it seems incontestable that it served that purpose.

Finally, the whites' deep-seated racial prejudices prevented them from seeing blacks as rational beings. Viewing the blacks more as brutes than men, they assumed that the only behavior they could expect from them was violence. Jefferson's "wolf by the ears" analogy had become too much a part of the Southern mentality to be questioned. Obviously, it appeared, that if you let the beast go, it will attack you. Therefore, self-preservation demanded that you tighten your grip. It did not enter the Southern consciousness that if you released the beast, it might peaceably go about its own business without ever molesting its former tormentor.

Dr. Smith's opinion notwithstanding, it was the slave masters and mistresses (and, it would seem, the historians who have promulgated their version of the story) who cultivated and encouraged this vision of racial destruction, not the abolitionists. While the abolitionists may have inspired slaves to resistance that ultimately proved dangerous to Southern whites, one cannot claim that acts of violence were their primary motives (The possible exception being the latter-day fanatic John Brown).

Writing from Boston in that very first issue of *The Liberator*, Garrison declared that he was "determined, at every hazard, to lift up the standard of emancipation in the eyes of the nation," literally "within sight of Bunker Hill and in the birth place of liberty. That standard is now unfurled." He vowed to continue "till every chain be broken, and every bondsman set free! Let Southern oppressors tremble, let their secret abettors tremble—let their Northern apologists tremble—let all the enemies of the persecuted blacks tremble."

> Assenting to the "self-evident truth" maintained in the American Declaration of Independence, "that all men are created equal, and endowed by their Creator with certain inalienable rights—among which are life, liberty, and the pursuit of happiness," I shall strenuously contend for the immediate enfranchisement of our slave population. In Park Street Church, on the Fourth of July, 1829, in an address on slavery, I unreflectingly assented to the popular but pernicious doctrine of gradual abolition. I seize this opportunity to make a full and unequivocal recantation, and thus publicly to ask pardon of my God, of my country, and of my brethren the poor slaves, for having uttered a sentiment so full of timidity, injustice and absurdity....
>
> I am aware, that many object to the severity of my language, but is there not cause for severity? I will be as harsh as truth, and as uncompromising as justice. On this subject, I do not wish to think, or speak, or write, with moderation. No! no! Tell a man whose house is on fire, to give a moderate alarm; tell him to moderately rescue his wife from the hands of the ravisher; tell the mother to gradually extricate her babe from the fire into which it has fallen;—but urge me not to use moderation in a cause like the present. I am in earnest—I will not equivocate—I will not excuse—I will not retreat a single inch—and I will be heard....
>
> It is pretended, that I am retarding the cause of emancipation by the coarseness of my invective, and the precipitancy of my measures. The charge is not true. On this question my influence,—humble as it is,—is felt at this moment to a considerable extent, and shall be felt in coming years—not perniciously, but beneficially—not as a curse, but as a blessing; and posterity will bear testimony that I was right.

Four • 1831

It would be interesting to know exact figures on the *Liberator*'s press run. Dr. Smith—who does not seem to be overly sympathetic towards the abolitionists in general, or Garrison in particular—claims that during "its first year... [*The Liberator*] had [only] six subscribers; the next year, fifty-three." In view of how notoriously well known Garrison and his paper soon became, these figures appear unrealistic.

Henry Mayer, who has written a complimentary biography of Garrison, claims that "Black subscribers [in Boston] proved to be the sustaining force of *The Liberator's* first year, with over five hundred subscriptions sold by midsummer." Mayer further claims that "*The Liberator* could boast the names of forty-seven agents on its masthead and several thousand subscribers ... by spring 1832," its second year of publication. It can only be assumed that readership, as in the case of most printed material in those days, was extended beyond just those who purchased it. Additionally, Southern efforts to repress his message quite often had the exact opposite effect, as is so often the case with censorship.

One way or another, Garrison was beginning to get noticed.

However, as the warm summer months waned, it was not the abolitionists that posed the biggest threat to the security of the South. In the early morning hours of August 22, the illusion of safety was brutally torn from the eyes of the slaveholding South, as, for a short but frightening period of time, it appeared that the "most terrible possibility of all" had become a reality. On that morning, a band of eight slaves, led by a black lay preacher named Nat Turner, initiated a reign of terror in Southampton County, Virginia, as they systematically combed the countryside for victims. Their numbers soon swelled to over 60. During a 36-hour period, the band was responsible for the deaths of 55 or more whites, many of them women and children.

Most of the violence occurred around the small town of Jerusalem, Virginia, about 70 miles east of Richmond. As terrified citizens huddled together, militia units from surrounding counties arrived in the area. By August 31, almost all of the insurgents had been captured except for Turner himself. Armed vigilante groups began combing the countryside. Untold hundreds of blacks, many with no connection to Turner or the incident, were brutally murdered. One man bragged that he had personally slaughtered over a dozen blacks.

At about the same time, independent of events in Southampton, plans were being developed in New Haven, Connecticut, to assist the much-maligned free blacks of the North. Simeon Jocelyn was the white pastor of a black congregation. Having briefly attended Yale, which did not enroll black students, Jocelyn saw the need for a black college. He envisioned an institution that would allow free blacks to "cultivate habits of industry and obtain a useful mechanical or agricultural profession, while pursuing classical studies." He had enlisted the aid of Arthur and Lewis Tappan who had purchased land in the Southern part of New Haven with the intention of establishing what would be the country's first institution of higher education for blacks.

Announced on September 7, 1831, this plan met almost immediate public disapproval. Mayor Dennis Kimberly (an 1812 Yale graduate) called a town meeting at city hall to be held on September 10. A 13-member committee was hastily assembled to present resolutions at the meeting opposing the plans.

"So great was the interest to hear the discussions," reported the *New Haven Advertiser*, that "the hall was crowded through the afternoon." Lewis Tappan recalled, "The opposers of the measures rallied in strong force and were vociferous in opposition. Several of them belonged to the legal profession, and by their inflammatory speeches, added greatly to the excitement."

The first resolution declared:

> WHEREAS in the opinion of this meeting, Yale College, the institutions for the education of females, and the other schools, already existing in this city, are important to the community and the general interests of science, and as such have been deservedly patronized by the public, and the establishment of a College in the same place to educate the colored population is incompatible with the prosperity, if not the existence of the present institutions of learning, and will be destructive of the best interests of the city:
> THEREFORE, RESOLVED ... that we will resist the establishment of the proposed College in this place, by every lawful means.

The committee used the particular situation as an opportunity to voice their general attitudes towards the abolitionists in the second motion, which stated:

> RESOLVED, ... that the propagation of sentiments favorable to the immediate emancipation of slaves in disregard of the civil institutions of the States in which they belong, and as auxiliary thereto the contemporaneous founding of Colleges for educating colored people, is unwarrantable and dangerous interference with the internal concerns of other States, and ought to be discouraged.

The joint resolutions were overwhelmingly approved by a vote of 700 to four. Simeon Jocelyn, James Donaghe and Roger Sherman Baldwin were three of the abstaining voters; the fourth man's name is not recorded. (Eight years later, Baldwin would join with Jocelyn in the defense of the *Amistad* captives.)

No minutes survive of the meeting, but the newspapers of the surrounding communities recorded their impressions of the event. It was obvious, commented one, that the "citizens entertain a very strong hostility to the idea of a Negro college being thrust into contact with... venerable Yale." It was plain to another that in the eyes of the local voters "the interest of the city, identified as it is with the prosperity of the institutions," would be made to "suffer material injury" if the proposed black institution was allowed to operate.

A Boston paper could not have been very far off the mark when it reported that the "real objection to the college appears to have been the apprehension of giving offense to the Southern patrons of Yale College." Ultimately it was the *Vermont Telegraph* that boldly complained:

> The Northern blacks must be bound to silence! Because slavery does not exist in Connecticut, therefore within the boundaries of Connecticut it must not be spoken against!... Because neither Connecticut nor Congress has any control over the laws of South Carolina, therefore the free people of color of the North must be doomed to perpetual ignorance and degradation! Such is the logic by which founding colleges for educating colored people is made out to be an interference with the internal concerns of other states.

Simeon Jocelyn was forced to relinquish his position in the black church as a result of the backlash from the New Haven meeting. According to one report, his personal residence was mobbed as well. Another report contends that after the meeting a mob of whites attacked Arthur Tappan's house. However, the literature of the period is so full of reports of attacks upon the Tappans, Jocelyn, Garrison, and other leading abolitionists that it is hard to distinguish which attacks followed which incidents. One thing, however, is certain: Men such as Jocelyn and Tappan who proclaimed their belief in abolitionism did so at great personal risk.

Naturally the South cannot be blamed directly for abuses such as these that abolitionists suffered at the hands of other Northerners. And yet, it seems certain that the fire of the Northern mobs was fueled by words from the South. The common Northern white had not yet seen that in yielding the issue of slavery to the South, they were placing their own rights in jeopardy.

Over the course of the next few years, many of these Northern whites would at last begin to sense that their own freedoms and rights were being threatened in order to protect the Southern right to own slaves. In many cases, it was undoubtedly this perception, more than empathy towards the slaves, that eventually gained a wider sympathy for the abolitionists.

In the meantime, voices in the South were quick and loud in blaming the abolitionists for the Turner revolt. Most of the abuse, it seems, was heaped upon Garrison's *Liberator*. In October, the town of Georgetown in the District of Columbia passed a law which prohibited free blacks from taking copies of the paper out of the post office. Violators could face a $25 fine and 30 days in jail, with the added threat of being sold into slavery for four months if the fine was not paid.

In Columbia, South Carolina, a reward of $1,500 was offered by a vigilance committee for the apprehension and conviction of any white person caught circulating copies of *The Liberator* or similar "seditious" publications.

Garrison himself was "horror-struck at the late tidings" from Southampton. He had always exerted his "utmost efforts to avert" scenes of violence, having "preached to the slave the pacific precepts of Jesus Christ." This was not what he had wanted to see happen. He had long "appealed to Christians, philanthropists and patriots to accomplish the great work of national redemption through the agency of moral power—of public opinion—of individual duty."

At the same time, he wouldn't deny that the uprising seemed to be "what we have long predicted.... [It is but the] first drops of blood, which are but a prelude to a deluge from the gathering clouds."

"What was poetry—imagination—in January," he lamented, "is now bloody reality." Yet he denied having been instrumental in any way in the incident. "Ye accuse the pacific friends of emancipation of instigating the slaves to revolt," he observed. "Take back the charge as a foul slander. The slaves need no incentive at our hands."

The historical record supports Garrison's defense. There is no indication that Turner had been influenced by Garrison or *The Liberator*. Yet if the South agreed to this, then it would be forced to accept the responsibility for its own slave problems.—which of course it was unwilling to do that. Therefore, the abuse continued to pour forth towards Garrison.

The state legislature of Georgia offered a $5,000 reward to anyone who arrested Garrison and brought him to the state to be tried for libel. Upon hearing of this, Garrison's righteous anger was aroused. "A bribe to kidnappers," he exclaimed, "a price set upon the head of a citizen from Massachusetts! Where are the immunities secured to us by our Bill of Rights?"

The *National Intelligencer* of Washington, D.C. (which was every bit as much slave territory as South Carolina or Mississippi), called upon the country to suppress and punish the paper and its editor. The article was heavily reprinted all over the country. Garrison wrote a rebuttal, in which he reminded readers that his efforts were "to prevent rebellion," not to cause it. His desire was to save lives "by moral power, by truth and reason," not to embroil the South in violence. Yet he insisted that

Four • 1831

slavery must be discussed. "Tell me not that an evil is cured by covering it up," he wrote, or "that if nothing be said, more will be done."

The *Intelligencer* refused to run his rebuttal; nor did any of the other papers that had published the article attacking him do so. He was left to defend himself within the pages of his own paper.

Around the same time, Garrison was approached by a young black woman with a manuscript. Twenty-eight year-old Maria Stewart had been married to James Stewart, a wealthy black Boston shipping agent. Her husband had died two years earlier, and she had been defrauded out of her inheritance by a group of white businessmen. Maria Stewart is not very well known today, but she holds the distinction of having been the first black woman in American history to speak out in public and to leave written texts of her writings. The work she presented to Garrison, and which he published in pamphlet form in October 1831, was entitled *Religion And The Pure Principles Of Morality, The Sure Foundation On Which We Must Build.* In it she argued that the black race must rise up and demonstrate its worth to the whites through good deeds and good works. She called upon her brothers and sisters to do so:

> All the nations of the earth are crying out for Liberty and Equality. Away, away with tyranny and oppression! And shall Africa's sons be silent any longer? *Far be it from me to recommend to you, either to kill, burn, or destroy.* [Emphasis added.] But I would strongly recommend to you, to improve your talents; let no one lie buried in the earth. Show forth your powers of mind. Prove to the world that
> Though black your skins as shades of night,
> Your hearts are pure, your souls are white.
> This is the land of freedom. The press is at liberty. Every man has a right to express his opinion. Many think, because your skins are tinged with a sable hue, that you are an inferior race of beings; but God does not consider you as such.... [A]ccording to the Constitution of these United States, he hath made all men free and equal. Then why should one worm say to another, "Keep you down there, while I sit up yonder; for I am better than thou?" It is not the color of the skin that makes the man, but it is the principles formed within the soul.
> Many will suffer for pleading the cause of oppressed Africa, and I shall glory in being one of her martyrs; for I am firmly persuaded, that the God in whom I trust is able to protect me from the rage and malice of mine enemies, and from them that will rise up against me; and if there is no other way for me to escape, He is able to take me to Himself, as He did the most noble, fearless, and undaunted David Walker.

She argued that blacks must not wait patiently, leaving it up to the whites to free them, for "never, no, never will the chains of slavery and ignorance burst, till we become united as one, and cultivate among ourselves the pure principles of piety, morality and virtue." Nor was the task to be left only to the men. "O, ye daughters of Africa, awake! awake! arise! no longer sleep nor slumber, but distinguish yourselves," she wrote. She optimistically predicted that the moment "knowledge would begin to flow" within individuals of the black race, then "the chains of slavery and ignorance would melt like wax before the flames."

Stewart admitted there were "very few" among the majority of white Americans "that bestow one thought upon the benighted sons and daughters of Africa, who have enriched the soils of America with their tears and blood: few to promote their cause, none to encourage their talents." For that reason she declared "let us promote ourselves and improve our own talents." She reminded her readers that " 'I can't' is a great barrier in the way; I hope it will soon be removed, and 'I will' resume its place." For she was "of a strong opinion, that the day on which we unite, heart and soul, and turn our attention to knowledge and improvement, that day the hissing and reproach among the nations of the earth against us will cease."

Of course, this was just so much wishful thinking on her part, for the last thing whites wanted was to see was the black race improve itself and be lifted up. Perhaps she realized as much, for she continued by suggesting "let us make a mighty effort, and arise; and if no one will promote or respect us, let us promote and respect ourselves."

She contrasted the blacks' apathetic acceptance of slavery with what white attitudes would be under similar circumstances:

> Did every gentleman in America realize, as one, that they had got to become bondmen, and their wives, their sons, and their daughters, servants forever, to Great Britain, ... , their souls would recoil at the very thought, their hearts would die within them, and death would be far preferable. Then why have not Africa's sons a right to feel the same? Are not their wives, their sons, and their daughters, as dear to them as those of the white man's?... [W]hy should man any longer deprive his fellow-man of equal rights and privileges? Oh, America, America, foul and indelible is thy stain! Dark and dismal is the cloud that hangs over thee, for the cruel wrongs and injuries to the fallen sons of Africa. The blood of her murdered ones cries to heaven for vengeance against thee. Thou art become drunken with the blood of her slain; thou hast enriched thyself through her toils and labors; and now thou refuseth to make even a small return. And thou hast caused the daughters of Africa to commit whoredoms and fornications; but upon thee be their curse.
>
> O, ye great and mighty men of America, ... You have acknowledged all the nations of the earth, except Hayti; and you may publish, as far as the East is from the West, that you have two millions of negroes, who aspire no higher than to bow at your feet, and court your smiles.... We will not come against you with swords and staves, as against a thief; but we will tell you that our souls are fired with the same love of liberty and independence with which your souls are fired. We will tell you that too

much of your blood flows in our veins, and too much of your color in our skins, for us not to possess your spirits. We will tell you, that it is our gold that clothes you in fine linen and purple, and causes you to fare sumptuously every day; and it is the blood of our fathers, and the tears of our brethren that have enriched your souls. AND WE CLAIM OUR RIGHTS We will tell you that we are not afraid of them that kill the body, and after that can do no more.

She spoke once more to her own color, reminding them that

> God hath raised you up a Walker and a Garrison. Though Walker sleeps, yet he lives, and his name shall be had in everlasting remembrance.... *Prove to the world that you are neither ourang-outangs, nor a species of mere animals, but that you possess the same powers of intellect as those of the proud-boasting Americans....* turn your attention to knowledge and improvement; for knowledge is power.... Arm yourselves with the weapons of prayer.

It is interesting to note that Stewart's message did not seem to receive the same amount of attention as did Walker's *Appeal*. Doubtless there are many reasons for this, though a primary one must be that her pamphlet was not as challenging as his. Her words were much more subdued and less threatening. If they were noticed at all in the South, it is unlikely that they stirred up as much concern as his did.

On October 31, a farmer named Benjamin Phipps accidentally stumbled upon the hiding place of the notorious Nat Turner. With very little drama or danger, the mastermind of the most violent slave revolt on the American continent quietly surrendered. The entire region must have breathed a collective sigh of relief when the news of his arrest was announced in the *Norfolk Beacon*. Turner was immediately brought before the justices.

> ... and after 1½ or 2 hours close examination was committed to Prison.—During the examination, he evinced great intelligence and much shrewdness of intellect, answering every question clearly and distinctly, and without confusion or prevarication. He acknowledges himself a coward and says he was actuated to do what he did, from the influence of fanaticism...—he is now convinced that he has done wrong, and advises all other Negroes not to follow his example.

A suspicious person might wonder whether this account was accurate reporting or simply official propaganda.

On Tuesday, November 1, Turner was visited in his cell by physician Thomas R. Gray. Later, Gray released what was purported to be Turner's dictated "confession" from their interview. The interview is very candid and matter-of-fact, though grisly in its details.

Turner began by relating an incident of his childhood. "Being at play with other children, when three or four years old, I was telling them something, which... had happened before I was born." [O]thers being called on were greatly astonished, ... and [it] caused them to say in my hearing, I would surely be a prophet, as the Lord had shewn me things." Surely, they exclaimed, the boy "was intended for some great purpose."

He related how later, as a young man, he "was praying one day at my plough, [and] the Spirit spoke to me, saying 'Seek ye the kingdom of Heaven and all things shall be added unto you.'" When asked by Gray what he meant by the spirit, he responded "The Spirit that spoke to the prophets in former days." He was "greatly astonished," but now fully "confirmed... in the impression that I was ordained for some great purpose in the hands of the Almighty."

He began to tell the other slaves that "something was about to happen," as he had had "a vision."

> ... I saw white spirits and black spirits engaged in battle, and the sun was darkened—the thunder rolled in the Heavens, and blood flowed in streams... [and again] the Spirit... appeared to me, and reminded me of the things it had already shown me, and that it would then reveal to me the knowledge of the elements, the revolution of the planets, the operation of ideas, and changes of the seasons.
>
> ...And from the first steps of righteousness until the last, was I made perfect; and the Holy Ghost was with me, and said "Behold me as I stand in the Heavens"... and shortly afterwards, while labouring in the field, I discovered drops of blood on the corn, as though it were dew from heaven... And now the Holy Ghost had revealed itself to me, ... For as the blood of Christ had been shed on this earth, ... it was plain to me that the Savior was about to lay down the yoke he had borne for the sins of men, and the great day of judgement was at hand.
>
> ...And on the 12th of May, 1828, I heard a loud noise in the heavens, and the Spirit instantly appeared to me and said the Serpent was loosened, and Christ had laid down the yoke he had borne for the sins of man, and that I should take it on and fight against the Serpent, for the time was fast approaching, when the first should be last and the last should be first.

When Gray asked Turner if he did not, now, believe that he was mistaken, his response was: "Was not Christ crucified?"

It may be noteworthy to point out that, prior to Turner's uprising, many slaveowners considered regular lessons in religion to be one of their beneficent obligations to their charges. They were particularly fond of passages that admonished servants to obey their masters. They also favored the aspect of Christianity that reminded the meek that they would be rewarded in the afterlife; and therefore, by implication, they should not be unduly concerned about their lot in this life.

Four • 1831

This changed drastically after Turner's *Confessions* became more well known in the South. Religion and spirituality in the blacks was now perceived as a bad thing, which led them to discontentment and instigated uprisings. In the aftermath of the Southampton tragedy, state after state passed ever-stricter laws to repress the blacks. Many of these laws focused upon education, or, more precisely, the restriction of education. It became illegal to teach the blacks to read or to write, or to provide them with religious instruction.

As evidence of this is an incident in the life of Frederick Douglas that occurred at about the same time as the Southampton incident and which he recounted years later in his autobiography. As a young slave child living in Maryland, Douglas was sent to be a servant in the house of Hugh Auld, who was his master's brother-in-law. Hugh's charming young wife, Sophia, was impressed with the young black's sense of curiosity, and took it upon herself to teach him how to read and write. As his abilities progressed, she boasted to her husband of the young slave's accomplishments. As Douglas continues the tale:

> Master Hughes was amazed at the simplicity of his spouse, and, probably for the first time, he unfolded to her the true philosophy of slavery, and the peculiar rules necessary to be observed by masters and mistresses, in the management of their human chattels. Mr. Auld promptly forbade the continuance of her instruction; telling her, in the first place, that the thing itself was unlawful; that it was also unsafe, and could only lead to mischief. To use his own words, further, he said, "if you give a nigger an inch, he will take an ell;" "he should know nothing but the will of his master, and learn to obey it." "Learning would spoil the best nigger in the world;" "if you teach that nigger... how to read the bible, there will be no keeping him;" "it would forever unfit him for the duties of a slave;" and "...learning would do him no good, but probably, a great deal of harm—making him disconsolate and unhappy." "If you learn him how to read, he'll want to know how to write; and, this accomplished, he'll be running away with himself."

The reading lessons were over, but Douglas had learned an even more important lesson that day: whites did not want blacks to be educated.

Of particular concern to many Southerners in 1831 was the manner in which Turner's narrative focused on ideas and concepts from Christianity. It was obvious that he had received a lot of "Bible learning." But where such education was supposed to make the slave more docile and manageable, it had instead inspired him to rise up against whites. Many slave-owners began questioning the value of religious education for their slaves. It may not even be too much to say that the established churches of the South soon found themselves under suspicion. The time would soon arrive when the religious members of Southern society would have to take a definite stand either for or against slavery. As shall be seen, great efforts were made by religious leaders over the course of the next few years to convince the slaveowners that the church was "on their side."

Turner continued his story, having been told by the Spirit that "by signs in the heavens... it would be made known to me when I should commence the great work... [that] on the appearance of the sign, [there was a solar eclipse in February 1831, which fit Turner's vision of "the sun was darkened"] I should arise and prepare myself, and slay my enemies with their own weapons."

Enlisting the aid of a few trusted accomplices, they started out on that fateful early morning of August 21. Quite methodically he described the murder of whites in their homes. The first was that of J. Travis, where they "determined to enter the house secretly, and murder them whilst sleeping." He related how, once inside, "the murder of this family, five in number, was the work of a moment, not one of them awoke; there was a little infant sleeping in a cradle, that was forgotten," but two of the accomplices "returned and killed it."

At another house they "entered, and murdered Mrs. Reese in her bed, while sleeping; her son awoke, but it was only to sleep the sleep of death." A good portion of his *Confession* relates the way in which his victims were dispatched, with no words of remorse or pity for any of the deaths. The total, by his reckoning, amounts to 55 deaths, though some sources list more.

Eventually the group—which had grown in numbers to 40 or more (again, depending upon what source you refer to)—soon encountered some of the white groups that had been seeking them out since the initial alarm had been given. At each confrontation, his band of followers was reduced in numbers. Eventually the group just melted apart under the white assaults. Turner managed to hide out in the woods for six weeks before his chance encounter with farmer Phipps led to his undoing.

Justice was swift and sure. Apprehended on October 31, he was immediately brought to trial. On November 5, he was

> ... convicted of one of the highest crimes in the criminal code. You have been convicted of plotting in cold blood, the indiscriminate destruction of men, of helpless women, and of infant children. The evidence before us leaves not a shadow of doubt.... [You were] the original contriver of a plan, deep and deadly, one that never can be effected, [but] you managed so far to put it into execution, as to deprive us of many of our most valuable citizens; and this was done when they were asleep, and defenceless; under circumstances shocking to humanity.
>
> ...Borne down by this load of guilt, your only justification is, that you were led away by fanaticism. If this be true, from my soul I pity you; and

while you have my sympathies, I am, nevertheless called upon to pass the sentence of this court.

The time between this and your execution, will necessarily be very short; and your only hope must be in another world. The judgment of the court is, that you be taken hence to the jail from whence you came, thence to the place of execution, and on Friday next, between the hours of 10 AM and 2 PM be hung by the neck until you are dead! dead! dead! and may the Lord have mercy upon your soul.

On November 11, as so ordered, the sentence was carried out.

Two days later, William Lloyd Garrison met with a small group of other abolitionists in an effort to establish an anti-slavery group that would be pledged to immediate emancipation, the first of its kind in America. The resultant New England Anti-Slavery Society (or NEAS) would not officially come into being until the first day of the new year. Yet there were still many details to be decided.

The first major problem was what to express as the aims of the group. Garrison insisted "they put their movement on the ground of immediate, in distinction from gradual, emancipation." Some of the others feared that they would alienate many potential anti-slavery supporters by taking such a radical and unpopular position. Despite these objections, Garrison was firm in the conviction that the vitality of the movement depended upon a frank avowal of fundamental principles, however unpopular they might be; and the vote upon the question showed that nine were in favor of organizing under his plan, while six were opposed."

The group met again on Friday, December 16th, at which time a committee composed of, Garrison, David Lee Child (husband of Lydia Maria Child), Samuel E. Sewall, Ellis Gray Loring and Oliver Johnson were appointed to draft a constitution for the society, which would be reported upon at its first meeting of the new year.

As the dust from the Turner affair settled, many people in Virginia, particularly in the more rural western section, began to question the utility of perpetuating slavery. It was beginning to seem that perhaps Garrison was right that the holding of slaves was endangering the welfare of the state. As a consequence, the state legislature in December began receiving petitions advocating the adoption of a gradual plan of emancipation. While sources disagree as to the actual number of petitions received, they agree that the most significant one seemed to be that forwarded from the Society of Friends (Quakers). This petition openly advocated gradual emancipation and the ultimate removal of blacks from the state.

At first, it appears the petitions were given a decent and respectful reception. Many delegates agreed with the senders of the petitions that the time had arrived to remove slavery. However, as time went by, an unfortunate backlash resulted. Many others thought that talk of emancipation was dangerous, as it gave credence to the recent insurrection and might tend to stir up more trouble. As the new year arrived and discussion continued, it was still not clear which way events would turn.

Popular folklore has it that a slave named Tice Davids fled Kentucky in 1831 and was pursued into Ohio by has master. When recapture seemed imminent, Davids suddenly vanished without a trace. According to the story, the frustrated master proclaimed that his property had disappeared so absolutely, it was as if he had been carried away on some "underground railroad." And the rest, as they say, is history.

Or is it? There are so many myths and legends about the underground railroad that one wonders what is fact and what is fiction. However, it is certain that by 1831 the illegal practice of assisting escaped slaves was already well established, if not common. If the story of Tice Davids may be suspect, the same can not be said about the better-documented story of Thornton and Lucie Blackburn.

The widow Susan Brown moved to Louisville in 1831, taking with her 19 year-old Thornton. Here he met and fell in love with 28-year-old Lucie. Fearing a separation if either should be sold, they decided to escape together. They made their way across the Ohio River where they presented papers to Captain John Quarrier of the steamboat *Versailles* that convinced him they were free. Through this ruse they were able to stay ahead of their pursuers and ultimately made their way to Detroit.

At this point, most fugitives exited the country into Canada. However, the Blackburns decided to settle comfortably in the Michigan city. The rest of their tale comes later.

The Cherokee Indians had taken their battle to the courts, but had been unsuccessful. In *Cherokee Nation vs. Georgia*, Chief Justice John Marshall ruled that the Supreme Court has no jurisdiction to hear the Cherokee's requests, as they are a "domestic, dependent nation," not a "sovereign nation." Plans to remove the Indians proceeded.

Samuel Francis Smith wrote the words to the song "America" (popularly known as "My Country, 'Tis of Thee"). The song was first sung in public on July 4, at a service in the same Park Street church outside of which Garrison had delivered his anti-slavery speech just two years previously.

Lydia Maria Child published another best-seller, *The Mother's Book*. The first of its kind in America, it was a manual covering childbirth and childrearing from infancy through the teen years. It was the precursor of Dr. Spock and various other family help guides. The book was very well received and graced the tables of prominent families throughout the nation.

A minor French dignitary named Alexis de Tocqueville arrived in

Newport, Rhode Island, on May 9. The 25-year-old Tocqueville and his 28-year-old traveling companion, Gustave de Beaumont, had journeyed to America to conduct an official study of the United States prison system on behalf of the government of France. While in the country, Tocqueville would unofficially study the character and government of the United States and its citizens as well.

Five

1832

Twenty-nine-year-old Prudence Crandall had every reason to be pleased with herself. She had been invited to Canterbury, Connecticut, to open an academy for the daughters of the local families of wealth. The generous support of the community had allowed her to purchase a handsome house on the village green as a site for what promised to be a fashionable center of eduction. She started her duties as headmistress in January, no doubt a little nervous, but confident that she would be successful.

Her confidence would have been severely shaken had she foreseen how much her situation would soon change.

During the first few weeks of January, members of the nascent NEAS debated the wording of their constitution. The original proposed preamble stated:

> We, the undersigned, hold that every person, of full age and sane mind, has a right to immediate freedom from personal bondage of whatsoever kind, unless imposed by the sentence of the law, for the commission of some crime. We hold that man cannot, consistently with reason, religion, and the eternal and immutable principles of justice, be the property of man. We hold that whoever retains his fellow-man in bondage is guilty of a grievous wrong. We hold that a mere difference of complexion is no reason why any man should be deprived of any of his natural rights, or subject to any political disability. While we advance these opinions as the principles on which we intend to act, we declare that we will not operate on the existing relations of society by other than peaceful and lawful means, and that we will give no countenance to violence or insurrection.

It's hard to believe that even this statement, which by modern standards appears rather weak, was considered too strong for adoption by the majority present. Garrison's bid for immediate emancipation was given token notice in the first sentence, but this would be replaced in the final version by a weaker plea for the immediate abolishment of slavery. (Note the fine difference here: Emancipation implied the actual release from a condition of slavery of individual slaves, whereas abolishing slavery only required pending legislation that might ultimately, at some future date, provide relief for individuals.) Also, the third sentence must have been seen as too strong an indictment against the slaveowning Southerners since it also would be dropped.

The final reported version, as published in the February 18, 1832 *Liberator*, read:

> Whereas, we believe that Slavery is contrary to the precepts of Christianity, dangerous to the liberties of the country, and ought immediatelyto be abolished; and whereas, we believe that the citizens of New-England not only have the right to protest against it, but are under the highest obligation to seek its removal by a moral influence; and, whereas, we believe that the free people of color are unrighteously oppressed, and stand in need of our sympathy and benevolent co-operation...; we agree to form ourselves into a Society, and to be governed by the following
> CONSTITUTION
> ARTICLE 1. This Society shall be called the New-England Anti-Slavery Society.
> ARTICLE 1. The objects of the Society shall be, to endeavor, by all means sanctioned by law, humanity and religion, to effect the abolition of slavery in the United States; to improve the character and condition of the free people of color, to inform and correct public opinion in relation to their situation and rights, and obtain for them equal civil and political rights and privileges with the whites.

That was it. That was what the group stood for. (The rest of the constitution dealt with memberships, duties and obligations, and other business concerns.) It's difficult to believe that this position was found so offensive to so many in the country. Quite likely, most of those who complained most strongly about them never took the time to read this document.

Meanwhile, the debate in Virginia had taken a turn for the worse. Too many delegates found talk of abolition threatening on too many levels. It threatened generations of accepted practice and belief. It threatened the sanctity of personal property. Many thought that even a discussion on abolishing slavery would encourage more violence within those enslaved.

Thomas R. Dew was professor of political economy at the College of William and Mary. Not long after the debates ended, he published a pamphlet describing the course of deliberation. "Upon the impropriety of this debate, we beg to make a few observations," he wrote. "Any scheme of abolition proposed so soon after the Southampton tragedy, would necessarily appear to be the result of the most inhuman massacre."

In other words, we must not give blacks the impression that we are afraid of them and that they can obtain their freedom through violence. "[W]ould not the extraordinary effect produced on the legislature by the Southampton insurrection, in all probability, have a tendency to excite another?" he stated.

In Professor Dew's mind, this was not the time to deliberate on such important issues because the tragedy was still too fresh. "Waiting, one year or more, until the excitement could be allayed and the empire of reason could once more ... [be] established, would surely ... [be] productive of no injurious consequences," he concluded.

Injurious, one might ask, to whom? For as the legislature deliberated and sober minds came to contemplate the results of the proposed emancipation, the climate of the discussions began to change. No longer were influential Southern slaveowners deploring the hideous legacy that their ancestors had bequeathed to them. A new generation of landowners had arrived who felt no need to apologize for their region's "peculiar institution." The illustrious Hayne had been reluctant to call slavery an evil. This new group of lawmakers had no qualms about going even further, and praising the system and its benefits to them.

These rising young Southern statesman were represented by men such as Mr. Gholson, who sarcastically remarked that "he really had been under the *impression* that he *owned* his slaves. He had lately purchased four women and 10 children, in whom he thought he had obtained a great bargain; for he supposed they were his own property, *as were his brood mares*." The speaker was supported by Mr. Roane who assured the legislative body that he "own[ed] a considerable number of slaves, and am perfectly sure they are mine; and I am sorry to add that I have occasionally, though not often, been compelled to make *them* feel the *impression* of that ownership. I would not touch a hair on the head of [another] gentleman's slave, any sooner than I would a hair in the *mane of his horse*."

Roane continued by observing "I think slavery as much a correlative of liberty as cold is of heat. History, experience, observation and reason, have taught me that the torch of liberty has ever burned brighter when surrounded by the dark and filthy, yet *nutritious* atmosphere of slavery!"

He spoke for many young planters when he remarked, "I do not believe in the fanfaronade that all men are by nature equal. But these abstract speculations have nothing to do with the question, which I am willing to view as one of cold, sheer state policy, in which the safety, prosperity, and happiness of the *whites alone* are concerned."

Apparently many of his listeners shared the same view. When the vote was finally taken, emancipation lost.

However, there was much more lost in the bargain, though it was not immediately apparent. By publicly debating the issue of slavery, Virginia and, by extension, the South had convinced itself of the danger not only of emancipation, but of even the consideration or discussion of emancipation. Indeed, the time when forthright Southern gentlemen could publicly question slavery had come to a close. "We must satisfy the consciences," editorialized an influential Southern paper. "We must allay the fears of our own people. We must satisfy them that slavery is of itself right—that it is not a sin against God—that it is not an evil, moral or political.... In this way, and this way only, can we prepare our own people to defend their institutions."

And that is where the significant change would come. No longer would the Southern politician try to excuse slavery as an undesirable wrong. Now he could stand up proudly and proclaim it good, both for the whites and the blacks of the South.

One would like to hope that the majority of white Southerners never actually believed this. However, the sad truth was that it was so believed by most of the whites who made the decisions and guided the courses of the states, and who tended to be those large slaveowners with political and economic influence and power. For the next 30 years, it was the rare Southerner who would brave the wrath of his neighbors by speaking out against slavery.

The pro-slavery minority was aided in its arguments by the same professor Dew who deplored the rash behavior of the Virginia state legislature. His words would be a major source of inspiration for a rising generation of fireeaters.

Where many Southern theologians had waffled on the issue, Dew came right to the point: "[T]here is no rule of conscience or revealed law of God which can condemn us" as slaveowners. He felt confident that he could "deny most positively that there is anything in the Old or New Testament which would go to show that slavery ... ought at all events to be abrogated, or that the master commits any offense in holding slaves."

He cited a number of cases of Biblical patriarchs who were slaveowners: "Abraham had more than 300; Isaac had a "great store" of them; and even the patient and meek Job himself had 'a very great household.' He went even further with his argument: "When we turn to the New Testament, we find not one single passage at all calculated to disturb the conscience of an honest slaveholder." This passage must have pleased his audience.

It is impossible to read the New Testament, stated Dew, "without seeing and admiring that the meek and humble Savior of the world in no instance meddled with the established institutions of mankind; he came to save a fallen world, and not to excite the black passions of men and array them in deadly hostility." Dew is, of course, suggesting that the abolitionists had misinterpreted the words of Jesus and had no right trying to turn their slaves against them.

In his view, Jesus accepted all, including "the monarch and the subject, the rich and the poor, the master and the slave." The abolitionists should try to be more like Christ and simply accept the institution as it is, without challenging it. Christ had been born into "a world in which the most galling slavery existed, a thousand times more cruel than the slavery in our own country."

Of course, the abolitionists would rightly refute this claim. The historical record makes it quite clear that in no period of time was slavery ever as despotic as it was under the Southern slaveholders. In fact, many of the abolitionists would go to great pains to examine the historical record, and it becomes almost tedious to read and reread their historical arguments.

The modern reader needs to understand why so much of the antislavery literature seems to focus on this issue. It was precisely because men such as Dew kept insisting that what was happening in the South was no different than what had happened in all the ages of man. But it *was* different, in two fundamental respects. First, it seems clear that much of the basis of Southern slavery was racial prejudice, which was not the case in other slave cultures. But the more damning difference was that the nineteenth century slaveowner could not plead ignorance as an excuse. It seems nothing short of barbaric that modern men, living in an enlightened age and in a civilized society, were willing to perpetuate practices that had been out-dated centuries earlier in most of the world.

Yet Dew was more than willing to defend the practice. And, in case it wasn't clear that he was criticizing the abolitionists, he made it even plainer: "What a rebuke does the practice of the Redeemer of mankind imply upon the conduct of some of his nominal disciples, who seek to destroy the contentment of the slaves, to rouse their most deadly passions, to break up the deep foundation of society, and to lead on to a night of darkness and confusion!" According to his interpretation of the Bible, each man is to "abide in the same calling wherein he is called." Meaning, of course, that if it is your place to be a slave, then no one else should try to change that.

And what of the slaves? "Servants are even commanded in Scripture to be faithful and obedient to unkind masters," he noted. Dew was quite satisfied that numerous "passages in the New Testament" most convincingly prove that slavery in the Roman world was nowhere charged as a fault or crime upon the holder, and everywhere is the most implicit obedience enjoined."

To further ease the conscience of the slaveholder, Dew asked him to "but recollect the exhortation of the apostle, 'Masters, give unto your servants that which is just and equal; knowing that ye also have a Master in heaven;' and in the final day he shall have nothing on this score with which his conscience need be smitten, and he may expect the welcome plaudit, 'Well done thou good and faithful servant, thou hast been faithful over a few things, I will make thee ruler over many things; enter thou into the joy of thy Lord.'"

It would be wrong to give the false impression that Dew's arguments were the first from the South to use religion to justify slavery. Such opinions had been around as long as slavery itself. However, coming as they did so close upon the aborted Virginia attempt to abolish slavery, they can be seen as a landmark of pro-slavery debate. Dew's writing systematized and validated many of the beliefs that had been accepted for generations by slaveowners in the South.

They also came at the time when anti-slavery arguments in the South virtually disappeared under the pressure of public sentiment. As such, they can be seen as having a profound influence on the Southern religious community. Had someone else of Dew's stature been willing to disagree with his conclusions, perhaps things would have been different. As it was, many of the South's religious leaders found themselves in the position where they were almost obligated to accept the pro-slavery view.

Not to excuse this behavior, but their position was certainly an awkward one. The simple truth is that the "Church" did not play as integral a role in the life of the typical Southern slaveowner as it did in that of his neighbors to the North. This is not to imply that the latter was any "better" or more virtuous than the Southerner. However, due to the Northerner's more urban lifestyle, he was more likely to live or work in sight of a church. Therefore, it was a constant part of his daily consciousness.

The Southerner, particularly the politically powerful large slaveowner on his plantation, tended to spend more time isolated from the presence of established religion. Though the South is often thought of as the "Bible Belt" today, records of the antebellum period suggest that religious leaders in the region were not accorded the same prestige and recognition as were their counterparts to the North. It may not be too much to say that those of the more rural South were often struggling for the attention of their prospective constituents.

As time went by, the success of this struggle seemed to depend upon acceptance of chattel slavery. To have fought against the mores and values of the communities in which they lived would have been of questionable value to the enslaved, and certainly would not have endeared them to their flocks.

It is unfortunate that the church leaders of the South lacked the moral fortitude to reject slavery. Perhaps, with their support, abolition might have been realized. However, it appears that they were more than willing to accept the oppression of the blacks. Sources suggest that as many as two-fifths of the ministers in South Carolina owned slaves themselves.

It should also be mentioned that, prior to this period, very few Northern preachers had been willing to speak out against slavery either. However, as the abolitionists's arguments came to receive more attention, many of the Northern churches began to examine their unquestioned acquiescence of slavery. Soon, religious debate between the two regions of the country would become almost as acrimonious as the political debate had always been. This would lead, in a few years, to schisms in the American churches.

Dew went to great lengths to convince his readers that slavery was the ideal situation for the blacks themselves. All needs, cares and concerns were provided for them. To emancipate him would be to throw him "into the hands of those who have no scruples of conscience—those who will not perhaps treat him so kindly" as does his master. To even suggest doing so was, in Dew's estimation, "not philosophy, it is not morality." Admitting that there "may be many cruel masters," he observed that "there are unkind and cruel fathers, too; but both the one and the other make all those around them shudder with horror."

"We are well convinced," he continued, "that there is nothing but the mere relations of husband and wife, parent and child, brother and sister which produce a closer tie than the relation of master and servant.... [The slaves have become] accustomed to look up to [their master] as their supporter, director, and defender."

Of course, the abolitionists could produce numerous slave accounts that were in contradiction to this claim.

But Dew was not interested in the slave side of the story: He had strong evidence to support his claim from the recently concluded Virginia debate. During those proceedings "no speaker *insinuated even*, we believe, that the slaves in Virginia were not treated kindly. [A]nd all, too, agree that they were most abundantly fed; and we have no doubt but that *they form the happiest portion of our society. A merrier being does not exist on the face of the globe than the Negro slave of the United States*" (emphasis added).

In Dew's appraisal of the situation, the problem with the abolitionists was that, like too many people, they were "prone to judge of the happiness of others by ourselves—we make *self* the standard and endeavor to draw down everyone to its dimensions.... We might rather die than be the obscure slave that waits at our back ... and [this] disposes us to look upon the slave as unsusceptible of happiness in his humble sphere, when he may indeed be much happier than we are, and have his ambition too...; to please and to gratify his master."

To Dew, it seemed sublimely obvious that the poor dumb brute was perfectly happy with his lot; that is, unless or until "the wily philanthropist" or abolitionist "but come and whisper into the ears of such a slave that his situation is degrading and his lot a miserable one." It takes the interference of an outsider to "light up the dungeon in which he persuades the slave that he is caged, and that moment ... he destroys his happiness and his usefulness."

It's easy to agree with Dew that a discontented slave would be less useful than a contented one to his master. But this argument seems so transparently self-serving that it's hard to believe even the writer himself actually believed it. Yet believe it he must have, as did the vast majority of the pro-slavery population of the South. (Not excluding many who were not themselves slaveowners.) The depth of racial prejudice contained within these words is appalling, particularly coming as they did from an educated individual.

Dew left no doubt that the issue was primarily one of rank and privilege since "the whole population of Virginia, consisting of three castes, of free white, free colored and slave colored population, is the soundest and most moral of any ... in the whole world."

But this was the way the world was meant to be. It was the ideal situation, as the greatest civilizations of old had recognized. "In the ancient republics of Greece and Rome, where the spirit of liberty glowed with most intensity, the slaves were more numerous than the freemen. Aristotle and the great men of antiquity believed slavery necessary to keep alive the spirit of freedom," Dew wrote. "In modern times, too, liberty has always been more ardently desired by slaveholding communities ... and "the Southern states have always borne this same honorable distinction." He finished his essay with an explanation of why the presence of slavery was such an integral part of Southern society. Slavery was the cause of "the perfect spirit of equality so prevalent among the whites of all the slaveholding states," and:

> We believe slavery in the United States has accomplished this, in regard to the whites, as nearly as can be expected or even desired in this world. The menial and low offices being all performed by the blacks, there is at once taken away the greatest cause of distinction and separation of the ranks of society.... But go to the South, and you will find that no white man feels such inferiority of rank as to be unworthy of association with

those around him. Color alone is here the badge of distinction, the true mark of aristocracy, and all who are white are equal in spite of the variety of occupation.... And it is this spirit of equality which is both the generator and preserver of the genuine spirit of liberty.

It's hard to imagine a more barefaced lie than this. That men like Calhoun, or Clay or any of the other Southern aristocratic families would consider the poor white trash Southern commoner their social equal borders upon the ludicrous. It's even more preposterous to think that poor white would consider himself the equal of a Clay or a Calhoun. But they all believed they were better than the blacks; and, in the final accounting, that was all that really mattered. It was likely this, more than any other factor, that allowed a slaveowning minority to manipulate the white majority of the South for so many years.

William Lloyd Garrison's role in the newlyfounded NEAS was to disseminate information to the uninformed masses; through the pages of *The Liberator* and also through personal speeches. He spoke often that summer, though the abolitionists were finding it hard to secure the use of locations for their speeches. "Although the most strenuous exertions have been made by a committee to procure a meeting house "in which he could speak, Garrison informed a friend in a private letter. "They have not been able to succeed , and probably we must resort to a hall. Tell it not at the South!"

Despite the fact that their numbers were indeed growing, they were still a decided and unpopular minority. The Southern propaganda had convinced many in the North there was nothing wrong with slavery, but that the problem was with the anti-slavery agitators. It was similar to convincing a cancer patient that it was his doctor's fault that he was ill, that there were no problems as long as no one mentioned the disease or brought it to your attention. Many Northerners didn't appreciate the fact that men like Garrison were "rocking the boat."

As the third anniversary of his Park Street address approached, he lamented the apathy of his fellow whites:

> The mockery of mockeries is at hand—the Fourth of July! By many, the day will be spent in rioting and intemperate drinking—by others, in political defamation and partisan heat—by others, in boasting of the freedom of the American people and unhazardous denunciations of the mother country. The waste of money, and health, and morals, will be immense. Another party will seize the occasion (many of them with the best motives) to extol the merits of the Colonization Society, and increase its funds. Mistaken men! A very small number will spend the day in sadness and supplication, on account of the horrible oppression which is exercised over the bodies and souls of two millions of the rational creatures of God, in this boasted land of liberty.

Later in July he spoke to a group of free blacks about the slow but steady advance of the fight against slavery. "Last year, I felt as if I were fighting single-handed against the great enemy," he told them. "Now I see around me a host of valiant warriors ... who are pledged to the end of the contest."

Yet he could not help minimizing his own role in the movement. "As for myself, whatever may be my fate—whether I fall in the springtime of manhood by the hand of the assassin, or be immured in a Georgia cell, or be permitted to live to a ripe old age—I know that the success of your cause depends nothing upon my existence. I am but as a drop in the ocean, which, if it be separated, cannot be missed."

On July 14, the Tariff Act of 1832 was passed against the protests of the South. It eliminated some of the more objectionable aspects of the earlier tariff of 1828, but clearly indicated that the federal government was still dedicated to a protective policy for manufacturers. As had happened four years previously, the South viewed this as an attack against the region. The legislature of South Carolina called for a special convention to meet in November to address the problem.

That fall, Prudence Crandall was anxiously looking forward to the opening of another school year. Things had gone very well so far for her academy, and she saw no reason for things not to continue that way.

Twenty-year-old Sarah Harris had dreams of being a teacher herself and asked to be admitted to the academy. One wonders what inspired Crandall to accept her because Sarah was not like the other girls in the school. Sarah was black.

It didn't take long for the families of the fashionable young ladies of Canterbury to make their displeasure known. Parents began withdrawing their daughters. Crandall was faced with a tough choice: remove Sarah from the school or see her institution flounder due to low enrollment. The former choice seemed a violation of good conscience; the latter could be economic ruin.

As she struggled to make a decision, a third alternative presented itself to her. Could there be enough students in New England's free black communities to fill her school? There were plenty of other options for the departing white students. They would not do without a good education if she changed the focus of her academy. But if she didn't help the young daughters of Africa, who would?

And how would she go about finding out if such a plan was even feasible?

On November 19, the special South Carolina convention began. It didn't take long to accomplish its work. On November 24, it adopted what is known as the South Carolina Ordinance of Nullification, by a vote of

136 to 26. This document was a direct challenge to the authority of the national government.

> Whereas the Congress of the United States ... hath exceeded its just powers under the Constitution, ... and hath violated the true meaning and intent of the Constitution....
>
> We, therefore, the people of the State of South Carolina in Convention assembled, do declare and ordain ... that the several acts and parts of acts of the Congress of the United States [which comprise the Tariff of 1832] are unauthorized by the Constitution of the United States ... and are null, void, and no law, nor binding upon this State, its officers, or citizens....

The ordinance insisted that its citizens adhere to its militancy:

> And it is further ordained, that all persons now holding any office of honor, profit, or trust, civil or military, under this State ... shall ... take an oath well and truly to obey, execute, and enforce, this ordinance, ... and on the neglect or omission of any such person or persons so to do, his or their office or offices shall be forthwith vacated.

That a group of elected officials could so cavalierly threaten their own associates speaks much for the political atmosphere of the time. Many apologists have claimed this convention was dominated by a few radicals and did not actually represent the will of the people. In view of the overwhelming support this ordinance received in convention, such an interpretation seems suspect. The people of South Carolina knew when they elected their representatives that such were the intentions of its members. This ordinance was not an unexpected aberration arising from within the convention. It was what the people wanted.

Or, if it wasn't, it certainly appeared to be that way to people of the Northern states.

Of course, the members knew that nullification would not be well-received, and they anticipated a negative reaction:

> And we, the people of South Carolina ... [who] are determined to maintain this, our ordinance and declaration, at every hazard, do further declare that we will not submit to the application of force, on the part of the Federal Government, to reduce this State to obedience; but that we will consider the passage, by Congress, of any act authorizing the employment of a military or naval force against the State of South Carolina ... as inconsistent with the longer continuance of South Carolina in the Union; and that the people of this State will thenceforth hold themselves absolved from all further obligation to maintain or preserve their political connexion with the people of the other States.

South Carolina was determined to do whatever it pleased, and, if the rest of the country didn't approve, that was too bad.

A lengthy discussion on nullification may seem out of place in a work dedicated to abolitionism. Yet the significance of this movement cannot be overlooked. It was obvious to all that the South was losing its political influence and its control of the country. If this trend continued, and there was no reason to suppose that it would not, the South might soon be losing control of its internal destiny as well. Though the issue now was the tariff, the handwriting was on the wall. If the North could manage to pass tariff regulations against the South's wishes, what might be next? To many Southerners, it was apparent that their entire way of life, including their "peculiar institution," was at stake. Better to strike a blow now, than to wait until it was too late.

In the eyes of the abolitionists, the nullification crisis and its underlying political theory was nothing other than a subterfuge, a smokescreen to cloud the issues or, more precisely, the issue of slavery. By turning the argument into an abstract political theory, the South managed to distract the country's attention from what was really at stake here: slavery must be protected. They did the job so well that many Americans today still believe that slavery was not the fundamental cause of the Civil War. The argument of states rights still sounds a clarion call to many listeners who are often so absorbed in what the South was saying that they don't hear the absurdity of their position.

Andrew Jackson was an unusual sort of president. Many may disagree with this observation, but it doesn't appear Jackson ever had a well-developed political system in operation. He was a crusty old man who operated primarily at the gut-level. If he didn't like you, he'd do everything in his power to oppose you. A strong ally if he was on your side, he was an indomitable enemy when aroused.

Jackson was a slaveowner himself, and the pro-slavery faction probably assumed that he would see things their way. His dealings with the Cherokee in Georgia seemed to make it clear that he was true-blue Southern. Perhaps the members of the South Carolina convention thought that Jackson's background would make him sympathetic towards their cause? If they did, they were in for a rude awakening. Because the nullification crisis aroused "Old Hickory" like few other things ever had.

On December 10, Jackson delivered his "Proclamation to the People of South Carolina." Written by Secretary of State Edward Livingston, it is a masterful document that should have ended the argument of states' rights for all time. It behooves the Civil War enthusiast to be familiar with it, as it refutes most of the claims of that insidious doctrine.

Following a straightforward account of the events that led up to the passing of the ordinance and a discussion of the ordinance's key features, he moved into the heart of his argument:

> I, Andrew Jackson, President of the United States, have thought proper to issue this my proclamation, stating my views of the Constitution and ... declaring the course which duty will require me to pursue, and warn [the people of South Carolina] of the consequences that must inevitably result from an observance of the dictates of the convention.
> The ordinance is founded, not on the indefeasible right of resisting acts which are plainly unconstitutional and too oppressive to be endured but on the strange position that any one state may not only declare an act of Congress void but prohibit its execution...; that the true construction of that instrument permits a state to retain its place in the Union and yet be bound by no other of its laws than those it may choose to consider as constitutional.... [I]t is evident that to give the right of resisting laws of that description ... is to give the power of resisting all laws[.]

He was quick to point out that the theory of nullification did not allow for any check against its abuse. Where within this ordinance was there contained any device to protect the public from its misapplication? The Constitution allowed for "two appeals from an unconstitutional act passed by Congress—one to the judiciary, the other to the people and the states." However, the manner in which this doctrine was framed allowed for no such appeal, since "the courts are closed against" any "application to review it," by reason of "both judges and jurors" having been "sworn to decide in its favor."

For the state of South Carolina to explicitly demand that its citizens adhere to this doctrine was in direct contradiction to the Constitution, which declared "that the laws of the United States" are "the supreme law of the land," and specifically contends "that the judges in every state shall be bound thereby, anything in the constitution or laws of any state to the contrary notwithstanding." So the claim that there was an implied constitutional right to nullification was a self-evident inconsistency.

Despite this objection, if a state somehow continued to maintain this position, it would lead to the utter negation of any act that the federal government tried to accomplish. If "every law" that operated "injuriously upon any local interest" was thought, and consequently "represented, as unconstitutional," then what law could be upheld, particularly since "there is no appeal" from the nullification doctrine? Jackson placed the situation into its historical prospective:

> If this doctrine had been established at an earlier day, the Union would have been dissolved in its infancy. The excise law in Pennsylvania, the embargo and nonintercourse law in the Eastern states, the carriage tax in Virginia, were all deemed unconstitutional, and were more unequal in their operation than any of the laws now complained of; but, fortunately, none of those states discovered that they had the right now claimed by South Carolina.... Hardly and unequal as those measures bore upon several members of the Union, to the legislatures of none did this efficient

and peaceable remedy, as it is called, suggest itself.... To the statesmen of South Carolina belongs the invention, and upon the citizens of that state will unfortunately fall the evils of reducing it to practice.

Bear in mind that as he was delivering these words, the primary South Carolinia advocate of these policies, John C. Calhoun, was Jackson's own vice-president.

Admitting there might be defects in the Constitution, he could not see this as an acceptable solution to any of them, for the "present happy Constitution was but formed in vain if this fatal doctrine prevails."

Jackson left no doubt of his position when he emphatically stated

> I consider, then, the power to annul a law of the United States, assumed by one state, incompatible with the existence of the Union, contradicted expressly by the letter of the Constitution, unauthorized by its spirit, inconsistent with every principle on which it was founded, and destructive of the great object for which it was formed.

"Our Constitution," he added, "does not contain the absurdity of giving power to make laws and another to resist them. Nor did the states, when they severally ratified it, do so under the impression that a veto on the laws of the United States was reserved to them or that they could exercise it by implication." Jackson challenged South Carolina to find any such idea contained anywhere within the historical records of the constitutional debate.

To make matters even worse, the doctrine suggested that even a fair law could be nullified if its intentions were suspect. To even suggest that a state such as South Carolina was justified in nullifying a federal law based solely upon its perception that the law had been intended so as to act unfairly towards it was a "miserable mockery of legislation!—if a bare majority of the voters in any one state may, on a real or supposed knowledge of the intent with which a law has been passed, declare themselves free from its operation."

To add insult to injury, the state goes to the extreme of declaring its right to "enforce" nullification "by a threat of seceding from the Union if any attempt is made to execute" these laws. Twenty-eight years later the same state would make the same threat to another president, and war would be the result. One can picture the 23-year-old future president sitting in Illinois quietly nodding his head in agreement as he read these words:

> This right to secede is deduced [by the State of South Carolina] from the nature of the Constitution, which, they say, is a compact between sovereign states who have preserved their whole sovereignty and therefore are subject to no superior; that because they made the compact they can

break it when in their opinion it has been departed from by the other states. Fallacious as this course of reasoning is, it enlists state pride and finds advocates in the honest prejudices of those who have not studied the nature of our government sufficiently to see the radical error on which it rests....

The Constitution of the United States, then, forms a government, not a league; and whether it be formed by compact between the states or in any other manner, its character is the same. It is a government in which all the people are represented, which operates directly on the people individually, not upon the states; they retained all the power they did not grant. But each state, having expressly parted with so many powers as to constitute, jointly with the other states, a single nation, cannot ... possess any right to secede, because such a succession does not break a league but destroys the unity of a nation...;

To say that any state may at pleasure secede from the Union is to say that the United States are not a nation[.]... Secession, like any other revolutionary act, may be morally justified by the extremity of oppression; but to call it a constitutional right is confounding the meaning of the terms, and can only be done through gross error or to deceive those who are willing to assert a right, but would pause before they made a revolution or incur the penalties consequent on a failure.

Because the Union was formed by a compact, it is said the parties to that compact may, when they feel themselves aggrieved, depart from it; but it is precisely because it is a compact that they cannot. A compact is an agreement or binding obligation.... A government, [as opposed to a mere league of independent nations], always has a sanction [or penalty for its breach; which sanction may be] express or implied; and in our case it is both necessarily implied and expressly given. An attempt by force of arms to destroy a government is an offense, by whatever means the constitutional compact may have been formed; and such government has the right by the law of self-defense to pass acts for punishing the offender.

...Men of the best intentions and soundest views may differ in their construction of some parts of the Constitution; but there are others on which dispassionate reflection can leave no doubt.

Of this nature appears to be the assumed right of secession. It rests ... on the alleged undivided sovereignty of the states and on their having formed in this sovereign capacity a compact which is called the Constitution, from which, because they made it, they have the right to secede. Both of these positions are erroneous....

The states severally have not retained their entire sovereignty.... [I]n becoming parts of a nation ... they surrendered many of their essential parts of sovereignty.... The allegiance of their citizens was transferred ... to the government of the United States; they became American citizens and owed obedience to the Constitution of the United States and to laws made in conformity with the powers it vested in Congress.

Of course, here was the weak point in Jackson's argument. Many Southerners did nor feel that their primary allegiance was to the United States, as was evidenced when the conflict ultimately came. It seemed, at least to many Northerners, that the South was only willing to claim primary allegiance to the United States when it was in its own best interest to do so. For the first few decades of the country's existence, when the South virtually monopolized control of the nation, such allegiance seemed manifest. But as the South's ability to manipulate the country's fortunes to its own advantage declined, so did its willingness to participate in the federal experiment.

To many Northerners, it must have seemed that now that it was finally their turn to run things their way, the South was no longer willing to participate. One is reminded of the youngster who is willing to be part of the group as long as they're playing by his rules. But as soon as someone else wants to play a different game, he wants to run off and abandon the group, regardless of any adverse consequences his leaving may have upon the others. It seems clear that Jackson had such a view of South Carolina's behavior:

> A small majority of the citizens of one state in the Union ... has ordained that all the revenue laws of the United States must be repealed, or that they are no longer a member of the Union. The [newly-elected] governor of that State [former senator Robert Y. Hayne] has recommended ... the raising of an army to carry the secession into effect[.]... No act of violent opposition to the laws has yet been committed, but such a state of things is hourly apprehended. And it is the intent of this instrument to proclaim, not only that the duty imposed on me by the Constitution "to take care that the laws be faithfully executed" shall be performed to the extent of the powers already vested in me by law, ... but to warn the citizens of South Caroline who have been deluded into an opposition to the laws of the danger they will incur by obedience to the illegal and disorganizing ordinance of the convention...; and to point out to ... the good people of that state ... that the course they are urged to pursue is one of ruin and disgrace to the very state whose rights they affect to support.

Jackson ended his proclamation by calling upon the rest of the nation and those citizens of the state of South Carolina who were still loyal. "On your undivided support of your government depends the decision of the great question it involves—whether your sacred Union will be preserved and the blessing it secures to us as one people shall be perpetuated."

Two weeks later on December 26, Governor Hayne issued a proclamation in response to Jackson's, in which he called for volunteers to defend the state's right to nullify the tariff. Over 25,000 men responded. Just two days afterward, Calhoun resigned as vice-president of the United States in order to fill the seat in the Senate that had been vacated by Hayne. Calhoun thus became the first man in the country's history to voluntarily relinquish this elected position. In doing so, he would be in a position to more strongly support the nullification ordinance that the president had so strongly opposed.

During the year, Maria Stewart published a collection of religious meditations. She delivered a few speeches as well. But, like her published works, these were more concerned with the religious conversion of her race than with its emancipation. These works also emphasized the role of women in society who, as a group, were fully as disenfranchised as the blacks.

The year 1832 saw the Supreme Court, in *Worcester vs. Georgia*, reverse its earlier opinion and rule that the Cherokee nation was sovereign. The constitutional implication was that the state of Georgia was not allowed to pass any laws concerning the coveted Cherokee lands. This offered the Indians a faint ray of hope in their struggle. President Jackson was quoted as saying, "Marshall has made his decision. Now let him enforce it."

Also in 1832, the last surviving signer of the Declaration of Independence, Charles Carroll, passed away.

Margaret Morgan, a slave and the property of Margaret Ashmore of Maryland, in 1832 joined the growing ranks of fugitive slaves by stealing herself and her children across the border into Pennsylvania. She quietly located herself in York county, fully confident that her mistress would not expend the time, money, and energy to come looking for her. Rural Pennsylvania had a growing population of runaways, and undoubtedly others already living there helped her settle in. Her respite from enslavement would be short-lived.

As an indication of the rapid growth of the railroad industry, Pennsylvania by this time had 67 different lines, ranging in size from a few hundred yards to a maximum of 22 miles. The B & O Railroad, chartered just four years previously, has already carried 140,000 people between Baltimore and Washington City.

The year 1832 was both the start and the finish of "Black Hawk's War." Black Hawk was the 67-year-old chief of the Sac (or Sauk) tribe that had lived for generations in the land that was now Northwestern Illinois, until the U.S. government relocated them west of the Mississippi River in 1804. Unsatisfied with their new lands, they returned to their ancestral home in the spring, setting off panic among the whites. When frightened settlers killed two Indians who had come bearing a white flag, the enraged Sac began killing white settlers. Hopelessly outnumbered and burdened with the presence of their women and children, the tribe was virtually annihilated during a massacre in early August at a time when Black Hawk himself was away trying to enlist the aid of other Indian allies. Military participants in the war included Albert Sidney Johnston, Zachary Taylor, Winfield Scott, and sons of Alexander Hamilton and Daniel Boone. A young captain in the Sangamon County volunteers, a group that never actually saw any action, was a clerk named Abraham Lincoln.

The proud old chief was captured later in the month by a group of rival Winnebagos. These Indians delivered him to Colonel Zachary Taylor. Taylor placed the Indian chief and others captured with him under the supervision of Lieutenant Jefferson Davis. Many sources list Davis as a participant in the Black Hawk War, but it seems that his only real involvement was in this role as a supervisor of prisoners. Black Hawk was eventually sent to Washington D.C. as a prisoner.

Though a minor historical incident, the Black Hawk War seemed to assume a larger significance due to the involvement of many individuals who would later become significant in the nation's future, including two future U.S. presidents and a president of the Confederacy.

Forty-year-old James Gillespie Birney was a successful lawyer living in Huntsville, Alabama. The wealthy, slaveholding son of a famous Kentucky plantation family, he began to question the South's acceptance of slavery, going so far as to consider the possibility of gradual emancipation. These radical ideas and his interest in the Colonization Society led him to abandon Alabama, and return to the relatively more free atmosphere of his native state.

On February 20, 1832, Alexis de Tocqueville and Gustave Beaumont left New York City to return to France. During the 271 days he had spent in America, Tocqueville had managed to visit 17 of the then 24 states. His experiences would provide the background for a monumental work on the young nation.

In an effort to recoup the declining fortunes of his family, British actor Charles Kemble traveled to America in the company of his daughter Fanny, who was still at the height of her career. They arrived in New York in September and began a series of performances that would extend to Philadelphia, Washington and Boston. By all accounts, Miss Kemble was enthusiastically received by the public and was soon attracting the attention of many eligible young bachelors.

Six

1833

In January, William Lloyd Garrison received a letter in Boston from Prudence Crandall in Canterbury. Crandall had made the decision to seek advice from the nation's leading abolitionist on her proposed school for black girls. Even before Garrison had an opportunity to respond to her communication, she arrived in Boston to speak with him privately about her plans.

While he wholeheartedly welcomed and approved of her idea, he cautioned her that she might be preparing herself for trouble. She declared herself willing to face the consequences if he deemed the prospects worthy. Upon her return to Canterbury, she informed her white students that their arrangement would be terminated at the end of February. In the meantime, ads appeared in *The Liberator* announcing the opening of the school to black candidates on April 1.

On January 16, President Jackson delivered a message to Congress that detailed the proceedings of the South Carolina Nullification Convention and his December 10 response to it. He observed in his message to Congress that "[i]t appears ... the State authorities are actively organizing their military resources" in preparation for opposition. "A recent proclamation of the present governor of South Carolina has openly defied the authority of the Executive of the Union" in calling up volunteers. "Thus South Carolina presents herself in the attitude of hostile preparation, and ready even for military violence if need be to enforce her laws for preventing the collection of the duties within her limits."

While admitting there had, as yet, been no actual violence or act of public outrage, Jackson expressed the opinion that "aggression may be regarded as committed when it is officially authorized and the means of enforcing it fully provided." He recorded the steps South Carolina had undertaken in preparation for defending itself against any federal encroachment, including calling up and organizing volunteer militia.

As if to meliorate the situation, South Carolina had suggested that Congress should "submit a plan of taxation" upon which it could "acquiesce in a liberal spirit of concession," as long as it was "met in due time and in a becoming spirit" by the Northern states. This vague proposal was tantamount to political blackmail, suggesting that the federal government should capitulate to demands in order to not see the union torn asunder.

Such a threat was the worst possible approach to take with the president. Jackson continued by observing that "these conditions" under which the state might be willing to retreat from its position were "so undefined ... and are so directly opposed to the known opinions and interests of the great body of the American people as to be almost hopeless of attainment." Consequently, Jackson called upon Congress to approve discretionary powers that would allow him to use force, if necessary, to see that the tariffs were duly collected.

The date South Carolina had set was February 1. As of that date, if the offending tariff had not been abrogated or rescinded, then the state would not consider itself obligated to comply.

Debate in Congress began in earnest late in January. Meanwhile, Henry Clay had stepped forth as the moderator, working behind the scenes to hammer together an alternate tariff compromise that would allow both parties to back down without losing face. Even as the compromise tariff was being introduced, Jackson's so-called "Force Bill" was passed on February 20. Clay's compromise was hurriedly pushed through, and ultimately passed on March 1.

Ironically, on March 3—his last day of his first term in office—Jackson signed both the Force Bill and the compromise tariff. Both sides were able to claim a victory. Jackson had refused to be intimidated by the recalcitrant state and had demonstrated his willingness to fight if the need arose. However, with the passage of the new tariff, South Carolina backed down from its position of noncompliance with Federal authority. In a letter to James Buchanan, Jackson described his success. "I met nullification at its threshold," he bragged. "My proclamation was well timed. It opened the eyes of the people to the wicked designs of the nullifiers."

The president informed Buchanan "that South Carolina has repealed the ordinance of secession and all laws based upon it." In what surely counts as one of the worst predictions in all of recorded history, Jackson exclaimed, "Thus dies nullification and the doctrine of secession, never more to be heard of." South Carolina viewed itself as having triumphed against federal encroachment by forcing Congress to replace the ill-fated 1832 tariff with Clay's more palatable compromise. It agreed to abide by the federal authority, though in a last gesture of defiance it voted to nullify the recently passed (and no longer relevant) Force Bill. It had demonstrated to its own satisfaction the ability to manipulate the rest of the nation through the use of threats, specifically the open threat of secession. Twenty-seven years later, under different circumstances and a different president, South Carolina would again resort to the same sort of bravado and threats of secession. Only this time it would push the game too far, against an opponent willing to risk all to perpetuate the union as it was.

Almost as soon as Prudence Crandall made her announcement concerning her school for blacks, the community leaders of Canterbury, Connecticut, called a town meeting for March 9. Reverend Samuel May and George W. Benson attended on behalf of the NEAS, virtually alone in their support of the beleaguered Crandall. May's journal of the meeting presents a view of Northern bigotry at its most horrendous. "On entering the village," May wrote, "we were warned that we should be in personal danger if we appeared there as Miss Crandall's friends." They were told that since her announcement Miss Crandall "had been grossly insulted and threatened with various kinds of violence." Despite these dire forebodings, May agreed to represent Crandall. Resolutions were introduced at this meeting that stated:

> Whereas it hath been publicly announced that a school is to be opened in this town on the first Monday in April next, using the Language of the advertisement, "for young ladies and little misses of color" or in other words for the people of color, the obvious tendency of which would be to collect within the town of Canterbury, large numbers of persons from other states, whose character and habits might be various and unknown to us, thereby rendering insecure, the persons, properties and reputations of our citizens. Under such circumstances, our silence might be construed into an approbation of the project.
>
> Thereupon it is Resolved—that the location of a school for the people of color at any place within the limits of this town for the admissions of persons of foreign jurisdictions meets with our unqualified disapprobation and it is to be understood that the inhabitants of Canterbury protest it in the most earnest manner.
>
> It is Further Resolved—that a committee be now appointed to be composed of the Civil Authority and Selectmen, who shall make known to the persons contemplating the establishment of said school, the sentiments and objections entertained by this meeting, in reference to said school, pointing out to her, the injurious effects and incalculable evils resulting from such an establishment within this town and to persuade her to abolish the project.

After the resolutions were duly noted, Rufus King elaborated upon them in a short speech in which he "grossly misrepresented what

Miss Crandall had done, her sentiments and purpose and threw out several mean and low insinuations against the motives of those who were encouraging her enterprise." By which, of course, he meant the abolitionists.

The Honorable Andrew T. Judson spoke next. May described Judson as "a great man in town, a leading politician in the state and much talked of by the Democrats as soon to be Governor." Judson's house was close to Miss Crandall's school, and the "idea of having a school for nigger girls so near him was insupportable."

> [Judson] vented himself in a strain of reckless hostility to his neighbor, her benevolent self-sacrificing undertaking and its patrons and declared his determination to thwart the enterprise. He twanged every chord that could stir the coarser passions of the human heart and with such success that his hearers seemed to be filled with the apprehension that a dire calamity was impending over them, that Miss Crandall was the author or instrument of it, that there were powerful conspirators engaged against them in the plot and that the people of Canterbury should be roused by every consideration of self-preservation as well as self-respect to prevent the accomplishment of the design, defying the wealth and influence of all who are abetting it.

Having allowed Judson to have his say, May presented himself as representing Crandall and requested to be heard on her behalf. At that point, Judson

> ... instantly broke forth with greater violence than before; accused us of insulting the town by coming there to interfere in its local concerns. Other gentlemen sprang to their feet in hot displeasure; poured out their tirade upon Miss Crandall and her accomplices and with fists doubled in our faces roughly admonished us that if we opened our lips THERE, they would inflict upon us the utmost penalty of the law if not a more immediate vengeance. Thus forbidden to Speak, we of course sat in silence and let the waves of invective and abuse dash over us.

When the meeting was adjourned, May endeavored to have his say. However, "the trustee of the church to which the house belonged came in and ordered all out, that the doors might be shut." If Prudence Crandall had been at all unaware of the risk she intended to take by opening her school, this meeting certainly must have disillusioned her. Yet, despite the opposition, she was determined to continue with her plans.

Had there yet remained even the slightest uncertainty of the community's attitude, a letter appeared in the *Norwich Courier* on March 27 that removed all doubt. It was signed by nine prominent citizens of Canterbury, including Andrew Judson.

> ... We might ask the citizens of any town in New England wherever situated would it be well for that town to admit blacks from slave states or other states to an unlimited extent? Once open the door and New England will become the Liberia of America.... [W]e appeal to every Christian and every philanthropist—we appeal to the enlightened citizens of our native state and the friends of our country; ... we ask them to apply to these facts those wholesome principles which we believe are universally cherished in New England and the issue, we will abide.

It's likely that this group of civic-minded individuals felt confident that the Northern majority would agree with them. And they were probably correct in assuming as much. But the winds of change were beginning to blow, and the persecution of Prudence Crandall would be just one of many incidents that would drive more and more people into the abolitionist camp.

On March 29, the *Brooklyn Advertiser Press* carried an open letter from May to Judson. May expressed his exasperation that

> ... so large a number of persons could be so completely misled by the art and influence of a few individuals; and ashamed that in Connecticut (which claims to be the most enlightened and moral state in our Union) a community of free men could be found who would thus yield themselves to be the instruments of such injustice and cruelty. From your high official standing, Sir, ... it was to have been expected that you would have endeavored to allay the popular excitement[.] ... So far from it, however, you were the prominent actor on the occasion; and exerted yourself ... to enkindle [the] bitterest feelings against Miss Crandall and her friends[.] [The decisions reached at the town meeting] can reflect no honor upon the town, [and] may indirectly affect the happiness of millions in our land.

Judson did, in fact, respond to May. His sentiments were probably more in line with the typical Northern attitude towards blacks then were May's:

> We are not merely opposed to the establishment of that school in Canterbury, we mean that there shall not be such a school set up anywhere in the state. The colored people can never rise from their menial condition in our country; they ought not to be permitted to rise. They are an inferior race of beings, and never can or ought to be recognized as the equals of the whites. Africa is the place for them. I am in favor of colonization. Let the niggers and their descendents be sent back to their fatherland[.] ... You and your friend Garrison have undertaken what you cannot accomplish. The condition of the colored population can never be essentially improved on this continent.... You are violating the Constitution of our Republic which settled forever the status of the black man in this land. They belong to Africa. Let them be sent there or kept as they are here. The sooner you Abolitionists abandon your project the better for our country, the niggers and yourself.

Canterbury wasn't the only place where confrontation was brewing that summer. In Detroit, Michigan, Thornton and Lucie Blackburn had been quietly living a free life since their escape from Kentucky. Unfortunately for them, a friend of Susan Brown, Thornton's owner, recognized him on the street while visiting the city. The widow Brown was contacted, and soon her lawyer and a nephew were in town demanding the pair be turned over. A Detroit judge agreed that, according to the Federal Fugitive Slave Act, such was his duty. They were jailed pending their removal back to the South.

Fortunately for the Blackburns—but unfortunately for widow Brown and, as it turned out, the city of Detroit—there was a large and fairly militant black population in the city. Leaders of the black community concocted a plan to save the pair.

Lucie was the easier one to free. The wives of two Baptist ministers visited her in jail, where one of them changed clothes with the fugitive. Lucie then walked undetected out of the jail and was quietly carried away to Canada. Thornton Blackburn, however, was heavily guarded, and his escape could not be accomplished through subterfuge. Instead, a mob of blacks estimated at between 200 and 400 stormed the jail and forcibly removed him.

Through the intervention of his rescuers, Thornton made it across the Detroit river into Canada, where he rejoined his wife. During the assault upon the jail, one of the guards was so badly beaten that he later died of the injuries. This event received national attention and has been memorialized as the "Blackburn Riots of 1833." It holds the dubious distinction of having been the first race-related riot in the city of Detroit.

Northern abolitionists were no doubt enchanted to hear that another pair of blacks had escaped from the South's evil institution. It is also safe to assume that their "former" owners were less pleased. Susan Brown's reactions are unrecorded, though it is said that she spent 15 years in litigation against the steamboat company whose vessel provided them their original getaway from Kentucky. Ultimately, she won a judgment in 1846 of $400.

While the escape of the Thorntons could be considered an antislavery triumph, things were not going quite so well in Connecticut. Despite the strong public protest, Prudence Crandall continued with her plans and opened her school as scheduled. Town officials decided that their best means of attack depended upon an old, though seldom used, vagrancy law that was still on the books. Since most of Crandall's students were not residents of Canterbury, the law could be made to apply to them. (Examination of the city's town meeting resolutions makes it clear that they had already decided at that time to utilize this approach.) According to this law, if any of her students was warned by a town official to leave town, she had to prove that she was not a vagrant by posting a bond. Failing to do so, she could be subject to a fine for each additional week which she remained. If the fine was not paid, she could receive ten lashes with a whip.

Eliza Hammond, who was from Providence, Rhode Island, was the first student so warned by the city officials. She refused to cooperate and was only spared her punishment when Samuel May posted the required bond in her behalf.

The next step against Crandall was the passage of a state bill that required any school to get permission from local officials before accepting any out-of-state pupils. Denouncing the law as unjust, Crandall refused to comply. On June 27, 1833, she was incarcerated for her disobedience. Though she spent only one night in a cell before she was released pending her trial, it drew a great deal of attention and sympathy to her case.

Lydia Maria Child was at the pinnacle of her success. Her books were bestsellers, and her name was gaining respect and recognition throughout the country. It could not have been easy, then, for her to associate her name so strongly with the unpopular cause of abolitionism. But that is exactly what she did with the publication, on August 5, of her latest book, *An Appeal in Favor of that Class of Americans Called Africans*.

Child's book was the first full-scale assault on slavery. Though the language seems rather stiff by today's conventions, it remains an interesting piece. That she was aware of the risk she was taking in putting her name to such a work is obvious from the preface in which she said, in part: "I am fully aware of the unpopularity of the task I have undertaken; but though I *expect* ridicule and censure, I cannot *fear* them."

That such was indeed the case was almost immediately realized. Sales on her previous books plummeted. Her publishers allowed her formerly popular works to quietly go out of print. Even the highly successful *Juvenile Miscellany* folded as readers withdrew their subscriptions. For all intents and purposes, her literary career was finished.

None of this, however, could have been totally unexpected. But the fact that she released the book even while anticipating that there would be a negative reaction to it is a measure of how strongly she believed in black rights. What little support she got came from the abolitionists, who unanimously hailed the work as a great piece.

To say that she accomplished something extraordinary seems like an understatement. Her book was the first to bring to many Northern minds the true conditions of slavery in America. Meticulously researched and lavishly sprinkled with true life anecdotes, it allowed many of its readers the chance to experience slavery up close. To the knowledgeable modern reader it may hold few surprises. But to her contemporaries it certainly must have.

The book was divided into eight chapters. The first outlined the progress of slavery in the New World. It included ghastly descriptions of the "middle passage" aboard slave ships from Africa, as well as scathing depictions of slavetraders and slave auctions. It offered her audience a portrait quite different from the bucolic scenes of pastoral splendor that the South painted of plantation living.

The second chapter, the longest in the volume, compared modern American slavery with historical accounts of slavery, stressing that the institution as it existed in the "Land of the Free" was more repressive than at any previous time. The chapter is amply loaded with citations of Southern slave laws demonstrating the absolute control Southerners had over the blacks. Any modern reader who has been deluded by accounts sympathetic to the Southern cause into thinking that slaves were treated well is advised to read this section carefully. Many contemporaries of Child, laboring under similar misconceptions, were rudely awakened by the stark realities portrayed within it.

The book, not surprisingly, created an uproar in the South. However, it seems significant that no major work ever emerged from the slaveholding states to refute her claims. There can be little reason to doubt the veracity of her words.

The third chapter addressed many of the Southern arguments against emancipating the slaves, particularly those dealing with the danger that would result from doing so. It is a veritable catalogue of the history of emancipated slaves throughout the New World. She sums up the results by observing that "as far as it can be ascertained ... it appears that in every place and time in which emancipation has been tried, *not one drop of white blood has been shed, or even endangered by it.*"

In the midst of addressing the typical pro-slavery defenses, Child suggested that the whole issue could be avoided if only people would "*simplify* their arguments—let them confine themselves to one single question, 'What right can a man have to compel his neighbor to toil without reward, and leave the same hopeless inheritance to his children, in order that *he* may live in luxury and indolence?'"

In this single question she articulated the entire abolitionist argument. If one agreed with her implication that no man does possess such a right, than all other arguments were superfluous. What does it matter that somebody's ancestors started the problem, or that it would be an economic hardship to abandon the practice now? Or that "the *laws* acknowledge these vested rights in human flesh? I answer, the laws themselves were made by individuals, who wished to justify the wrong and profit by it. We ought never to have recognised a claim, which cannot exist according to the laws of God."

"Must our arguments be based upon justice and mercy to the slaveholders *only*?" she demanded to know. "Have the negroes no right to ask compensation for their years and years of unrewarded toil? The Southerners are much in the habit of saying they really wish for emancipation, ... but I search in vain for any proof that these assertions are sincere."

There was "no doubt" in her mind "that the majority" of the people in the South "wish to perpetuate slavery. They support it with loud bravado, or insidious sophistry, or pretended regret." But most significantly, "they never abandon the point."

In the short fourth chapter, she described the influence that slavery and its representation had on the political course of the country. As she pointed out, this "slave representation is always used to protect and extend slave power; and in this way, the slaves themselves are made to vote for slavery: they are compelled to furnish halters to hang their posterity."

Some of her most powerful arguments were reserved for chapter five in which she contrasted the goals of the Colonization Society with those of the NEAS. The Colonization Society owed its nationwide popularity not to its deeds, or even its intentions, but to the misconceptions of the general public. "The public takes it for granted that slavery is a 'lamentable *necessity*.' [S]o long as the South insists that slavery is *unavoidable*, and say they will not tolerate any schemes *tending* to its abolition—and so long as the North take the *necessity* of slavery for an unalterable truth, ... what remote hope is there of emancipation?"

Therein lay the power of the Colonization Society. People in the North could support it because to them it represented well-intentioned benevolence. People in the South could accept it as well, for to them it represented noninterference. There was nothing the South was so adverse to than interference in its own affairs.

"If by political interference" wrote Child, "is meant hostile interference, or even a desire to promote insurrection, I should at once pronounce it to be most wicked; but if by political interference is meant the liberty to investigate this subject, as other subjects are investigated—to inquire into what has been done, and what may be done—I say it is our sacred duty to do it."

She provided some startling statistics that may have surprised her Northern readers. The Colonization Society had "been in operation more than fifteen years, during which it has transported between two and three thousand *free* people of color. There are in the United States two million of slaves, and three hundred thousand free blacks; and their numbers are increasing at the rate of seventy thousand annually. While the Society have removed less than three thousand,—five hundred thousand

Six • 1833

have been born. While one hundred and fifty *free* blacks have been sent to Africa in a year, two hundred *slaves* have been born in a *day*.... So far as this gradual removal has *any* effect, it tends to keep up the price of slaves in the market, and thus perpetuate the system." This is why so many Southerners favored the Society, and likewise, why all those who sincerely deplored slavery would oppose it.

She went on to observe the fact that many people in the country were "adverse to giving the blacks a good education."

> Now I would ask any candid person why colored children should *not* be educated? Some say, it will raise them above their situation; I answer, it will raise them *in* their situation—not *above* it. When a high school for black girls was first talked of in this city, several of the wealthy class objected to it; because, said they, "if everybody is educated, we shall have no servants." This argument is based on selfishness, and therefore cannot stand.... Lord Brougham said very wisely, "If the higher classes are afraid of being left in the rear, they must likewise hasten onward."
>
> With our firm belief in the natural inferiority of negroes, it is strange we should be so much afraid that knowledge will elevate them quite too high for our convenience....
>
> Besides, like all selfish policy, this is not true policy. The more useful knowledge a person has, the better he fulfils his duties in any station; and there is no kind of knowledge, high or low, which may not be brought into use.

Many people seemed to be concerned that educated blacks wouldn't know their place in society, that they would intrude themselves upon the whites. Child assured them that "one thing is certain, the blacks will never come into your house, unless you *ask* them; and you need not ask them unless you choose."

This seemingly innocuous statement has more significance to it than the modern reader may be aware, as it appears to be Child's attempt to refute one of the strongest arguments in the pro-slavery arsenal: namely, white fears of black improprieties. While the comment as it is made directly concerns educated blacks, it could also refer to the ignorant black slave who, if emancipation was realized, would be "set loose" upon white society. Without delving too deeply into the psychological issues involved, it would be safe to say that whites felt "threatened" by their perception of the animal sensuality of the black race. This threat operated on two distinct levels.

First, as the Southern male constantly reminded Northerners, the South's white women were particularly vulnerable to the unrestrained passions of freed blacks. If the slaves were emancipated, the argument went, hordes of black men would roam the countryside at will, looking for innocent, defenseless white girls and women upon which they could release their animal lusts. (Particularly since, as Jefferson had already pointed out in *Notes on Virginia*, black men preferred white women to "their own kind.") In the South's finely developed code of chivalry, no act was so heinous as the rape of a white woman by a black man. The perpetrator of such a vile act would be lucky to receive a death sentence from the courts; more often, mob violence and lynch law would carry out the punishment.

Child seems to be reassuring her Southern readers (if any) that emancipated blacks would not be entering their homes unbidden, that is, in search of sexual conquests. Their women would be safe from unwanted black encroachments upon their liberties.

Yet there is a second level upon which these sexual fears were played, and it was this second point which was the more potent ammunition to use against Northerners. During the Civil War, it would be referred to as "miscegenation." However, in the 1830s it was called "amalgamation," defined as the sexual "mixing" of the two races. In the eyes of most white Americans, there was nothing quite as repugnant as the idea of whites and blacks breeding together. As the years progressed, the cry of "amalgamist" was one of the easiest and most surefire ways of inciting a crowd against the abolitionists. What white man could stomach the vision of his daughter marrying a black man? But such a possibility existed if blacks were received as social equals with whites, as Garrison and his gang of "Nigger lovers" wanted them to be. Most states had laws against such "unnatural" couplings.

Nor was such legislation a purely antebellum phenomenon. At one point as many as 40 states prohibited the practice. In fact, in 1964, the state of Virginia upheld such a law, declaring:

> Almighty God created the races white, black, yellow, malay, and red, and he placed them on separate continents. And but for the interference with his arrangements there would be no cause for such marriages. The fact that he separated the races shows that he did not intend for the races to mix.

It was not until 1967 that the Supreme Court finally overturned such interracial bans, stating that the "freedom to marry" was a basic right of all Americans.

It seems ironic that, despite such prohibitive laws and the "universal" disapproval of racial mingling, the practice was not altogether uncommon. As witness to this fact is the specialized terminology that developed over the years. A *mulatto* was a person of half black blood; that is, the direct offspring of a black/white liaison. A *quadroon* was one-quarter black, or, specifically, the mixing of a white with a mulatto. An *octoroon* was one-eighth black, or a white with a quadroon. Presumably other mixes were conceivable, such as mulatto with mulatto, mulatto with quadroon, and so forth. However, as the dominant race, the whites were only concerned enough to have a special word for it when the union involved one of their own.

It would probably be impossible to determine how many individuals of each racial mix were present at any given time, though a guess can be made by examining the works of Abraham Lincoln. On June 27, 1857, he made a speech in Springfield, Illinois. Within that speech he remarked.

> ... In 1850, there were in the free States 56,649 mulattos; but for the most part they were not born there—they came from the slaves states, ready made up. In the same year the slave States had 348,874 mulattos, all of home production. The porportion of free mulattos to free blacks—the only colored classes in the free States—is much greater in the slave than in the free States. It is worthy of note, too, that among the free States those which make the colored man the nearest equal to the white have proportionably [sic] the fewest mulattos, the least of amalgamation. In New Hampshire, the State which goes farthest toward equality between the races, there are just 184 mulattos, while there are in Virginia—how many do you think?—79,775, being 23,126 more than in all the free States together.
>
> These statistics show that slavery is the greatest source of amalgamation[.]

One could perhaps argue with Lincoln's conclusions, but there is no reason to suppose that his statistics were faulty. With a total "black" population of 3,638,808 in 1850, Lincoln's 405,523 mulattoes translate into just over 11 percent of the country's black population. Assuming that the same proportion held true in 1835, the country's mulatto population that year would have numbered almost 300,000 individuals. And each one of these mixed individuals represented an instance of black and white amalgamation.

This, of course, leads to the inevitable question: Where were these mulattos, quadroons and octoroons all coming from if "everyone" was against racial mingling?

Many of them, it seems, must have been the offspring of white slaveowners and their property. There were various explanations as to how such unions might occur. One reason may have been simply an economic one. In the slave culture of the South, the offspring of a slave woman was considered a slave, regardless of who the father was. Therefore, it is not beyond the realm of possibility that some slaveowners impregnated their chattel in order to replenish or augment their working stock.

For example, Sally Hemmings, it has been generally asserted, was the daughter of Thomas Jefferson's father-in-law and his mulatto slave,

Betty. Therefore, Sally was a quadroon. But she was also, in effect, the step-sister of Jefferson's wife.

Another explanation, paradoxically, revolved upon the chivalrous notion of idolizing Southern women. Ladies were expected to be virgins when they wed, and, as a result, were inexperienced and perhaps unsatisfying to their mates. Men, on the other hand, viewed sexual prowess as an essential component of their virility. What could be more natural than that they should exercise their passions upon the captive female portion of their population? It is not unreasonable to assume that "Southern hospitality" towards one's male guests often extended to the free use of master's female property. Many a young man no doubt was introduced to the pleasures of the flesh in the arms of a black woman. (As, irrefutably, they had been nursed by black woman in their infancy.)

As the young Southern gentleman became established in the world, he may have found himself saddled with a mate who was unequal to the task of satisfying his desires. After all, Southern women were notorious for their long bouts of "confinement" and incapacity. Why deny himself when the opportunity was as close as his own backyard?

In her famous *Civil War Diary*, Mary Chesnut wrote:

> Like the patriarchs of old our men live all in one house with their wives and their concubines, and the mulattoes one sees in every family exactly resemble the white children—and every lady tells you who is the father of all the mulatto children in everybody's household, but those in her own she seems to think drop from the clouds, or pretends so to think.

While Chesnut's diary was written almost 30 years after the period covered here, there is no reason to believe that such attitudes had not been just as true in the earlier period.

Of course, availing oneself of a black woman's charms was not the same as marrying her. Therefore, the Southern "gentleman" saw no hypocrisy in a system that deplored amalgamation, but allowed each planter to maintain his own personal brothel. At the same time, he could, and often did, argue vehemently without the slightest twinge of self-consciousness against the abolitionists whose theories suggested social equality. His relations with black women were certainly not predicated upon equality.

It should not be misinterpreted as suggesting that all Southern slaveowners took sexual advantage of their female charges. No doubt many did not. However, the sheer numbers of mulattos, quadroons and octoroons in Southern society give evidence that many did. Countless Southern families knew, who were the half-brothers and half-sisters, though many times admissions of such were reserved to death-bed confessions or ultimately revealed in wills.

Nor were all such unions strictly between master and slave. It seems that Southern males often sought out women of mixed blood. It is rare that a mulatto, quadroon or octoroon woman is mentioned without some notice being given of her attractiveness. Occasionally it may be only the simple adjective "comely"; at other times it was the ultimate compliment, "so light as to be almost white." The brothels of the large cities were well-stocked with comely mulattos, quadroons and octoroons.

Throughout the antebellum South particularly attractive femal slaves sold for premium prices due to their sexual desirability, often bringing double the price of a choice fieldhand. Once purchased, the slave had no real defense against her owner's advances, since the law did not recognize them as rape. The unfortunate woman had two options: to resist, and thus to risk beatings, abuse, or being sold; or to yield and thus possibly receive a certain amount of protection, even special privileges. It seems fair to suppose that, given such a choice, many would pretend the role of the willing partner, if only for the sake of self-preservation.

Though records of course do not show how many slave women were cajoled into becoming sexual partners of their masters, common folklore suggests that the number must have been significant. Paradoxically, each such occurrence contributed to the growing perception that black women were wanton, lustful creatures whose passions were unquenchable. This, in turn, strengthened the allure of the black female to those who could afford such forbidden fruits.

And if one couldn't afford to purchase his own private brother, there were alternatives available. The mulatto prostitutes of Charleston were legendary for their beauty. And in New Orleans, light-skinned free black women sometimes became the willing concubines of white men as part of a system called "placage." It all started with the social highlight of the season, the Quadroon Ball. Such balls originated as early as 1805. At the ball, the prospective mistress would mingle with the wealthy white men who attended specifically looking to establish a semi-permanent arrangement with one of the ladies. There was a certain amount of consensus involved: the woman was under no obligation to accept the advances of anyone who did not please her. However, if the "suitor" met with her approval—as well as that of her mother, who was also in attendance—arrangements would be made for the white man to set her up on her own, usually in an apartment or small cottage. He would be responsible for her financial support (as well as that of her children, if any resulted from the arrangement). In return, she would be available to him whenever he was in town.

Apparently there was a little stigma for whites who participated in this system. Some men, even after they became married, continued to maintain their quadroon family in New Orleans while having a separate white family back home. Presumably, it made out-of-town travel more bearable to have all the luxuries, and pleasures, of home awaiting one's arrival.

This system, like other examples of interracial mingling, is difficult to assess in terms of numbers or time period. It appears to have lasted at least until the verge of the Civil War, if not well into the war years. One can only assume that such longevity was evidence of the system's popularity, at least with those who could afford it. Yet it seems possible that even those whites who could not afford it found the mere existence of such a system tittillating, thereby making the black female even more desirable to the white, slaveowning males of the South.

Perhaps it is implying too much of Child to think that she had this entire sexual argument behind her casual statement. However, genteel woman that she was, she could never come right out and address such issues, even though she was no doubt aware they existed. Doubtless, she viewed the sexual crimes committed upon black women as another strong argument against slavery, even if she was unable to address this directly in her work. But she does seem to be reassuring her readers that the (popularly undesirable) amalgamation of the races is not an inevitable result of freeing (or educating) blacks.

Returning to her discussion of the Colonization Society, Child's "greatest objection" to it was that "its members write and speak ... as if the prejudice against skins darker colored than our own, was a fixed and unalterable law of our nature."

"[W]e are constantly told by this Society, that people of color must be removed ... because they *must* always be in a state of degradation here— that they never *can* have all the rights and privileges of citizens—and all this is because the *prejudice* is so great." Child had, of course, reached the same conclusion that Garrison and so many other abolitionists had already come to: in fighting slavery, one had also to combat white prejudice.

"Our prejudice against the blacks is founded in sheer pride; and it originates in the circumstance that people of their color only, are universally allowed to be slaves," Child penned. "We made slavery, and slavery makes the prejudice. No Christian, who questions his own conscience, can justify himself in indulging the feeling. The removal of this prejudice is not a matter of opinion—it is a matter of *duty*. We have no right to palliate a feeling, sinful in itself, and highly injurious to a large number of our fellow beings. Let us no longer act upon the narrow-minded idea, that we must continue to do wrong, because we have so long been in the habit of doing it."

She illustrated the depth of white prejudices with an anecdote about "a gentleman originally from the South" who entered into a conversation between her and another Abolitionist:

Six • 1833

"Whatever you may think. Mrs. Child," said he, "the slaves are a great deal happier than either of us; the less people know, the more happy they are." ...["Anyway," he continued,] "why do you concern yourself about the negroes? Why don't you excite the horses to an insurrection, because they are obliged to work, and are whipped if they do not?" "One *horse* does not whip another," said I; "And besides, I do not wish to promote insurrections. I would, on the contrary, do all I could to prevent them."

As this story demonstrated, "the planter tells us that the slave is very happy, and bids us leave him as he is." But the truth of the matter was that "the negro may often enjoy himself, like the dog when he is not beaten, or the hog when he is not starved; but let not this be called happiness."

She continued by contrasting the views of the Colonization Society with those of the Anti-Slavery Society:

> The Colonization Society are always reminding us that the *master* has rights as well as the slave: The Anti-Slavery Society urge us to remember that the *slave* has rights as well as the master....
>
> The abolitionists think it a duty to maintain at all times, and in all places, that slavery *ought* to be abolished, and that it can be abolished.... They propose no *plan*—they leave that to the wisdom of Legislatures.— But they never swerve from the *principle* that slavery is both wicked and unnecessary. Their object is to turn the public voice against this evil, by a plain exposition of facts....
>
> The Anti-Slavery Society is loudly accused of being seditious, fanatical, and likely to promote insurrections. It seems to be supposed, that they wish to send fire and sword into the South, and encourage the slaves to hunt down their masters. Slave owners wish it to be viewed in this light[.] ...
>
> This Society do not wish to see any coercive or dangerous measures pursued. They wish for universal emancipation, because they believe it is the only way to prevent insurrections....
>
> If there were any apparent wish [on the part of the South] to get rid of this sin and disgrace, I believe the members of the Anti-Slavery Society would most heartily and courageously defend slave owners from any risk that they might incur in a sincere effort to do right. They would teach the negro that it is the Christian's duty meekly and patiently to *suffer* wrong; but they dare not excuse the white man for continuing to *inflict* the wrong.
>
> They think it unfair that all arguments on this subject should be founded on the convenience and safety of the master *alone*. They wish to see the white man's claims have their due weight; but they insist that the negro's rights ought not to be thrown out of the balance.
>
> At the time a large reward was offered for the capture of Mr. Garrison, on the ground that his paper excited insurrections, it is a fact, that he had never sent or caused to be sent, a single paper South of Mason and Dixon's line. He *afterwards* sent papers to some of the leading politicians there; but they of course were not the ones to promote insurrec-

tions.... Are we then forbidden to publish our opinions upon an important subject, for fear somebody will send them somewhere? If so, we live under an actual censorship of the press....

If insurrections do occur, they will no doubt be attributed to the Anti-Slavery Society. But we must not forget that there were insurrections ... long before the ... abolitionists began their efforts; and that masters were murdered in this country, before the Anti-Slavery Society was thought of.

The sixth and seventh chapters dealt primarily with the intellectual and moral accomplishments of members of the black race. Within these pages, Child showed her readers that there were many examples of blacks who had attained as much or more than any white men, in an effort to disprove any supposed natural inferiority of the race.

The eighth and final chapter dealt with the duties, or obligations, the white man owed to the suffering black race. She cited examples—such as Prudence Crandall's on-going struggle in Canterbury—that showed the kind of opposition well-meaning whites encountered when they tried to uplift the blacks.

It can safely be assumed that the majority of the readership of Child's book consisted of those who were already favorably—or, at least, not adversely—inclined towards abolitionism. However, many of those who would step forward in support of abolitionism in the period between its publication and the Civil War would comment upon the significance of her book in shaping their beliefs. Few other anti-slavery volumes would have its impact on the general public.

In August, Prudence Crandall's trial approached. Lawyers for the state based their argument upon the well-accepted "fact" that blacks were not considered legal citizens, and, therefore, did not possess the same rights as whites. Crandall's defense, not surprisingly, took the contrary view.

Her first trial ended on August 23, with the jury unable to reach a verdict. The case went to court again. At this second trial, which ended in October, she was found guilty. "It would be a perversion of terms," stated Judge David Daggett, "and the well-known rule of construction to say that slaves, free blacks or Indians, were citizens within the meaning of that term as used in the Constitution. God forbid that I should add to the degradation of this race of men; but I am bound by my duty, to say they are not citizens."

Crandall's lawyers immediately appealed the case to the Supreme Court of Errors of Connecticut. In the meantime, the school had remained open, though not without its share of persecution. Many merchants in the town refused to sell food or supplies to the school. The building was pelted with rotten eggs and stones. At one point during the summer, the school's well was contaminated with manure. The future of both Crandall and her school rested upon the upcoming appeal.

Meanwhile, plans were preceding for the organization of a national anti-slavery group, spearheaded by the Tappans and Garrison. The group met in Philadelphia and announced the establishment of the American Anti-Slavery Society (AAS) on December 4, 1833. Almost immediately, they met opposition, primarily from those who never took the time to find out what they actually stood for. For those whose knowledge of the group comes from secondhand sources, their "Declaration of Sentiments" may seem less incendiary than would be expected.

It began by contrasting the grievances of the British colonies, "great as they were," with those of the blacks:

> Our fathers were never slaves—never bought and sold like cattle—never shut out from the light of knowledge and religion—never subjected to the lash of brutal taskmasters.
>
> But those, for whose emancipation we are striving—constituting at the present time at least one-sixth of our countrymen—are recognized by law, and treated by their fellow-beings, as brute beasts; are plundered daily of the fruits of their toil without redress; really enjoy no constitutional nor legal protection from licentious and murderous outrages upon their persons; and are ruthlessly torn asunder—the tender babe from the arms of its frantic mother—the heartbroken wife from the weeping husband—at the caprice of irresponsible tyrants. For the crime of having a dark complexion, they suffer the pangs of hunger, the infliction of stripes, the ignominy of brutal servitude....
>
> It is piracy to buy or steal a native African, and subject him to servitude. Surely, the sin is as great to enslave an American as an African.
>
> Therefore, we believe and affirm—that there is no difference, in principle, between the African slave trade and American slavery.

To this point, the group was enumerating a policy that would have been moderately agreeable to most Americans. However, as they continued, they made it clear that they were losing their sympathy for those Southerners who deplored slavery in theory, yet continued to practice it. They firmly declared their conviction that "every American citizen, who detains a human being in involuntary bondage as his property, is ... a manstealer." They further insisted "that the slaves ought instantly to be set free, and brought under the protection of law."

In perhaps the most-quoted portion of their declaration, they stated "That all those laws which are now in force, admitting the right of slavery, are therefore, before God, utterly null and void...." This statement has been used against them for 170 years as an indication of their lawlessness and disregard of their obligations towards society. Yet seldom is the remaining portion of the statement included: [These laws] "being an audacious usurpation of the Divine prerogative, a daring infringement on the law of nature, a base overthrow of the very foundations of the social compact, a complete extinction of all the relations, endearments and obligations of mankind, and a presumptuous transgression of all the holy commandments; and that therefore they ought instantly to be abrogated."

These words are not the radical cry of lunatic anarchists, calling out for lawlessness and violent rebellion as they are often portrayed to be. They are, instead, the impassioned pleas of devoutly sincere individuals, who are not advocating the disobedience of the laws, but are calling for change. While it can be understand why pro-slavery Southerners of the time were displeased with these words, it's difficult to understand why so many modern writers continue to disparage the abolitionist groups. To say that the laws of the country were grossly unfair to the blacks—which, in effect, is all that these words try to say—seems hard to debate.

The next target of the AAS was white prejudice. "We further believe and affirm—that all persons of color, who possess the qualifications which are demanded of others, ought to be admitted forthwith to the enjoyment of the same privileges, and the exercise of the same prerogatives, as ... persons of a white complexion." In the context of nineteenth-century America this was a contention that could easily be seen as offensive by the majority, though from a modern perspective of basic human rights it hardly seems "incendiary." If the pro-slavery, anti-black South was repulsed by such words, how is it fair to blame the abolitionists for the former group's narrow-minded bigotry?

Probably the South's biggest criticism of the AAS came in the following statement: "We maintain that no compensation should be given to the planters emancipating their slaves." One can imagine the affronted slaveowner throwing up his hands in disgust at such an outlandish idea.

Why, if such a farfetched notion caught on, it could mean financial ruin. The AAS, however, had strong arguments for its proposition. In its opinion, to compensate the slave-owners.

> ... would be a surrender of the great fundamental principle, that man cannot hold property in man:
> Because slavery is a crime, and therefore is not an article to be sold:
> Because the holders of slaves are not the just proprietors of what they claim; freeing the slave is not depriving them of property, but restoring it to its rightful owner, it is not wronging the master, but righting the slave—restoring him to himself:
> Because immediate and general emancipation would only destroy nominal, not real property; it would not amputate a limb or break a bone of the slaves, but ... would make them doubly valuable to the masters as free laborers; and

Because, if compensation is to be given at all, it should be given to the outraged and guiltless slaves, and not to those who have plundered and abused them.

The AAS "Declaration of Sentiments" contained words of criticism for the Colonization Society as well: "We regard as delusive, cruel and dangerous, any scheme of expatriation which pretends to aid, either directly or indirectly, in the emancipation of the slaves or to be a substitute for the immediate and total abolition of slavery."

In what may have been the weakest portion of their strongly framed manifesto, the abolitionists tried to mollify the pro-slavery politicians. They expressed themselves as still being willing to "fully and unanimously recognize the sovereignty of each State, to legislate exclusively on the subject of the slavery which is tolerated within its limits." They would even go so far as to "concede that Congress, under the present national compact, has no right to interfere with any of the slave States, in relation to this momentous subject." They would, however, "maintain that Congress has a right, and is solemnly bound, to suppress the domestic slave trade between the several States, and to abolish slavery in those portions of our territory which the Constitution has placed under its exclusive jurisdiction." This referred to Washington, D.C.

They categorically denied they were interfering in a subject that did not concern them, for there were "the highest obligations resting upon the people of the free States to remove slavery by moral and political action, as prescribed in the Constitution of the United States." Notice that they were not suggesting extra-legal or illegal methods, as has been traditionally ascribed to them. They still wished to arrive at a workable solution to the slavery issue within the limited structure the Federal government provided. Perhaps they were naive in doing so. But to describe their position as "threatening" to the South is to accept the slaveowner view of the situation without giving the words of the AAS full consideration.

In contrast to these high moral standards, there was at the same time a group of Southern gentlemen whose goal was the "immediate preparation for future emancipation," which sounds remarkably like continued procrastination on the issue. Perhaps the most telling feature of this group was that it called itself the "Kentucky Society for the Gradual Relief of the State from Slavery." Notice that it is not the slave who they are trying to relieve. In their view, it was the white state that needed saved from the evils of the black horde within their borders.

The AAS "*Declaration of Sentiments*" brought renewed abuse upon the abolitionists. The strongest criticisms seemed to be against their demand for immediate abolition, as opposed to some gradual or long-range plan. Garrison was quick to elaborate upon this within the pages of *The Liberator*:

> Immediate abolition does not mean that the slaves shall immediately exercise the right of suffrage, or be eligible to any office, or be emancipated from law, or be free from the benevolent restraints of guardianship. We contend for the immediate personal freedom of the slaves, for their exemption from punishment except where law has been broken, for their employment and reward as free laborers, for their exclusive rights to their own bodies and those of their children, for their instruction and subsequent admission to all the trusts, offices, honors and emoluments of intelligent freemen.

Fuel was added to the abolitionists' fire in 1833 when Great Britain abolished slavery throughout the empire, going into effect the following summer. Once this was accomplished, the United States would be the sole slaveowning nation in North America.

Twenty women, dismayed at their inability to actively participate in the AAS, formed their own group called the Philadelphia Female Anti-Slavery Society. It was one of the first groups of its kind in America in which women would take an active role. Soon, similar groups sprung up all over the country, giving women an opportunity to make a difference in a society that had disenfranchised them almost as completely as it had the blacks.

Maria Stewart, discouraged by strong public opposition to her views, gave her last speech on September 21. Frustrated at the lack of acceptance given blacks and women in society, she quietly retired from the public spotlight. She settled down as a school teacher in New York. As the years went by, she often quietly assisted the newly forming women's anti-slavery groups, but she was no longer willing to suffer personal ignominy for her beliefs.

The advance of technology continued. By the end of the year, South Carolina led the nation with 137 miles of railroad line. The Canadian steamship S. S. *Royal William* completed the Atlantic crossing in just 25 days.

While in Philadelphia, British actress Fanny Kemble was introduced to Pierce Butler. Butler was that uniquely American byproduct of the Southern slave "aristocracy": no job, no trade, no vocation, no goals, little education, but filled with a sense of his own self-importance. His family was one of the richest in the state of Georgia thanks to large plantations and slaveholdings, which Butler would soon inherit. He would be condsidered by most American women to be a "fine catch," but Fanny was at least initially unimpressed. Undaunted, Butler pursued the object of his attentions with single-minded determination.

Six • 1833

President Jackson continued an ongoing attack against the Bank of the United States by ordering Secretary of the Treasury William J. Duane to withdraw all government deposits. Jackson's campaign against the bank was prompted as much by a personal vendetta against the bank's president, Nicholas Biddle, than by any sound fiscal policy. Duane refused to comply and resigned in protest. Jackson appointed Maryland lawyer Roger B. Taney, who complied with the president's directive despite the fact that Congress never officially approved Taney's appointment.

Sometime during 1883 a U.S. army surgeon living in St. Louis, named Dr. John Emerson, purchased a slave named Sam from Peter Blow. No record was kept of the transaction—which is not very surprising, as there was no need to do so. There was nothing out of the ordinary about this particular sale or this particular slave. However, a quarter century later Sam would be the most widely-known slave in the nation. Though by that time, he had changed his name to Dred Scott.

In October, Emerson received orders to relocate to Fort Armstrong. This army post was located on an island in the Mississippi River three hundred miles north of St. Louis. Fort Armstrong was situated in the free state of Illinois. Dr. Emerson arrived at the fort on December 1, 1833, accompanied by his human property, Sam. It can be assumed that Dr. Emerson did not inform Sam that the constitution of Illinois prohibited slavery within its borders.

SEVEN

1834

Outside of Cincinnati, Ohio, stands the Lane Seminary. Mention has already been made of Cincinnati's location as a hot spot for anti-slavery activity. Therefore, it should not be surprising that there was a great deal of interest among the seminary students concerning slavery. As in many places in the country where well-meaning individuals were concerned about slavery but unsure how it could be dealt with, the Colonization Society was popular at Lane. However, that was about to change. In March, against the wishes of the faculty, the students organized a debate upon the issues involved.

At the time, the majority of those involved were decidedly sympathetic towards the goals of the Colonization Society, or, more precisely, towards what were perceived to be the goals of the society. There were very few decided abolitionists among the debaters. However, the questions posed for debate were:

> 1st: "Ought the people of the Slaveholding States to abolish Slavery immediately?"
> 2nd: "Are the doctrines, tendencies, and measures of the American Colonization Society, and the influence of its principal supporters, such as render it worthy of the patronage of the Christian public?"

According to the prepared report of the debates:

> Each question was debated nine evenings of two hours and a half each; making forty-five hours of solid debate. We possessed some facilities for discussing both these questions intelligently. We are situated within one mile of a slaveholding State; eleven of our number were born and brought up in slave States, seven of whom were sons of slaveholders, and one of them himself a slaveholder, till recently; one of us had been a slave, and

had bought his freedom, "with a great sum," which his own hands had earned; ten others had lived more or less in slave States.

It was deemed important to provide such a detailed description of the participants in order to convince readers they were not predisposed towards abolitionism, yet were familiar enough with the peculiar institution to speak about it first-hand. Besides their personal expertise, they had at their disposal "nearly all the Annual Reports of the Colonization Society, and the prominent documents of the Anti-Slavery Society."

After the first few nights of discussion, the group established as basic facts the following:

> That slaves long for freedom; that it is a subject of very frequent conversation among them; that they keenly feel the wrong, the insult and the degradation which are heaped upon them by the whites; they feel no interest comparatively in their master's affairs, because they know he is their oppressor; they are indolent, because nothing they can earn is their own; they pretend to be more ignorant and stupid than they really are, so as to avoid responsibility, and to shun the lash for any real or alleged disobedience to orders; when inspired with a promise of freedom, they will toil with incredible alacrity and faithfulness; they tell their masters and drivers they are contented with their lot, merely through fear of greater cruelty if they tell the truth; no matter how kind their master is, they are dissatisfied[.]

All of these conclusions are in direct contradiction to the lot of the slaves as usually described by the slaveowners. One suspects that many of those listeners with Southern backgrounds felt their faith in the region's domestic institutions being shaken.

One of the high points of the debates must have been the testimony of James Bradley:

> James Bradley, the emancipated slave above alluded to, addressed us nearly two hours; and I wish his speech could have been heard by every opponent of immediate emancipation, to wit: first, that "it would be unsafe to the community;" second, that "the condition of the emancipated negroes would be worse than it is now; that they are incompetent to provide for themselves; that they would become paupers and vagrants, and would rather steal than work for wages." This shrewd and intelligent black, cut up these *white objections* by the root[.] ... I wish the slanderers of negro intellect could have witnessed this unpremeditated effort. I will give you a sketch of this man's history. He was stolen from Africa when an infant, and sold into slavery. His master, who resided in Arkansas, died, leaving him to his widow. He was then about eighteen years of age. For some years, *he managed the plantation for his mistress*. Finally, he purchased his time by the year, and began to earn money to buy his freedom. After five years of toil, having paid his owners $655, besides supporting himself during the time, he received his "free papers," and

emigrated to a free State with more than $200 in his pocket. Every cent of this money, $865, he earned by labour and trading. He is now a beloved and respected member of this institution.

Now, Mr. Editor, can slaves take care of themselves if emancipated? I answer the question in the language employed by brother Bradley, on the above occasion. "They have to take care of, and support themselves *now, and their master, and his family into the bargain*; and this being so, it would be strange if they could not provide for themselves, *when disencumbered from this load.*" He said the great desire of the slaves was "*liberty and education.*"

At the end of the ninth evening of debate on the first question, "every individual voted in the affirmative except four or five, who excused themselves from voting at all, on the ground that they had not made up their opinion."

The next nine evenings were devoted to the second question. However, many of those who had planned on supporting the Colonization Society were quite surprised at what they found when they actually came to examine its documents.

> *Most of the Colonizationists who expressed any opinion on the subject, declared their ignorance of the doctrines and measures of the Society until this debate.* They cannot find words to express their astonishment that they should have been so duped into the support of this Society, as a scheme of benevolence towards the free blacks, and a remedy for slavery. They now repudiate it with all their hearts....
>
> At the close of the debate, the [2nd] question was taken by ayes and noes, and decided in the negative with only one dissenting voice.

Many of the Southern participants, as a direct result of these debates, dedicated themselves to "immediate emancipation" as the only reasonable solution to the slavery problem. The students became convinced that if they could carry their message to the slaveowners, then their "brethren from the slave states" could be educated to the reasonableness of the abolition position. The slaveowners "have somehow got the opinion that *abolition* is an infuriated monster, with a thousand heads and ten thousand horns, panting after blood, and ready to gore to death every slaveholder in the Union." It's amazing that many today still have the same mistaken impression.

Upon the completion of the debates, the students involved were told by the heads of the college that if they continued their support of abolition there would be no place for them at Lane. In the words of Theodore Dwight Weld, one of the students who had originally orchestrated the debates, "it was left for the students either to sacrifice their duty to God and remain; or to maintain it and leave. They nobly chose the latter, and the result was that about forty of the most pious and talented were thus compelled to quit Lane Seminary." Weld was among the group. Temporarily denied a place of their own, many of them would become "wandering evangelists" for abolitionism.

While most white Americans celebrated July 4th as Independence Day, blacks in New York celebrated it as "Emancipation Day." It had been on that date in 1827 that the last slaves in the state of New York were officially freed. New York City alone had a black population of 14,000 who often observed the occasion parading drunkenly through the streets, banging drums and blowing trumpets. Much, it must be assumed, to the disgust of the city's whites.

Lewis Tappan offered the blacks an alternative by sponsoring a special service for them at the Chatham Street Chapel. Many blacks showed up, as well as a number of white abolitionists. Unfortunately, so did an unruly mob of pro-slavery whites who, though uninvited, filled the upper galleries. As the blacks and whites on the floor attempted to sing their hymns, insults and prayers books began to fly from the balconies. The assistance of a hastily dispatched squad of watchmen was needed to temporarily restore order, though the peace would be shortlived.

Three days later, the black parishioners refused to disperse upon the demands of a white group that called itself the Sacred Music Society. Soon rioting broke out. When Tappan received word of the altercation, he rushed from his home to the chapel, only to discover that the mob had already been broken up by the police. However, many of the whites had assembled at Tappan's home in his absence. He was forced to push his way through to his besieged wife "amidst a tremendous noise, mingled groans, hisses, and execrations." It required the services of privately hired guards to finally persuade the mob to leave.

William Leggett, in his position as editor of the *Evening Post*, editorialized the events the next morning. "The story is told in the morning journals in very inflammatory language, and the whole blame is cast upon the negroes; yet it seems to us, from these very statements themselves, that, as usual, there was fault on both sides, and more especially on that of the whites." Leggett's words are particularly telling once it is realized that he was not sympathetic towards the abolitionists:

> It seems to us, also, that those who are opposed to the *absurd and mad schemes* [emphasis added] of the immediate abolitionists, use means against that scheme which are neither just nor politic.... It is the duty of the press to discriminate; to oppose objectionable measures, but not to arouse popular fury against men; ... persecution will inevitably have the effect of prolonging its existence and adding to its strength.
> ... That the whole scheme of immediate emancipation, and of promiscuous intermarriage of the two races, is preposterous, and revolting alike to common sense and common decency, we shall ever be ready, on all occasions, to maintain. Still, this furnishes no justification for

invading the undoubted rights of the blacks, or violating the public peace[.]

Leggett had, quite unintentionally, articulated what was quickly becoming one of the strongest weapons of the abolitionists: the desire of the common American, regardless of his personal feelings towards the blacks or their supporters, to see them treated fairly. As the next few years rolled along and abuses against the abolitionists increased in frequency and intensity, many people who might otherwise have disagreed with them and their policies began to defend them and their rights against pro-slavery attacks.

Fearful of his family's safety, Tappan left with them the following afternoon to a more secluded place outside of the city. That night, a mob of rowdies descended upon the unoccupied Tappan home. Windows were smashed, and furniture and personal belongings were tossed into the street to become fuel for the mob's bonfire.

The Tappans returned the next day to inspect the damage to their property. Lewis Tappan later commented: "When my wife saw the large chimney-glass—which we purchased eighteen years ago and which I often said looked too extravagant—was demolished, she laughed and said, 'you got rid of that piece of furniture that troubled you so much.'"

A touching piece of bravado, but no doubt they were both terribly concerned about the cost of their beliefs. But Tappan refused to be bullied. In fact, he decided to forego for the summer repairs to the damaged house, preferring to let it stand as it was so it would be "a silent Anti-Slavery preacher to the crowds who will flock to see it."

Popular legend has it that after that night, members of the free black community took turns standing silent watch outside the house, their presence unknown to the Tappans inside.

Prudence Crandall's case finally came before the Connecticut Supreme Court that same month. Perhaps mindful of the violence that had erupted in nearby New York City, the court was apparently afraid to make a decisive ruling. To avoid doing so, it ruled that an error had been committed in Crandall's second court case and thus threw the ruling out on a technicality. In the eyes of the courts, she was free to keep her school open. In the eyes of the community, however, the verdict was still out.

That August saw additional anti-black rioting, this time in Philadelphia. Over the course of three nights, 40 or more black homes were burned by the mobs, many blacks were injured, and one black man drowned in the Schuykill River while trying to escape from the hostile crowd.

Late that summer, Prudence Crandall married Calvin Philleo, a Baptist minister. Her story had become a familiar one throughout the country and she was something of a national celebrity. Though many disagreed with what she was doing, many applauded her determination to continue. Unfortunately, it would take more than just moral support to continue the fight against popular prejudice.

On the night of September 9 a band of whites broke into the school in Canterbury. Furniture was broken amid threats and the yelling of crude oaths against the black students. Crandall realized that she could no longer guarantee the safety of her charges. With profound regret, she decided that she would have to close the school.

With her capitulation, another anti-slavery martyr was added to the ever-increasing list.

Within just a few years, Crandall would separate from her husband, and retire to an uneventful life in Illinois. In 1866, in belated recognition of her great courage and moral strength—and as a result of a public campaign spearheaded in part by Samuel L. Clemens—the Connecticut legislature honored her with an annual pension of $400, which she received until her death in 1890. Finally, on October 1, 1995, by an act of the General Assembly, Prudence Crandall was officially named as Connecticut's State Heroine.

A new national party was formed, consisting of a varied group of individuals who had very little in common apart from their opposition to President Jackson. They adopted the name Whigs.

Thirty-two year-old British authoress Harriet Martineau decided to visit America to accumulate information for a planned work. Little-known today, Martineau was both financially and critically successful, and was at the peak of her world-renown at the time of her trip. She was perhaps the most significant foreign visitor to the United States since the Marquis Lafayette. She was a bit of an eccentric. The tragic death years earlier of her fiance had left her unmarried, and a childhood illness left her so deaf as to require a hearing tube.

In 1832, she published a novel, *Demerara*, which was a passionately sympathetic portrayal of slave life in the West Indies. This novel revealed her to the world as an abolitionist sympathizer. However, she had no personal exposure to slavery, relying instead upon second-hand accounts and romanticized fancies for her work. Many in the South looked forward to her visit as a golden opportunity to promote slavery and disillusion her of false sentimental notions. She arrived in New York in September and spent the rest of the year traveling through the New England states. As cold weather arrived, she headed south where she spent most of the next spring and summer.

Close upon her heels was another Briton, abolitionist George Thompson, who arrived in America in October to speak at the invitation of the AAS. Thompson had been one of the prime movers in the recent battles in Parliament for abolition of slavery in the British Empire. He was not as well-received as Martineau; his presence in New England was viewed as "foreign interference" by many pro-slavery and anti-abolitionist Americans. His lectures were often preceded by sharp attacks in the press and from the pulpits, they were usually accompanied by jeering taunts and threatening mobs. Such opposition no doubt often contributed to the interest in his presentations, where he generally denounced gradualism and recommended immediate emancipation along the lines adopted by England.

Fully committed to his beliefs of gradual emancipation, Kentucky slaveowner James Birney freed his own slaves from their bondage this year. By now, Birney was actively engaged in his work with the Kentucky Colonization Society. He would soon come to the realization that more needed to be done to fight the evils of slavery.

The social event of that summer in Philadelphia may have been the marriage of the dashing, debonair Pierce Butler of Georgia to the celebrated British actress Fanny Kemble. The match must have appeared to onlookers as the stuff of romance, the union of two of society's "beautiful people." However, the marriage between the fiercely-independent Kemble and the headstrong Butler would prove to be a difficult union, and one that would in many ways reflect the larger story developing around them. Butler's entire essence was based upon his family's slaveholdings, and Fanny would soon find herself at odds with his vision of Southern male dominance.

Eight

1835

Robert Hayne had been elected mayor of Charleston, South Carolina. His replacement as governor of the state was George McDuffie. McDuffie wasted no time expressing his feelings in an address to the state legislature early in the year. He tried to make it clear—presumably for the benefit of his Northern neighbors—how important slavery was to the welfare of South Carolina, and how acceptable it was to him personally, as well as to the constituents he represented:

> No human institution, in my opinion, is more obviously in keeping with the will of God than slavery. No one of His laws is written in plainer letters than the law which says that this is the happiest condition for the African. That the African was meant to be a slave is clear. It is marked on his face, stamped on his skin, and proved by the intellectual inferiority and natural helplessness of this race. They have none of the qualities that fit them to be free men. They are totally unsuited both for freedom and for self-government of any kind. They are, in all respects, physically, morally, and politically inferior. From an excess of labor, poverty, and trouble our slaves are free. They usually work from two to four hours a day less than workers in other countries. They usually eat as much wholesome food on one day as an English worker or Irish peasant eats in two. And as for the future, slaves are envied even by their masters. Nowhere on earth is there a class of people so perfectly free from care and anxiety.

It seems doubtful that the abolitionists believed that slaves had it as good as McDuffie claimed they did. Likewise, there are plenty of slave narratives that make it clear that the blacks would have disagreed as well. What is significant, however, is that he spoke as the chief magistrate of his state, and, therefore, it can be assumed that many of the state's citizens would have agreed with him.

McDuffie also insisted that "domestic slavery is the corner-stone of our republican edifice." Without it, the state could not exist. It seemed clear that South Carolina prized its peculiar institution more than its union with the other states. He went even further, adding that those who labored in any country, whether "bleached or unbleached," were a dangerous element in the community. He predicted that the working class of the North would be "virtually reduced to slavery" within 25 years.

Not surprisingly, he was particularly harsh in his expressions of disgust towards the abolitionists. "The laws of every community," he declared, "should punish this species of interference with death without the benefit of clergy." He called upon South Carolina legislators to adopt a resolution requesting the "non-slaveholding states to pass laws to suppress promptly and effectively all abolition societies."

William Leggett responded to McDuffie's speech with an editorial in the New York *Evening Post* on February 10. Leggett's main concern seemed to be that McDuffie was wrongly judging the entire Northern democracy by the words and actions of "enthusiasts and fanatics in this quarter, and all their dangerous zeal for immediate emancipation." He went to great lengths to assure McDuffie that the governor had been "misled in his ideas of the part taken by the democracy of this and the eastern states in the mad and violent schemes of the immediate abolitionists, as they are called. He may be assured that the abettors and supporters of Garrison—and other itinerant orators who go about stigmatizing the people of the South as 'man stealers' are not the organs or instruments of the democracy of the North."

No doubt the editor spoke for many, perhaps even the majority of Northern whites when he assured McDuffie that Northerners were "not fanatics, nor hypocrites." He wished the South to know that it could count on the support of the Northern masses:

> They know well that admitting the slaves of the South to an equality of civil and social rights, however deeply it might affect the dignity and interests of the rich planters of that quarter, would operate quite as injuriously, if not more so, on themselves.... It is here the emancipated slaves would seek a residence and employment, and aspire to the social equality they could never enjoy among their ancient masters. If they cannot bring themselves up to the standard of the free labouring white men, they might pull the latter down to their own level, and thus lower the condition of the white labourer by association[.]
>
> Not only this, but the labouring classes of the North, which constitute the great mass of the democracy, are not so short-sighted to consequences, that they cannot see, that the influx of such a vast number of emancipated slaves would go far to throw them out of employment, or at least depreciate the value of labour to an extent that would be fatal to their prosperity. This they know, and this will forever prevent the democ-

racy of the North from advocating or encouraging any of those ill-judged, though possibly well-intended schemes for a general and immediate emancipation, or indeed for any emancipation, that shall not both receive the sanction and preserve the rights of the planters of the South, and at the same time, secure the democracy of the North against the injurious, if not fatal consequences, of a competition with the labour of millions of manumitted slaves.

... [W]e assure Governor McDuffie, and all those who imagine they see in the democracy of the North, the enemies to their rights of property, and the advocates of principles dangerous to the safety and prosperity of the planters of the South, that they may make themselves perfectly easy on these heads. The danger is not in the democratic [majority of the North, but] is a scheme of a few ill-advised men[.]

As the year continued, the "democratic majority" would match its actions to these words, as attacks against abolitionists intensified in the North. Many historians refer to the middle 1830s as the "Age of Martyrs," for reasons that will become apparent.

The South Carolina legislature dutifully followed McDuffie's recommendations. Soon a committee of the Massachusetts legislature had received the governor's request. Try to imagine the scene: The state of Massachusetts considering the repression of its own citizens so that the state of South Carolina can continue to enslave its. To many Northerners not otherwise sympathetic to the abolitionists, such a proceeding seemed outlandish. Many began to think that the South was going too far in its crusade against the anti-slavery element.

At first reluctant to allow the abolitionists to defend themselves, the committee ultimately decided to hear their side of the story. Their defense rested primarily upon their published reports that convincingly demonstrated they had no intention or desire to incite violence in the South. To the contrary, there was concern that any legislative censure of their proceedings might encourage the pro-slavery members of Northern society to even more violence and abuse.

Perhaps the most impassioned speaker was William Goodell. He argued that the demands from the South amounted to a veritable conspiracy against the liberties of the North. He characterized McDuffie's speech and the South Carolina documents as "the fetters of Northern freemen," and considered any proposed legislation as tantamount to attaching shackles to the wrists of the North. "Mr. Chairman, are you prepared to attempt to put them on?" he asked.

Apparently Massachusetts was not so prepared as it voted against enacting any such repressive laws. Nor did any other Northern state comply with the South's request to suppress anti-slavery groups. It seemed that the South would have to fight its battles on its own, leading to even more resentment against the North.

The rest of the spring of that year seemed subdued enough. In March, 28 white students and 14 black students, at least one of which seems to have been one of those evicted from Prudence Crandall's Canterbury school, quietly commenced classes at a newly established integrated school in Canaan, New Hampshire, called the Noyes Academy.

Also in that same month, Angelina Grimké attended her first anti-slavery meeting, which was a lecture by George Thompson at the Reformed Presbyterian Church on Cherry Street in Philadelphia. It seems likely that her sister, Sarah, did not attend with her, though in later years both girls would date this meeting as the beginning of their involvement in the struggle against slavery. Soon Angelina would be a member of the Philadelphia Female Anti-Slavery Society. And, before the summer was over, she would find herself drawn into the abolitionist camp as one of its strongest champions.

With the coming summer, the heat of anti-slavery passions seemed to rise as well. One noteworthy incident was described in the Buffalo, New York *Daily Commercial Advertiser* of July 13, 1835. Under the headline "Buffalo Fugitive Slave Case and Riot," it read:

> Yesterday afternoon our streets were thronged by a mob under considerable excitement, produced by the arrest of a slave family and their subsequent rescue. As far as we can learn the facts, they are briefly these. One Tait, a slave agent from the South, having learned a family of slaves, consisting of a man [Sanford], his wife, and a child, were living at St. Catharines, [Ontario, Canada], went over and brought them away in the night. They were followed to this city, when a party of Blacks organized and pursued the kidnappers as far as Hamburg, where they effected a rescue, and bore the liberated individuals off in triumph with the intention of placing them again on the Canadian side, but when at the ferry, at Black Rock, a reencounter took place between them and several citizens, who had been called by the police to assist in arresting them, which resulted in some severe injuries on both sides.... The slaves succeeded in making good their escape.

While it's difficult to ascertain the opinion of the writer of this article on the matter (though it seems significant that he referred to the slave agents as "kidnappers"), one thing is certain: instances such as this and the Detroit Blackburn riots were a wake-up call for many Northerners. It was one thing to talk in the abstract about the plight of slaves in the South; it was altogether different to see men legally seized within a Northern community for the crime of having black skins. The resultant disruption to the peace of the North seemed to be in direct contradiction to the oft-repeated claim that the issue of slavery was a purely Southern concern. It was becoming painfully obvious that, like it or not, the North was involved in the issue of slavery.

Eight • 1835

The plight of fugitive slaves, however, would not be the major issue that summer. The abolitionists managed, consciously or not, to bring abuse down upon themselves. It started in the form of a mail campaign conceived by the AAS and funded largely by Lewis and Arthur Tappan. The idea seemed forthright enough: What better way to help the blacks than to get the message of abolitionism to the slaveowners themselves? With that end in mind, a list was developed of those individuals in the South—politicians, civic leaders, members of the clergy, educators—whose influence, it was assumed, could make a difference in Southern communities. Why not send these important individuals some anti-slavery information, with the hope of peaceably persuading them to do something about the issue?

In retrospect, the idea seems either naive or lunatic. A huge, totally unsolicited mailing of abolitionist pamphlets, newspapers and documents was sent to the South where it entered the port city of Charleston, South Carolina.

On July 29, city postmaster Alfred Huger opened his mail sacks to discover the offensive mailings. To Huger, such an "appeal to white consciences" was in reality "a call for black revolution." To allow such mail to be delivered "would strew antislavery around Charleston's houses, where blacks could see it." Better to lock it up and contact Washington for instructions on how to handle it.

Such instructions, however, were too slow in coming. The next evening, a gang of "respectable" slaveholders—led, it was said, by mayor Hayne—accompanied a mob to the post office. The windows were forced open, the mail rifled and the offending materials removed. They were consumed in a public bonfire in the streets. A crowd estimated at 3,000 applauded the action and watched as effigies of Garrison and the Tappans were burned along with the insurrectionist materials.

President Jackson's private response to the situation is revealed in his correspondence to U.S. Postmaster General Amos Kendall. He told Kendall that any "suspicious-looking" materials coming through the mail should not be delivered unless specifically demanded by the addressee. If such requests were forthcoming, the local postmasters should take "their names down, and have them exposed thru the Publick journals as subscribers to this wicked plan of exciting the negroes to insurrection and to massacre." Doubtless any "moral and good" Southerners would ostracize such miscreants. Jackson was convinced there were few individuals who were "so hardened in villainry as to withstand the frowns of all good men" and bring upon themselves the disfavor of their neighbors.

As time went by, it appeared that Jackson was, indeed, absolutely correct. Most Southerners were quite unwilling to court such social disfavor. It was pro-slavery coercion such as this that increasingly quieted any open expression of anti-slavery sentiment in the South.

In the aftermath of the Charleston incident, many other Southern cities also saw their mails seized and destroyed by irate citizens often with the compliance of the acting postmasters. Postmaster General Kendall's official response to the situation did not go quite as far as to endorse Jackson's suggestion, though there was no doubt where he believed the fault lay. According to Kendall, the abolitionists had been asked "voluntarily to desist from attempting to send their publications into the Southern States ... and their refusal to do so ... is but another evidence of the fatuity of the counsels by which they are directed."

He described himself as being "confirmed in the opinion, that the Postmaster General has no legal authority ... to exclude from the mails any species of newspapers, magazines, or pamphlets." However, he informed the Southern postmasters that he "deterred from giving any order to exclude the whole series of abolition publications from the Southern mails only by a want of legal power; and that if I were situated as you are, I would do as you have done."

He enumerated some of the laws against the circulating of anti-slavery material in the South.

> ... If the abolitionists or their agents were caught distributing their tracts in Louisiana, they would be legally punished by death; if they were apprehended in Georgia, they might be legally sent to the penitentiary; and in each of the slaveholding States they would suffer the penalties of their respective laws....
>
> Upon these grounds a postmaster may well hesitate to be the agent of the abolitionists in sending their incendiary publications into States where their circulation is prohibited by law, and much more may postmasters residing in those States refuse to distribute them.... [O]f one thing there can be no doubt. If it shall ever be settled by the authority of Congress, that the post office establishment may be legally, and must be actually employed as an irresponsible agent to enable misguided fanatics or reckless incendiaries to stir up with impunity insurrection and servile war in the Southern States, those States will of necessity consider the General Government as an accomplice in the crime—they will look upon it as identified in a cruel and unconstitutional attack on their unquestionable rights and dearest interests, and they must necessarily treat it as a common enemy in their defense. Ought the postmaster or the department ... to hasten a state of things so deplorable?
>
> I do not desire to be understood as affirming that the suggestion here thrown out ... be considered as the settled construction of the law[.] ... It is only intended to say, that ... the safest course for postmasters and the best for the country, is that which you have adopted.

Acknowledging that it may have been less than discreet for the AAS to send unwanted anti-slavery material to the South, it must also be pointed out that the materials were not sent to slaves or to free blacks. They were sent to responsible members of Southern society, who, it could be assumed, would not be handing it out to the slaves. Therefore, the Southern claim that the postal barrage was intended to launch a slave insurrection loses some of its credibility. In fact, its only basis of truth lies in the South's own paranoia.

The South, it seems, was slowly losing its grip on the situation. And, as so often happens to both individuals and societies under exasperating circumstances, there was a tendency to lash out. In the case of the South, the lashing was not always simply metaphorical.

Amos Dresser was a member of the Ohio Abolition Society. He was one of the Lane debaters who had been ousted with Theodore Weld. He was also black. In his autobiography published the following year, he explained that he spent the summer traveling in a gig throughout the South, trying to sell Bibles to raise money for his education. And, perhaps, this was all that he was doing since the practice was not uncommon.

According to Harriet Martineau—who was in the South at the time though probably not present at the event—while Dresser was in Nashville, Tennessee, he "fell under suspicion of abolition treason; his baggage [was] searched, and a whole abolition newspaper, and part of another [were] found among the packing-stuff of his stock of bibles. There was also an unsubstantiated rumour of his having been seen conversing with slaves." The fact that he had abolitionists papers upon him should not have been considered a crime. There were no laws at that time in Tennessee forbidding their distribution, and Dresser claimed to have given "no person of color, bond or free any pamphlets."

Martineau would return to Dresser's story in her 1839 book *The Martyr Age of the United States*. In that book, she would state that the group that examined Dresser "acknowledged through the whole proceeding, that Dresser had broken no law; but pleaded that if the law did not sufficiently protect slavery against the assaults of opinion, an association of gentlemen must make law for the occasion."

It seems clear that regardless of Dresser's intentions, his possession of anti-slavery material at that time and place was ill-advised. Not surprisingly, the folks in Nashville did not take kindly to his presence among them. Martineau provides us with an account of what happened next.

> ... He was brought to trial by the Committee of Vigilance; seven elders of the Presbyterian church at Nashville being among his judges. After much debate as to whether he should be hanged, or flogged with more or fewer lashes, he was condemned to receive twenty lashes, with a cowhide, in the market-place of Nashville. He was immediately conducted there, made to kneel down on the flint pavement, and punished accord-

ing to his sentence; the mayor of Nashville presiding, and the public executioner being the agent. He was warned to leave the city within twenty-four hours: but was told, by some charitable person who had the bravery to take him in, wash his stripes, and furnish him with a disguise, that it would not be safe to remain so long. He stole away immediately, in his dreadful condition, on foot; and when his story was authenticated, had heard nothing of his horse, gig, and bibles, which he values at three hundred dollars.

As an indication of at least one reaction to the flogging, the *Cincinnati Whig* of August 15 commented upon the account it had published "of a Mr. Dresser's being well *dressed* in Nashville, for his incendiary interference with the Slave population of Tennessee." The newspaper noted that the affair had "excited a good deal of attention among our citizens. The punishment he received seems to give universal satisfaction".

Martineau, no doubt influenced by Dresser's ordeal, continued her American tour much more sympathetic with the abolitionists than when she had started out. As for Dresser, he became yet another abolitionist martyr whose experience tended to further alienate many Northerners who might otherwise have been sympathetic towards the South. It seemed that slavery and the fight to maintain it brought out the worst in the Southern culture.

It may appear ironic that many of the documented cases of violence and riot against abolitionism, with the exception of Dresser's, occurred in the North. There are two main reasons for this.

First, despite their strong sense of devotion to the cause and their often-expressed willingness to die in its behalf, few of the abolitionists were foolhardy enough to venture into the South. To have done so would have been quite literally courting death. As it was, it was often dangerous enough just being an abolitionist in Philadelphia or Boston, without adding the risk of discovery within a slave state.

Secondly, much of what happened in the South has been "lost" to the modern reader or researcher. A case in point is that of the "Vicksburg Gamblers."

Unfortunately, except for a few shadowy allusions, there's not much to factually report. One of the few "substantive" clues is contained within the text of an anti-slavery narrative published in Cincinnati in 1836:

> The REIGN OF TERROR was introduced into the South, last summer, by the sudden and public execution, without trial, of five American citizens, [by which they presumably meant *Northern citizens*] charged with being "professional" gamblers—whilst it was kept up by the plundering of the National Mail—by the pretence of slave-insurrections—by the most degrading inflictions—by numberless cruel and unauthorized *scourgings* of such as had been either removed from the free States to the South, or

were temporarily called thither on business—by the offering of REWARDS for the forcible abduction of peaceable and inoffensive citizens, with the avowed purpose of handing them over to the tender mercies of infuriated slaveholders—by the unconcealed, the open and illegal *hangings* of many of our [Northern] countrymen in the South, on whom popular suspicion had fastened the obnoxious sentiment, that they were opposed to the system of slavery as it existed there[.]

One thing seems clear here. Men were being lynched in the South for harboring anti-slavery ideals. How many, or when or where, is not so clear. However, the emphasis on the "professional" gamblers at the beginning of this litany of Southern cruelties implies that the contemporary readers of this document would understand that the true meaning behind the Vicksburg lynchings had nothing to do with gambling. Presumably, it had more to do with abolitionism.

Further evidence is found in Martineau's *Martyr Age* book. In it, she refers to one of the "events which attracted the most attention" during the summer of 1835: "a desperate and cruel massacre of upwards of twenty persons on the gibbet at Vicksburg on the Mississippi, on a vague and unfounded suspicion of an intended rising among the slaves." Allowing for the fact that she may have arrived at the number of "twenty" by erroneously compounding the Vicksburg incident with other lynchings, it seems irrefutable that some tragedy (or tragedies) occurred. Men were losing their lives in the South because they believed slavery was wrong. If this was indeed the case, where are the facts?

It would be easy to say that much of the documentation of such incidents that might have existed during the antebellum period was lost during the war. Quite likely there is some truth to such an assumption. However, it could be suggested with no hard evidence to support it, that the South had no desire to provide such evidence against itself. Therefore, material of this nature conveniently "disappeared" over the years.

The Civil War was barely over before Southern writers began rewriting the history of the years that led up to the conflict. It was Southern historians who popularized the notion that the war was not fought due to slavery. What would be more natural than that reports of Southern atrocities towards abolitionists, which would not fit in with their states rights myth, should be excluded from the Southern mythology? Certainly there are enough reports of threats and bitter recriminations rising up from the South against abolitionists to assume that the region was hostile towards them. Does it seem likely that Dresser's was the only instance of violence being done upon individual abolitionists? You would expect there to have been other incidents. But where are they?

One such incident may have been a case that summer in the Georgetown Section of Washington, D.C. Dr. Reuben Crandall, a botanist and the younger brother of Prudence, was jailed after a vigilant postmaster noticed that botanical samples he had received had arrived wrapped in antislavery newspapers. He was charged with "publishing seditious libels" with the "intent to distribute." In point of fact, there was no reason to think that he had any part in the publication of the materials he had received. His only actual offense was possession of them, which was not against any law at that time.

The chief prosecutor in Crandall's case was Francis Scott Key of "Star Spangled Banner" fame. Key was one of the founders and an important member of the local Colonization Society. He was also so virulently anti-abolitionist that he refused to allow Crandall to be released on bail while he awaited his court time. As a result, the young botanist languished in the Georgetown jail as the hot days of summer wore on.

While he was imprisoned awaiting trial, a white crowd infuriated at the presence of the abolitionist fanatic in their city descended upon the Washington County jail where he was incarcerated. According to many reports, the mob was cursed by a free black named Beverly Snow, who owned a fashionable tavern in town. Supposedly Snow "said some derogatory things" about the wives of the men in the crowd. This was just the spark needed to set off a riot. The immediate target of the mob's wrath was Snow's tavern, which they promptly demolished. Not being satisfied there, the spree of destruction continued through the black district where the whites smashed windows and vandalized churches, homes and schools. The unrest lasted for two days and three nights, and has been referred to as the "Snow Riot."

William Leggett, while not a particularly well-known or influential journalist, is interesting because the transformation in his thinking that his editorials display is representative of a type of metamorphosis that was occurring throughout the North. On August 8, again in the *Evening Post*, he took the South to task for the heavy-handed response to the threat of abolitionism. "We defy any man," he began, "to point to a single instance in which fanaticism has been turned from its object by persecution." So it was, he argued, that the more the South fought the abolitionists, the more likely they were to be "heated to more dangerous fervour by violence" against them. The correct response would be to treat them as you would any other lunatics: with kindness, reason and moderation.

He also cautioned the South against portraying the anti-slavery societies in a false light:

> While we believe most fully that the abolitionists are justly chargeable with fanaticism, we consider it worse than folly to misrepresent their character in other respects. They are not knaves nor fools, but men of wealth, education, respectability and intelligence. misguided on a single subject,

> but actuated by a sincere desire to promote the welfare of their kind.... Is it not apparent ... that invective, denunciations, burnings in effigy, mob violence, and the like proceedings, do not constitute the proper mode of changing the opinions and conduct of such men? The true way is, either to point out their error by temperate arguments, or better still leave them to discover it themselves. The fire, unsupplied with fuel, soon flickers and goes out, which stirred and fed, will rise to a fearful conflagration, and destroy whatever falls within the reach of its fury.
>
> With regard to the outrage lately committed in Charleston,—we do not believe it constitutes any exception to our remarks. The effects of all such proceedings must be to increase the zeal of fanaticism, which always rises in proportion to the violence it encounters.

Leggett's characterization of the abolitionists as "fanatics" and "misguided" makes it clear that he did not sympathize with their crusade. However, he begrudgingly rose to defend their rights.

> ... [I]t is the bounden duty of the Government to protect the abolitionists in their constitutional right of free discussion; and opposed, sincerely and zealously as we are, to their doctrines and practise, we should be still more opposed to any infringement of their political or civil rights If the Government once begins to discriminate as to what is orthodox and what heterodox in opinion, what is safe and what is unsafe in its tendency, farewell, a long farewell to our freedom.

In Canaan, New Hampshire, the presence of the integrated Noyes Academy had irritated white residents long enough. It seemed to many of them that it was about time to remove the blight from their community. On August 10, with the help of "nearly one hundred yoke of oxen," they did just that. Hitching the beasts to the building, they literally pulled it off its foundations. Some accounts claim that the students were still inside at the time. The building was dragged to the village commons where it was burned.

On August 19, the *New York Evening Star* published a letter written by James Henry Hammond of South Carolina. He attacked the Northern majority for providing the abolitionists with "an asylum from which to hurl their murderous missiles." In Hammond's opinion, Northern laws were too lax to deal with the fanatics living within their borders. He suggested that the anti-slavery element "can be silenced in but one way—*Terror—death*." Northern states owed it to their brethren of the South to pass laws that would deliver the offending individuals "on demand to those whose laws and whose rights they have violated." The very sake of the nation was at stake. If the North refused to extradite the incendiaries, then the South would by honor be forced to "dissolve the Union, and *seek by war* the redress denied" them.

It seems nothing less than a travesty of history that the abolitionists have so often been criticized for inciting trouble. Nor have they been spared the charge of spreading propaganda against the South. Garrison, it has been said, strove to convince the Northern majority that the people of the South were barbaric, ruthless, violent people. No words of Garrison's are needed to depict them in such a light. Their own actions and words give evidence enough. If either side was responsible for "stirring up passions," it seems most of the blame should be placed upon the pro-slavery South.

It appeared there were many Northerners who were ready to accept Hammond's suggestions. Anti-abolitionist meetings were held in many Northern cities. The streets of New York were filled with crowds protesting against the AAS. The city postmaster refused to receive any abolitionist material, and the offices of the AAS were barricaded with iron bars and wooden planks for protection from the mob.

In Boston, George Thompson had received numerous death threats, and, for his own safety, was surreptitiously hurried out of town. Meanwhile, civic leaders had called for an anti-abolition meeting to be held at Faneuil Hall on August 21. According to the account in the *Transcript*, the meeting was called to determine just how far the "guaranteed rights" of the South would be "marred, mutilated, and brought into contempt ... by infuriated madmen ... and reckless arguers on abstract principles."

Many in the crowd called for laws that would punish those who were threatening the South's property. It indeed appeared that the abolitionists were as friendless at home as they were in the South.

However, there were still a few brave people in the free states who, like Leggett, were willing to defend the abolitionists during that summer. From Philadelphia, Angelina Grimké had carefully followed the reports of the postal incident in Charleston. Perhaps the events touched her more deeply than they did most Northerners since her familiarity with the city of her birth must have made the impressions particularly poignant for her.

She knew about the anti-abolitionist sentiment brewing in the North. She also read Garrison's *Liberator*, that called upon the citizens of the North to repudiate the mob violence which seemed to be surrounding them.

She penned a letter to Garrison expressing her feelings as both a Southerner and a woman concerning the recent attacks against the abolitionists. She also implied that through her work with the Female Anti-slavery Society she knew about the plan to send materials to the South. "I can hardly express to thee the deep and solemn interest with which I have viewed the violent proceedings of the last few weeks. Although I had expected opposition, I was not prepared for it so soon—and I greatly feared abolitionists would be driven back in the first outset, and thrown into confusion."

She credited Garrison as being the rock that held the abolitionists so firm. "The ground upon which you stand is holy ground; never—never surrender it," she begged of him. "If you surrender it, the hope of the slave is extinguished.

"If persecution is the means which God has ordained for the accomplishment of this great end, EMANCIPATION; then ... I feel as if I could say, LET IT COME; for it is my deep, solemn deliberate conviction, that this is a cause worth dying for."

Grimké had not expected or intended Garrison to print her letter, yet that is exactly what he did. With its publication on August 25, and totally without her prior knowledge or consent, Grimké joined the ranks of those whose words would stir up displeasure in the South. At first self-conscious over the unwanted attention it brought upon her, she soon rose to the occasion.

On August 26, William Leggett published a scathing indictment of happenings in the South in the aftermath of the Charleston Post Office incident. It began to become clear that to Leggett, as to many Northerners, the abolitionists were not the only party in the confrontation that could rightly be referred to as "fanatics."

> The Southern presses team with evidences that fanaticism of as wild a character as that which they deprecate exists among themselves. How else could such a paper as the *Charleston Patriot* advert with tacit approval to the statement, that a purse of twenty thousand dollars has been made up in New Orleans as a reward for the audacious miscreant who should dare to kidnap Arthur Tappan,—and deliver him on the Levee in that city. Revolting to right reason as such a proposition is, we find it repeated with obvious gust and approbation by prints conducted by enlightened and liberal minds—by minds that ordinarily take just views of subjects, achieve their ends by reasoning and persuasion, and exert all their influence to check the popular tendency to tumult. Is the *Charleston Patriot* so blinded by the peculiar circumstances in which the South is placed as not to perceive that the proposed abduction of Arthur Tappan, even if consummated by his murder, as doubtless is the object, would necessarily have a widely different effect from that of suppressing the Abolition Association, or in anywise diminishing its zeal and ardour? Does it not perceive, on the contrary, that such an outrage would but inflame the minds of that fraternity to more fanatical fervour, and stimulate them to more strenuous exertions, while it would add vast numbers to their ranks through the influence of those feelings which persecution never fails to arouse.
>
> But independent of the effect of the proposed outrage on the abolitionists themselves, what, let us ask, would be the sentiments it would create in the entire community? Has the violence of the South, its arrogant pretensions and menacing tones so overcrowded our spirits, that we would

tamely submit to see our citizens snatched from the sanctuary of their homes, and carried off by midnight ruffians, to be burned at a stake, gibbeted on a tree, or butchered in some public place, without the slightest form of trial, and without even the allegation of crime? Are our laws so inert, are our rights so ill-guarded, that we must bear such outrages without repining or complaint? Is our Governor a wooden image, that he would look on such unheard of audacity and make no effort to avenge the insult? These are questions which it will be well for the South to ponder seriously before it offers rewards to ruffians for kidnapping citizens of New York. If the South wishes to retain its slaves in bondage, let it not insult the whole population of this great free state by threatening to tear any citizen from the protection of our laws and give him up to the tender mercies of a mob actuated by the most frantic fanaticism. Such a proceeding would make abolitionists of our whole two millions of inhabitants.

Some abolitionists apparently managed to convince Leggett to actually read some of their documents, for early in September, he began writing editorials much more sympathetic to them. In speaking of himself in the plural tense in the following passage, he seemed to feel he was speaking on behalf of many in the North:

It is quite time ... that we remember the maxim which lies at the foundation of justice, Hear the other side. We have listened very credulously to the one side. We have with greedy ears devoured all sorts of passionate invectives against the abolitionists, and received as gospel, without evidence, the most inflammatory and incendiary tirades against them. While appropriating to them exclusively the epithets of incendiaries and insurrectionists, we have ourselves been industriously kindling the flames of domestic discord, and stirring up the wild spirit of tumult. It is high time to pause, and ask ourselves what warrant we have for these proceedings? It is time to balance the account current of inflammatory charges, and see which side preponderates, whether that of the incendiaries of the North or of the South.

Having carefully read the "official address" of the abolitionists, Leggett felt that it "deserve[d] cordial approval." However, he still made it explicitly clear that "this expression we wish taken with a qualification" that: "we do not approve of perseverance in sending pamphlets to the south on the subject of slavery in direct opposition to the unanimous sentiments of the slaveholders." Having said this much in opposition to the abolitionists, he next felt obligated to admit that he did "approve of the strenuous assertion of the right of free discussion, and moreover we admire the heroism which cannot be driven from its ground by the maniac and unsparing opposition which the abolitionists have encountered."

The writer suggested that a "spirit of conciliation and compromise should govern in this matter," and that "paramount considerations of brotherhood and national unity should prevent [the free states] from stirring the question of slavery." However, he also warned the slave states that.

> ... their high and boastful language shall never deter this print from expressing its opinion that slavery is an opprobrium and a curse, a monstrous and crying evil, in whatever light it is viewed; and that we shall hail, as the second most auspicious day that ever smiled on our republic, that which shall break the fetters of the bondman, and give his enfranchised spirit leave to roam abroad on the illimitable plain of equal liberty.
> We have no right to interfere legislatively with the subject of slavery in our sister states, and never have arrogated any. We have no moral right to stir the question in such a way as to endanger the lives of our fellow human beings, white or black, or expose the citizens of the North, attending to their occasions in the South, to the horrors of Lynch law.... [W]e deeply deplore all intemperate movements on this momentous subject[.]... But while we truly entertain these sentiments, we know no reason that renders it incumbent on us to conceal how far our views are really opposed to slavery; and while we disclaim any constitutional right to legislate on the subject, we assert, without hesitation, that, if we possessed the right, we would not scruple to exercise it for the speedy and utter annihilation of servitude and chains.

In another article penned that same week, he went even further:

> If to believe slavery a deplorable evil and a curse, in whatever light it is viewed; if to yearn for the day which shall break the fetters of three millions of human beings, and restore to them their birth-right of equal freedom; if to be willing ... to do all in our power to promote so desirable a result, by all means ... not inconsistent with higher duty: if these sentiments constitute us abolitionists, then are we such, and glory in the name. But while we mourn over the servitude which fetters a large portion of the American people ... yet we defy the most vigilant opponent of this journal to point his finger to a word or syllable that looks like hostility to the political rights of the South, or conceals any latent desire to violate the federal compact, in letter or spirit.
> ... [Our] federal compact ... places an interdiction on the discussion of no subject whatever[.] ... If it is true that the people of the United States are forbidden to speak their sentiments on one of the most momentous subjects which ever engaged their thoughts; if they are so bound in fetters of mind that they must not allude to the less galling fetters which bind the limbs of the Southern slave; let the prohibitory passage, we pray, be quickly pointed out; let us be convinced at once that we are not freemen, as we have heretofore fondly believed[.]

In a third article, written the same week as the other two, he took offense with:

> ...the sentiments openly expressed by the Southern newspapers, that slavery is not an evil, and that to indulge a hope that the poor bondmen may be eventually enfranchised is not less heinous than to desire his immediate emancipation....
>
> Slavery no evil! Has it come to this, that the foulest stigma on our national escutcheon, which no true-hearted freeman could ever contemplate without sorrow in his heart and a blush upon his cheek, has got to be viewed by the people of the South as no stain on the American character? Have their ears become so accustomed to the clank of the poor bondman's fetters that it no longer grates upon them as a discordant sound? Have his groans ceased to speak the language of misery? Has his servile condition lost any of its degradation? Can the husband be torn from his wife, and the child from its parent, and sold like cattle at the shambles, and yet free, intelligent men, whose own rights are founded on the declaration of the unalienable freedom and equality of all mankind, stand up in the face of heaven and their fellow men, and assert without a blush that there is no evil in servitude? We could not have believed that the madness of the South had reached so dreadful a climax.
>
> Not only are we told that slavery is no evil, but that it is criminal towards the South, and a violation of the spirit of the federal compact, to indulge even a hope that the chains of the captive may some day or other, no matter how remote the time, be broken.... [T]hat unless we speedily pass laws to prohibit all expression of opinion on the dreadful topic of slavery, the Southern states will meet in Convention, separate themselves from the North, and establish a separate empire for themselves....
>
> If ... the political union of these states is only to be preserved by yielding to the claims set up by the South; if the tie of confederation is of such a kind that the breath of free discussion will inevitably dissolve it; if we can hope to maintain our fraternal connexion with our brothers of the South only by dismissing all hope of ultimate freedom to the slave; let the compact be dissolved, rather than submit to such dishonourable, such inhuman terms for its preservation.

Leggett's philosophy had changed remarkably in the course of just a little over a year, goaded, no doubt, by both the intemperate language coming out of the South and the acts of violence against the abolitionists. Like many other fair-minded Northerners, he was beginning to sympathize with those who sympathized with the slaves.

Wealthy New Yorker Philip Hone commented in his diary upon a rumored slave revolt in August in Vicksburg, Mississippi, (presumably the "professional gamblers" that have already been mentioned). According to Hone, "murder and violence [were] committed without the least color of the law upon the poor negroes and several whites who had been accused of being their instigators."

Nor was the North immune to the risk of violence. There were still many who opposed the anti-slavery movement and its leaders. Garrison knew that he was unpopular with many people both below and above the Mason Dixon line. Yet even he could not have expected to find what he woke up to on the morning of September 11. During the dark hours before dawn, someone had erected a macabre gallows upon his doorstep. It was made of five-inch thick joists of wood, and two nooses hung upon in it in dire warning. A note was affixed, announcing that it was compliments of "Judge Lynch."

Garrison tried to make light of it, joking that the nooses were intended for "those twin monsters, Slavery and Colonization." Yet he most certainly was aware that warnings such as this could very easily be followed by violence. Popular legend has it that, after this incident, sentinels from the free black community kept a protective watch on the house at night.

In what might seem like a totally unrelated event, revolution broke out during October in the Mexican province of Texas. It was most certainly inspired by the Americans living there. There were many reasons for their discontent, including lack of a stable government, trade restrictions, unfair taxation policies, and social, political, and religious differences.

But one of the most powerful reasons was slavery, or, more precisely, the Mexican government's policy prohibiting slavery. Texas at the time had a population of around 50,000. A scant majority of these were displaced Americans, most of them from Southern slave states. The second largest group consisted of about 14,000 Indians, slightly more than half of which were considered "civilized," the remainder were hostile to white encroachment. Only about 3,000 Texans were Mexican, and they were outnumbered by the 5,000 slaves the white Americans had brought with them.

Texas was coveted by the South. Its climate was perfect for cotton, and its territory was large enough to make three or four more states (slave states, of course, if the whites living there had their way). There is no doubt that one of the prime motivations for Texan independence was to augment the power of the slave states. The struggle for Texas was closely watched by both the North and the South, but supported and abetted primarily by Southerners. The South had the most to gain by the acquisition of Texas as a new slave territory.

The Boston Female Anti-Slavery Society announced that George Thompson would address its first anniversary meeting on October 14. Unfortunately for the women, tension from the unresolved anti-abolitionist meeting at Faneuil Hall two months earlier still lingered. It may have seemed like not just the South, but all the North as well was against them. The citizens of Hartford, Connecticut, had just passed "A Declaration of the Sentiments of the People of Hartford Regarding the Measures of the Abolitionists." In it they proclaimed that "the moral force of public opinion [is] the basis and primary elemental principle of our government, [and] the Citizens of Hartford cannot view with indifference the excitement which now prevails on the subject of slavery in the United States."

While the abolitionists would certainly have agreed that a certain amount of excitement prevailed in the country upon the subject, they would no doubt have strongly disagreed with the Hartford conclusion that "this excitement has been occasioned by the rash and reckless measures and proceedings of the abolitionists":

> We believe that these proceedings will result in no good, but much evil; that their direct and obvious tendency is to agitate and alarm the people of the slave States; endanger their peace and security, if not expose them to the evils and horrors of insurrection, massacre, and a servile war—to injure the slave population and subject them to restrictions and severities from which they have hitherto been exempt, and greatly defer, if not wholly extinguish the hope of the final amelioration of their condition—that they tend to destroy that reciprocal harmony and confidence which should prevail among the people of different sections of the Union; to embarrass commercial and social intercourse among them, to alienate their minds and to weaken those sacred ties which hold together its several parts.

In this document, it appears it was the abolitionists who were at fault for all of the problems between the two sections, rather than the existence of slavery, or the Southern desire to perpetuate or extend its influence. The citizens of Hartford further criticized the "conduct of the Abolitionists, in distributing their incendiary publications ... in the slave holding States, in violation of their laws and in contravention of the spirit of the constitution of the United States, which guarantees to each State the exclusive regulation of all local interests, including that of master and slave[.]"

In the opinion of these New Englanders, the behavior of the abolitionists was "wholly unjustifiable—a contempt of public opinion, a flagrant outrage against the society which affords them protection, and a high offense against the principles of morality, because their whole conduct is predicated on a total recklessness of consequences, which can only proceed from depravity of heart or desperate infatuation." The document concluded by "declar[ing] our solemn conviction, that it is the duty of all good citizens, by word, deed, and example, to condemn and discountenance the violent [?] measures of the Abolitionists, and to use all reasonable and peaceable means, consistent with their own rights, to put an end to them; to restore quiet to the public mind, and harmony and confidence among the people of every section of our happy confederacy."

There was no shortage of people in the North ready and willing to

Eight • 1835

attempt to "do their duty" and "put an end" to the abolitionists. But while the citizens of Hartford professed to be looking for peaceful means to quiet the fanatics, it was obvious that many Americans were willing to resort to less peaceable measures. Rumors of expected violence circulated in Boston, and no meeting hall or church would allow the Ladies Anti-Slavery Society the use of their facilities. Bowing to prudence, the women rescheduled their meeting for October 21, at their own headquarters on Washington Street. The situation was considered too volatile for Thompson to appear, though Garrison agreed to speak in the Englishman's stead.

As the morning arrived, concerned businessmen, fearing a riot and its consequent property damage, called on Mayor Theodore Lyman to prevent the meeting. Garrison assured the mayor's office that Thompson was not even in the city; yet his message went unheeded or unbelieved. Soon handbills were appearing throughout the city, calling upon "the friends of the Union" to rally in Washington Street "to snake out ... the infamous foreign scoundrel Thompson." A reward of $100 was said to be promised to the first man who laid "violent hands on Thompson, so that he may be brought to the tar-kettle before dark."

By the time Garrison arrived that evening, the crowd had turned decidedly ugly. Having learned that Thompson was not present nor expected, they seemed determined to find someone else upon whom to vent their displeasure. Sensing their mood, Garrison decided that "for the peace of the meeting and the safety of all" it would be best not to speak.

He made his way to one of the offices in the building, as Mayor Lyman arrived to implore the ladies to cancel their meeting. "Ladies," he said, "you must retire. It is dangerous to remain." When asked if he could guarantee their safety if they left, his response was, "If you go *now*, I will protect you."

The ladies, apparently unaware that Garrison was still in the building, quietly exited amidst the jeers and hisses of the disappointed mob. From within he heard the crowd screaming: "Out with him" and "Lynch him." Later in life, Garrison left his own account of what happened next:

> It was apparent that the multitude would not disperse until I had left the building; and as egress out of the front door was impossible, the Mayor and his assistants, as well as some of my friends, earnestly besought me to effect my escape in the rear of the building....
>
> [Accompanied by another Abolitionist, John Reid Campbell,] I dropped from a back window onto a shed, and narrowly escaped falling headlong to the ground. [Meanwhile, the Mayor tried to disperse the crowd by announcing that Garrison was not in the building.] We entered into a carpenter's shop, through which we attempted to get into Wilson's

Lane, but found our retreat cut off by the mob. They raised a shout as soon as we came in sight, but the workmen promptly closed the door of the shop, ... and thus kindly afforded me an opportunity to find some other passage.

I told Mr. C. it would be futile to attempt to escape—I would go out to the mob, and let them deal with me as they might elect; but he thought it was my duty to avoid them as long as possible. We then went upstairs, and, finding a vacancy in one corner of the room, I got into it, and he and a young lad piled up some boards in front of me to shield me from observation. In a few minutes several ruffians broke into the chamber, who seized Mr. C. in a rough manner, and led him out to the view of the mob, saying, "This is not Garrison, but Garrison's and Thompson's friend, and he says he knows where Garrison is, but won't tell." Then a shout of exultation was raised by the mob, and what became of him I do not know; though, as I was immediately discovered, I presume he escaped. [One source says that while the mob was pummeling Campbell to get him to talk, one of the shop lads silently pointed out Garrison's hiding place.]

On seeing me, three or four rioters, uttering a yell, furiously dragged me to the window, with the intention of hurling me from that height to the ground; but one of them relented, and said—"Don't let us kill him outright." So they drew me back, and coiled a rope about my body—probably to drag me through the streets. I bowed to the mob, and, requesting them to wait patiently until I could descend, went down upon a ladder that was raised for that purpose. I fortunately extricated myself from the rope, and was seized by two or three powerful men, to whose firmness, policy, and muscular energy I am probably indebted for my preservation. [These men have been identified as Daniel and Buff Cooley, truckmen in the city who were moved to pity upon seeing Garrison's plight. They did not consider themselves Abolitionists, but were motivated to succor the editor simply by anger at the activities of the lynch mob.]

They led me along ... through a mighty crowd, ... shouting "He shan't be hurt!! You shan't hurt him! Don't hurt him! He is an American," etc., etc. This seemed to excite sympathy among many in the crowd, and they reiterated the cry, "He shan't be hurt!" I was thus conducted through Wilson's Lane into State Street, in the rear of the City Hall[.]...

Orders were now given to carry me to the Mayor's office in the City Hall. As we approached the south door, the Mayor attempted to protect me by his presence; but as he was unassisted by any show of authority or force, he was quickly thrust aside—and now came a tremendous rush on the part of the mob to prevent my entering the hall. For a moment the conflict was dubious—but my sturdy supporters carried me safely up to the Mayor's room....

After a consultation of fifteen or twenty minutes, the Mayor and his advisors came to the singular conclusion, that the building would be endangered by my continuing in it, and that the preservation of my life depended upon committing me to jail, ostensibly as a disturber of the peace! A hack was got in readiness at the door to receive me—...

Now came a scene that baffles the power of description. As the ocean, lashed into fury by the spirit of the storm, seeks to whelm the adventurous bark beneath its mountain waves—so did the mob, enraged by a series of disappointments, rush like a whirlwind upon the frail vehicle in which I sat, and endeavored to drag me out of it. Escape seemed a physical impossibility. They clung to the wheels—dashed open the doors—seized hold of the horses—and tried to upset the carriage. They were, however, vigorously repulsed by the police—a constable sprang in by my side—the doors were closed—and the driver, lustily using his whip upon the bodies of his horses and the heads of the rioters, happily made an opening through the crowd[.] ... But many of the rioters followed even with superior swiftness, and repeatedly attempted to arrest the progress of the horses. To reach the jail by a direct course was found impracticable; and after going in a circuitous direction, and encountering many "hairbreadth 'scapes," we drove up to this new and last refuge of liberty and life, when another bold attempt was made to seize me by the mob—but in vain. In a few minutes I was locked up in a cell, safe from my persecutors, accompanied by two delightful associates, a good conscience, and a cheerful mind.

Twenty-four-year-old Boston lawyer Wendell Phillips was a silent spectator to Garrison's ordeal, watching the near-lynching from his office window. Phillips had never thought much about anti-slavery. Like most Northerners, he had always accepted the Southern contention that it was the abolitionists who were responsible for all the unrest and turmoil associated with slavery. Now, as he watched a Northern crowd lay violent hands upon Garrison simply because the editor had insisted upon speaking the truth as he saw it, Phillips began to question the beliefs he had always held. It would not be much longer before circumstances would force him to take a stand beside the besieged Garrison.

Even as Garrison was being "escorted" to jail for his own protection, more violence was unfolding 250 miles away in the town of Utica, New York. Local abolitionists were meeting that night at the Bleecker Street Presbyterian Church for the purpose of organizing a state anti-slavery society. Thirty-eight-year-old philanthropist Gerrit Smith, who considered himself a lukewarm colonizationist, happened to be staying overnight in Utica en route to Schenectady. More out of curiosity than for any other reason, he decided to attend and observe the meeting.

He had barely taken his seat when a mob of nearly a hundred men stormed the church doors. Amid their shouts, the meeting broke up in confusion. Smith, enraged by the mob's interference, called out an appeal for fairness and the right to free speech. He invited the delegates to his estate in Peterboro, about 14 miles away, to resume their deliberations.

Also that night, a mob, perhaps the same one, destroyed the offices and press of *The Standard and Democrat,* a local abolitionist press in Utica.

As he lay that night in his cell, Garrison inscribed the following message upon the building's wall:

> William Lloyd Garrison was put into this cell on Wednesday afternoon, October 21, 1835, to save him from the violence of a "respectable and influential" mob, who sought to destroy him for preaching the abominable and dangerous doctrine that "all men are created equal" and that all oppression is odious in the sight of God.

When taken before the magistrate the following day, Garrison discovered that the mayor had actually pressed criminal charges against him "and thirty or more unknown persons" for unlawful assembly and disturbing the peace. The charges were dismissed by the judge, but Garrison was warned to leave town until things settled down. He willingly complied, though he was soon back again to continue his crusade. However, his brush with the mob made it abundantly clear how dangerous it was to advance the cause of the slaves, even in the North.

Meanwhile, more than half of the Utica abolitionists reconvened as invited at Smith's estate. In his accidental position as host, Smith found himself forced into a leadership role in the newly forming anti-slavery group; a role which he readily accepted. In an address to the group, he had the following to say:

> It is not to be disguised, that a war has broken out between the North and the South.—Political and commercial men are industriously striving to restore peace: but the peace, which they would effect, is superficial, false, and temporary. True, permanent peace can never be restored, until slavery, the occasion of the war, has ceased. The sword, which is now drawn, will never be returned to its scabbard, until victory, entire, decisive victory, is ours or theirs; not, until that broad and deep and damning stain on our country's escutcheon is clean washed out—that plague spot on our country's honor gone forever;—or until slavery has riveted anew her present chains, and brought our heads also to bow beneath her withering power. It is idle—it is criminal, to hope for the restoration of the peace, on any other condition.

He further admonished his listeners to not seek their goal with "carnal weapons," but instead emphasized that "truth and love are inscribed on our banner, and 'By these we conquer.'" The Utica mobbing had been "an instructive providence" for Smith. He found himself no longer able to accept the philosophy of colonization, now preferring instead the ideals of "immediatism" that he had formerly considered too radical. They were still deserving of a fair hearing in a land where such liberties were supposed to be constitutionally protected. "The enormous and insolent demands of the South," he would later write, "sustained, I am deeply ashamed to say, by craven and mercenary spirits at the North, manifest beyond all dispute, that the question now is not merely, nor mainly, whether the blacks of the South shall remain slaves—but whether the whites at the North shall become slaves also."

While acknowledging that Southerners were not directly responsible for either Northern riot that October, it seems clear that the virulent anti-abolitionist rhetoric directed towards the North had indeed inspired those two events. At least, it certainly seemed that way to Smith, and presumably to many other observers. As long as Southerners would continue to rant against the enemies of slavery, there would be those in the North who would support their pro-slavery views, often with violence or the threat of violence.

But just as surely there would be those who would view such flagrant disregard of civil liberties as a threat against whites. And with the proliferation of such views, the numbers of the anti-slavery and abolitionist societies in the North would continue to grow.

On November 12, Gerrit Smith officially asked to have his name added to the roles of the American Anti-Slavery Society, and resigned all connection with the ACS. Over the next 10 years, he would personally contribute over $40,000 to the cause of immediate emancipation. (By 1858, appalled at the violence rampant in Kansas and no longer trusting to peaceful means to settle the conflict, he would become a member of the "Secret Six" who provided financial backing to John Brown's aborted invasion of the South.)

On November 18, despite the trouble that had erupted in October, the Boston Female Anti-Slavery Society assembled for its monthly meeting. Harriett Martineau, who had returned from the South in the middle of July, was an invited guest. Martineau had been in Massachusetts on the day of the riot that almost claimed Garrison's life. At least one account claims that she actually witnessed the mobbing from her coach. The troubling aspect of this event had more effect upon her beliefs than did the best efforts of pro-slavery Southerners to modify her opinions. She was now, more than ever, committed to abolitionism.

With no forewarning, she was asked that night to address the group about her feelings concerning slavery. She was under no delusions concerning the possible consequences of her response. "[T]he fury against 'foreign incendiaries' ran high ... and there was no safety for any one, native or foreign, who did what I was now compelled to do." She had witnessed slavery firsthand, had listened to the masters' arguments, and returned more fully convinced of its evils. Despite the very real potential of personal danger, her conscience would not allow her to avoid the issue. "I felt that I could never be happy again if I refused what was asked of me."

She addressed the group calmly, trying to be heard over the shouts of protestors in the street as they pelted the building with clods of mud and dirt:

> I will say what I have said through the whole South, in every family where I have been; that I consider Slavery as inconsistent with the law of God, and as incompatible with the course of His Providence. I should certainly say no less at the North than at the South concerning this utter abomination—and I now declare that in your *principles* I fully agree.

Having spoken out on behalf of the abolitionists, Martineau was almost immediately vilified in the South. Rumors reached her of mobs along the Ohio River watching for her approach. She was warned not to venture to Louisville, Kentucky—as she had originally planned to do the following spring—as "they mean to lynch you." Her status as a single woman and a visiting foreign celebrity appeared to be insufficient to assure her safety in the South, so she was forced to change her itinerary, remaining for the rest of her stay within the relative safety of the free states.

As the end of the year approached, it was clear that the controversy over sending abolitionist pamphlets to the South was not over. On December 7, President Jackson delivered his seventh annual State of the Union message, within which he referred to the anti-slavery mailings:

> I must also invite your attention to the painful excitement produced in the South by attempts to circulate through the mails inflammatory appeals addressed to the passions of the slaves, in prints and various sorts of publications, calculated to stimulate them to insurrection and to produce all the horrors of a servile war. There is doubtless no respectable portion of our countrymen who can be so far misled as to feel any other sentiment than that of indignant regret at conduct so destructive of the harmony and peace of the country, and so repugnant to the principles of our national compact and to the dictates of humanity and religion. Our happiness and prosperity essentially depend upon peace within our borders, and peace depends upon the maintenance in good faith of those compromises of the Constitution upon which the Union is founded. It is fortunate for the country that the good sense, the generous feeling, and the deep-rooted attachment of the people of the nonslaveholding States to the Union and to their fellow-citizens of the same blood in the South have given so strong and impressive a tone to the sentiments entertained against the proceedings of the misguided persons who have engaged in these unconstitutional and wicked attempts[.] ... But if these expressions of the public will shall not be sufficient to effect so desirable a result, not a doubt can be entertained that the nonslaveholding States, so far from countenancing the slightest interference with the constitutional rights of the South, will be prompt to exercise their authority in suppressing so far as in them lies whatever is calculated to produce this evil.
>
> ... [I]t is ... proper for Congress to take such measures as will prevent the Post-Office Department, which was designed to foster an amicable intercourse and correspondence between all the members of the Confederacy, from being used as an instrument of an opposite character. The General Government, to which the great trust is confided of preserving

inviolate the relations created among the States by the Constitution, is especially bound to avoid in its own action anything that may disturb them. I would therefore call the special attention of Congress to the subject, and respectfully suggest the propriety of passing such a law as will prohibit under severe penalties, the circulation in the Southern States, through the mail, of incendiary publications intended to instigate the slaves to insurrection.

To the embattled abolitionists who were facing both verbal and physical abuse from the South and the North, these words of Jackson's must have seemed particularly disheartening. The chief executive officer of the nation was blaming them for all the lawlessness and disorder. His words seemed to condone—indeed, perhaps even encourage—the abuse that was being heaped upon them. Now Jackson was calling for a legislative censor on their freedom of expression. It did not require any particular powers of prophecy to guess that even worse things were yet to happen.

And they soon would.

One of the most shameful and little-known incidents in the history of the United States Congress was about to unfold. It started innocently enough on Wednesday, December 16, as the first session of the Twenty-Fourth Congress opened. As per precedent, the opening days of the House of Representatives were devoted to the presentation of petitions. Following standard procedure, petitions were received starting with the most northerly state; therefore it fell to 38-year-old John Fairfield of Maine to unintentionally initiate what would become a nine-year assault upon fundamental American liberties.

On that day, Fairfield presented a petition from 172 ladies in his district asking for the end of slavery in the District of Columbia. There was nothing particularly novel about this. Conceding the accepted belief that Congress had no authority to legislate upon slavery in the states, the standard anti-slavery approach had become to agitate for Congressional removal of the institution in the federal city. And since petitions were one of the few ways that women could have their voices heard in Congress, various women's anti-slavery groups had been submitting such petitions for quite some time. The standard method of dealing with such requests was to politely receive them and then allow them to quietly expire in some unnoticed committee.

However, such a procedure afforded the possibility of discussion or debate on the issue, which was something that many members of the House would prefer to avoid. Congressman John Cramer, a Democrat from New York, moved that the petition be "laid on the table." This would prevent it even making it to committee; and, in effect, removing any possibility that it would receive any support on the floor. By a voice vote, the House agreed to Cramer's suggestion.

Fairfield had another anti-slavery petition. To save time and trouble, he himself moved that it be tabled as the first one had been, which was quickly agreed to by a vote of 180 to 31. In protest, William Slade of Vermont requested that "as a matter of common courtesy," the petitioners "were entitled ... to a respectable hearing." He therefore moved that the petition be printed.

In response to Slade's proposal, it was pointed out that there was no need to print the petition. Congress had already received many such petitions in the past, and nothing this one said could possibly be any different. Nor was it supposed that any action taken on it (or, more precisely, non-action) would be any different than any former petitions. The motion to print was laid on the table with the languishing petitions by a vote of 168 to 50.

Two days later, Congressman William Jackson of Massachusetts referred yet another anti-slavery petition to the House. By this time, some of the Southern members were becoming exasperated at the persistence of their Northern counter parts. In their efforts to ensure that slavery was not discussed on the floor of the House, the delegates spent the better part of the next few days debating the issue of whether Congress had the right to abolish slavery within the District of Columbia.

According to Eleazer W. Ripley of Louisiana, "There was no subject of deeper interest in the quarter of the country from whence he came. He had been sent here to oppose every effort of a certain class of citizens, in reference to slavery within the District." Henry A. Wise of Virginia agreed with Ripley on the significance of the issue. "If it was the opinion that Congress had the right to interfere in this question," said Wise, "let the South know it at once, and it would know what to do."

If Northern representatives sympathetic to the fanatic abolitionists were going to assert such a claim, then the Southerners "had no longer any business there. Their business was at home, to report to their people. He would go home, never to return again, if that House were to say, directly or indirectly, that Congress had that power."

James Henry Hammond of South Carolina felt he could no longer silently accept the intrusion of these fanatic petitions. His object in representing the citizens of his state was a "sacred one. It was to protect the rights of his constituents and his own. If they could not maintain them by the action of the House, they would maintain them by their own action.

> Mr. Hammond moved that the petition not be received. The large majority by which the House had rejected a similar petition [Fairfield's] a few days ago had been very gratifying to the whole South. He had hoped it would satisfy the gentlemen charged with such petitions, of the impropriety of introducing them here. Since, however, it had not had

that effect, and they still persisted in urging them upon the House and upon the country, he thought it was not requiring too much of the House, to ask it to put a more decided seal of reprobation on them, by peremptorily rejecting this [one as well.]

Speaker of the House (and future president of the United States) James K. Polk expressed his doubts as to the precedent for such an action. There were many parliamentary ways to defeat or ignore an undesirable petition, but what Hammond was suggesting was altogether new. Could the House simply refuse to even receive a petition?

> Mr. Hammond ... did think it due to the House and the country, to give at once the most decisive evidence of the sentiments entertained here upon the subject. He wished to put an end to these petitions. He could not sit there and submit to their being brought forward until the House had become callous to their consequences. He could not sit there and see the rights of the Southern People assaulted day after day, by the ignorant fanatics from whom these memorials proceed[ed].

His purpose was quite clear: the House should establish the fact that such petitions were no longer welcome. Once the anti-slavery fanatics found out that their memorials would not be received, then they would stop sending them. The threat of discussion upon slavery would cease, and harmony could return to the halls of justice.

Mr. Aaron Vanderpoel of New York agreed wholeheartedly with Hammond's suggestion:

> The refusal to consider the petition would be telling such petitioners, in language that could not and would not be misunderstood, to cease their abortive and incendiary efforts to disturb the rights of property recognised and guaranteed by those men of olden times, who were so much wiser and better than the fanatics of modern days.... Why not march directly to the point upon which all the true enemies of abolitionists would agree? Refuse to consider the petition, and you do what should be done, and that in the most prompt manner.

Most of the speakers voiced sentiments in agreement with Hammond and Vanderpoel. Hiram P. Hunt of New York remarked that "there was but one sentiment everywhere. He apprehended that gentlemen on all sides merely differed as to the means of effecting a general and desired end—an end they were all seeking, and which was to give quiet and composure to this republic, upon this exciting question." However, Hunt cautioned his listeners that "the quiet of the community could not be ensured by suppressing information and inquiry":

> [T]hey should give to all these petitions the usual parliamentary course, for this was not the last, in all human probability, that would be sent here.

> They could not conceal from themselves the fact that the public were advised of the existence of these memorials. They would [continue to] be sent to members there; and ... other gentlemen would also feel it to be their duty to present them. He asked, then, that they would show the South fairly the principles they maintained, by referring this and all similar petitions ... to some special committee, with instructions to report.

With, of course, the unstated implication everyone seemed to be in agreement on that the committee's report would prove unfavorable to the petitioners. By such a procedure, the House would appear to be recognizing the sacred right of petition, and yet at the same time put an end to them.

And there the issue would lie until the new year.

Even as the battle of the petitions was unfolding in the House, a different conflict was arising in the Senate. On December 21, Senator John C. Calhoun moved that the President's plea against incendiary materials being transmitted by the U.S. Mail be referred to a special committee. As the standing post office committee was composed primarily of Northerners, Calhoun thought that it "was earnestly to be desired" that any report upon the President's message should issue from a group "a majority of whom were of those most deeply interested in the matter." That is, from Southerners.

After the typical bout of legislative bickering, Calhoun's proposal was accepted. Calhoun was named chairman, and the other members were John P. King of Georgia, Willie P. Mangum of North Carolina, Lewis F. Linn of Missouri, and John Davis of Massachusetts, the Lone Northerner.

It appears that being an abolitionist had become quite dangerous by 1835. Besides the two October riots already discussed, historian Gerda Lerner (in her biography of the Grimké sisters) claims that "the mobbing and beating of antislavery speakers became commonplace. Charles Stuart was attacked in western New York; Amos Phelps was almost killed by a brickbat while he gave an abolitionist lecture in Farmington, Connecticut." According to Dr. Lerner:

> Every effort was made to deny [to the Abolitionists] a hearing, frighten their audiences away and keep free Negroes from attending their meetings. Usually the press prepared the ground for violence with a barrage of distorted interpretations of abolitionist views or outright lies. At their meetings hecklers abounded, sometimes drummers or other kinds of noisemakers invaded the hall and kept up a steady racket. Frequently the speakers were pelted with rotten eggs and vegetables. Occasionally they were tarred, feathered, and ridden out of town on a rail.... In time [the Abolitionists] came to consider a riot a part of their introduction to a community. Pacifists by conviction, they developed "non-violent resistance" into a working technique. On the first night in a new community

their main task was to stand up to the mob without fear. [Theodore] Weld discovered that by folding his arms across his chest and calmly staring down a mob, he usually could impress the crowd enough to escape serious injury. The next night (or perhaps the third, if resistance was particularly virulent), he would have found enough men curious to see what was the source of his courage to guarantee him a hearing. Often a few of these would form an escort and handle the disturbances. Once the audience was willing to listen, he would speak without further reference to the violence, using all his persuasiveness and oratorical skill. He would usually end up by making enough converts to form a committee to carry on the work after his departure. In town after town, village after village ... the foundation for abolition organization was laid in this painful manner.

Fifty-five-year-old William Ellery Channing, who had almost single-handedly founded Unitarianism in May 1819, published a volume called *Slavery*. While it is occasionally referred to as a "landmark" antislavery book, it had very little new or noteworthy to contribute to the issue. Channing began by emphasizing that "recent events" had "done much to unsettle and obscure men in regard" to slavery. He was quick to point out that the agitation could "be ascribed in part to the injudicious vehemence of those who have taken into their hands the cause of the slave."

Southerners must have been comforted by his assertion that "to the slaveholder belongs the duty of settling, and employing the best methods of liberation, and to no other. We have no right of interference." While claiming to deplore slavery, he insisted that "our proper and only means of action, is to spread the truth on the subject of slavery, and let none condemn this means because of its gradual influence."

As Channing saw it, it was the duty of all who were sincerely concerned for the bondsmen to patiently wait until "the great principle, that man cannot rightfully be held as property, should be *admitted by the slave-holder*. [emphasis added] The slave should be acknowledged [by his master] as a partaker of a common nature, as having the essential rights of humanity."

In view of Southern attitudes towards blacks, it was very unlikely that such admissions or acknowledgements would soon be forthcoming. Channing's advice, therefore, amounted to little more than sitting back and doing nothing.

A large portion of the volume was devoted to the abolitionists who had been "acting, however mistakenly, from benevolent and pious impulses." Though Channing's general tone was critical of their actions, he began by offering some words of defense in their behalf.

> That they have ever proposed or desired insurrection or violence among the slaves, there is no reason to believe. All their principles repel

the supposition. It is a remarkable fact, that, though the South and the North have been leagued to crush them, though they have been watched by a million of eyes, and though prejudice has been prepared to detect the slightest sign of corrupt communication with the slave, yet this crime has not been fastened on a single member of the body. A few individuals at the South have, indeed, been tortured or murdered by enraged multitudes, on the charge of stirring up revolt [Vicksburg again?]; but their guilt and their connection with the Abolitionists ... could not be established[.] ... The act, which caused the present explosion of popular feeling, was the sending of pamphlets by the Abolitionists into the slave-holding States. In so doing, they acted with great inconsideration; but they must have been insane, had they intended to stir up a servile war, for the pamphlets were sent, not by stealth, but by the public mail; and not to slaves, but to the masters; to men in public life, to men of the greatest influence and distinction. Strange incendiaries these! They flourished their firebrands about at noon-day; and, still more, put them into the hands of the very men whom it was said they wish to destroy.... The charge of corrupt design, so vehemently brought against the Abolitionists, is groundless. The charge of fanaticism I have no desire to repel.

Channing admitted that had they done wrong by the law, they should be made to suffer for it. "For all their errors and sins let the tribunal of public opinion inflict the full measure of rebuke which they deserve. I ask no favor for them. But they shall not be stripped of the rights of man, of rights guaranteed by the laws and Constitution, without one voice, at least, being raised in their defence."

He was, however, quick to point out that "the Abolitionists have done wrong, ... nor is their wrong to be winked at, because done fanatically or with good intention[.] The tone of their newspapers ... has often been fierce, bitter, exasperating. Their imaginations have been fed too much on pictures of the cruelty to which the slave is exposed, till not a few have probably conceived of his abode as perpetually resounding with the lash, and ringing with shrieks of agony."

Channing deplored their systematic policy of "agitation" as being "unfriendly to the spirit of Christianity, and as increasing, in a degree, the perils of the Slave-holding States." The abolitionists were either ignorant or naive if they hadn't foreseen the probable consequences of their words.

> Among the unenlightened, whom they so powerfully addressed, was there no reason to fear that some might feel themselves called to subvert this system of wrong, by whatever means? From the free colored people this danger was particularly to be apprehended.... And would it be wonderful, if, in a moment of passionate excitement, some enthusiast should think it his duty to use his communication with his injured brethren for stirring them up to revolt? Such is the danger from Abolitionism to the Slave-holding States.

He admonished the abolitionists: "Let not a good cause find its chief obstruction in its defenders. Let the whole truth, be spoken without faltering or fear, but so spoken as to convince, not inflame, as to give no alarm to the wise, and no needless exasperation to the selfish and passionate." While a great sentiment, it was an impossible one to put into practice. There was no way that anyone could speak against slavery—no matter how calmly or dispassionately—without arousing the anger of the South. To have followed Channing's advice, the abolitionists would have had to quit speaking out against slavery altogether. And this they were not prepared to do.

Upon careful assessment, it is hard to see how Channing's work could be considered a "landmark" in anti-slavery literature. Instead, it was little more than another attempt to mollify the outraged sensibilities of the slaveowners, with little genuine regard for the plight of the slaves.

This year saw the enactment in South Carolina and Louisiana of a series of laws that would soon become particularly obnoxious to the New England states. Popularly called "Black Seaman's Laws," they were an attempt by the harassed South to eliminate the dissemination of ideas of freedom between free black sailors and slaves. Under the terms of these laws, any black sailors on incoming vessels were immediately incarcerated for the duration of their ship's time in port, thereby effectively denying the free blacks any opportunity to incite the local slaves to insurrection. When the ship was ready to leave port, the captain was required to make payment to the local authorities for the black sailors' jail time. If the captain was unwilling or unable to do so, the free black was sold into slavery to recoup the state's losses.

There appear to be no records of how many, if any, free blacks were sentenced to this ultimate punishment. However, blacks comprised a significant portion of the crew on many Yankee vessels, and the terms and conditions of these laws were rightfully viewed as unconstitutional by the Northern states. It would, however, be many years before the North would be enraged enough to lodge any formal protests against these laws.

Notable deaths in 1835 included the venerable John Marshall, who had served as Chief Justice of the Supreme Court since 1801. The Liberty Bell was rung in Philadelphia to mourn the nation's loss. One popular, though undocumented, account has it that it was upon this occasion that the now famous crack appeared in the American icon.

Marshall was replaced on the court by Roger Taney of Maryland, who would be responsible for the infamous court ruling involving the slaves of Dr. Emerson. Taney would still be presiding over the court when the Civil War broke out.

Another significant death for the future of the young republic was that of Henry James Hungerford. Hungerford, it will be recalled, had been the recipient of James Smithson's fortune upon that man's death in 1829. A bachelor, Hungerford died "without issue," and, as stipulated in Smithson's will, the fortune he had received was now to go to the United States. Many Americans were loath to accept the gift, fearing to establish a precedent that would obligate them to recognize any bequest regardless of its origin or terms. "Every whippersnapper vagabond who has been traducing our country," complained William C. Preston of South Carolina, "might think proper to have his name distinguished in the same way. It was not consistent with the dignity of the country." Congress would spend a long time arguing over whether or not to accept Smithson's money.

President Jackson's frustrated desire to remove the Cherokees from Georgia finally received legitimacy with the signing of the Treaty of New Echoata on December 29. By the terms of this treaty, the Cherokees agreed to relinquish their claim to their Georgia Territory. The problem was that the group that signed the treaty represented less than 500 of the 17,000 Cherokee in the Cherokee Nation. Ignoring this minor inconsistency, Jackson sent the treaty, with his blessings, on to the Congress for ratification.

The government's Indian Removal Policy did not seem to be going quite as well in Florida. According to a treaty signed in 1832, the Seminole Indians, like so many other eastern tribes, were supposed to be removed to reservations west of the Mississippi. Resistance mounted among the natives, led by their chief, Osceola, and the Second Seminole War erupted in November.

The total miles of railroad in the country by the end of the year was 1,098.

The year 1835 saw what was perhaps the shortest and undoubtedly one of the most bizarre wars in the history of the United States. This was the comic "Toledo War" between the state of Ohio and the Michigan Territory over a small strip (approximately 468 square miles) of real estate between the two that now includes the city of Toledo and encompasses the mouth of the Maumee River. Michigan contended that the boundary should be shifted about eight miles farther south at Lake Erie, and tapering slightly to just five miles farther south at the Indiana border.

According to the original terms upon which Ohio had been admitted into the Union, Michigan was correct. However, recent erroneous surveys had established the line in the proximity of its present border, and Ohio was not about to give it up. The region was about to become prosperous as canals in Ohio inched their way towards the Maumee River.

A confrontation in April was avoided only because the Michigan and Ohio militia units sent to establish claim to the region got lost in the swamps near Perrysburg and were unable to find each other. The only bloodshed was by Michigan Sheriff Joseph Wood. When Wood attempted to arrest Major Benjamin Franklin Stickney of the Ohio militia, Stickney's younger son, Two Stickney (as opposed to the Major's older son, One Stickney) stabbed Wood with a penknife.

Ultimately, Congress would step in to settle the dispute, but its decision was not forthcoming until the following summer.

Alexis de Tocqueville assured his historical fame with the publication in 1835 of *Democracy in America*. This book is still recognized today as a significant exposition on American political theory. While the main emphasis of his volume dealt with the workings of the American institutions of government, Tocqueville did give notice to the existence of black slavery in America and many of the issues dealing with it. Much of what he said must have pleased his Southern readers, particularly when he proclaimed that "the Negro ... scarcely feels his own calamitous situation.... [H]e admires his tyrants more than he hates them, and finds his joy and his pride in the servile imitation of those who oppose him." He agreed with the Southern claim that if the slave "becomes free, independence is often felt by him to be a heavier burden than slavery." After he described the hardships the freeman dealt with on a daily basis, he could only conclude that the free black "is sunk to such a depth of wretchedness that while servitude brutalizes, liberty destroys him."

Significantly, however, Tocqueville recognized that "the most formidable of all the ills that threaten the future of the Union arises from the presence of a black population upon its territory; and in contemplating the cause of the present embarrassments, or the future dangers of the United States, the observer is invariably led to this as a primary fact."

Tocqueville's observations seemed particularly keen when he remarked that "in the South of the United States the whole race of whites formed an aristocratic body [.] ... This aristocracy contained many who were poor, *but none who would work*[.]" (emphasis added.)

It seems this idea is critical to an understanding of why non-slaveholding Southern whites were willing to fight to perpetuate slavery. Without the slaves to do the menial work, it would fall upon the backs of the lower-class whites.

He seemed also well aware of the secret fear of the bondsmen that "perpetually haunts the imagination of the Americans." He pointed out that "in the Southern States, the subject is not discussed: the planter does not allude to the future in conversing with strangers; he does not communicate his apprehensions to his friends; he seeks to conceal them from himself."

He concluded his remarks by observing:

> When I contemplate the condition of the South, I can discover only two modes of action for the white inhabitants of those States: namely, either to emancipate the Negroes and to intermingle with them, or, remaining isolated from them, to keep them in slavery as long as possible.... Such is the view that the Americans of the South take of the question, and they act consistently with it. As they are determined not to mingle with the Negroes, they refuse to emancipate them.

The next 25 years of the nation's history would demonstrate the accuracy of Tocqueville's conclusions.

James Birney had decided to publish a journal "devoted to a full and impartial discussion of the whole subject of slavery, as connected with emancipation." However, the opposition and persecutions of his neighbors compelled him to realize that even in Kentucky it would not be safe to do so. He moved with his family to Cincinnati, Ohio, and began publication of the contemplated anti-slavery newspaper, which he entitled the *Philanthropist*.

Nine

1836

On January 7, Thomas Morris of Ohio presented two petitions in the Senate requesting the abolition of slavery in the District of Columbia. Calhoun referred to them as "a foul slander on nearly one half of the States of the Union." he claimed "he did not fear these incendiary publications, but he dreaded the agitation which would rise out of the discussion in Congress on the subject. Every man knew that there existed a body of men in the Northern States who were ready to second any insurrectionary movement of the blacks."

The problem with these documents, as he saw it, was due to "the forbearance which had been exhibited towards them. Nothing can, nothing will, stop these petitions but a prompt and stern rejection of them."

Alexander Porter of Louisiana insisted that "the constitution was established, not merely in spirit, but in letter, in reference to this great interest of the South. The right to property which the petitioners sought to impair was solemnly recognised by that instrument." Like many other Southerners, he feared that the "boldness and illiberality" of the abolitionists "was increasing by the forbearance which had been existed towards them." In other words, Southerners had been too nice to them, and it was time to start getting tough.

Porter argued that there existed some "propositions so revolting that we cannot approach them for the purposes of investigation, and such, I consider, are those contained in the [anti-slavery] petition[s]." Porter complained that "the language" contained within these petitions was "most indecorous and insulting to a large portion of the members" of the Senate. "No men in this country have a right to come here, and, in the form of petition, accuse this body or any of its members of offenses against the laws of God or the laws of man." Porter rose to the defense of Southern slaveholders:

> They are neither tyrants nor murderers. They found relations existing in their country, either at the time of their birth or of their emigration to it, which they in no way contributed to establish, and for which they are not responsible. They feel that they cannot abolish them without utter ruin to themselves. So circumstanced, they have comported themselves in a manner which gives them no cause to blush....
>
> He firmly asserted, because he honestly believed, that so far *the domestic institutions of the South had worked no injury either to the white man or the black*[.] [Emphasis added]
>
> [The Southern slave-holders] should not, and with God's blessing they shall not, with impunity, be made the objects of vituperation. Year after year have they quietly [?] heard themselves, their wives, and daughters, denounced by miserable wretches[.] ... Aware of the danger which hangs over our glorious Union by agitating this subject, they have practiced forbearance until it has ceased to be a virtue. But I warn our estimable brethren in the non-slaveholding States that another feeling than that of patient endurance is rising rapidly among the people of the South, and that, unless provocation ceases, no man can contemplate without dismay the point to which that feeling rapidly tends.

Porter warmed to his argument:

> [T]he Southern mind has been already filled with agitation. Their property, their domestic relations, their altars, their lives, are in danger[.] ... Are we to behold our rights and privileges trampled upon? All upon which the permanence and security of our prosperity depends [has been] assailed by these blood-thirsty fanatics[.] ... Let me beseech them to weigh well the consequences which will follow the success of their mad and misguided efforts—insurrection and rebellion. A servile, not a civil war. A war upon women and children. A war that spares no sex, respects no age, pities no suffering; that consigns our hearths and altars to flame and blood, and fills our fields and woods with a foe at once savage, bloody, and remorseless....

Of course, an abolitionist, given an opportunity to do so, might reply to Porter that the peculiar institution that he so adamantly defended also "spares no sex, respects no age, pities no suffering." But, Porter was okay with that as long as such abuses were reserved solely for the blacks.

William C. Preston of South Carolina observed that it was up to Congress to:

> stay the desperate efforts of these stirrers up of bloodshed and murder.... [U]nless the plans and operations of the abolitionists are ... put down—unless Government stands as an impassable barrier between us and them—I fear ... that no adequate conception can be formed of the

tremendous consequences which will follow. I wish not to menace or threaten.... We exist under a necessity which cannot be touched or tampered with. Our property and lives may be in jeopardy.

Preston admitted that all citizens had the right to petition their grievances, yet he vehemently denied that such was the case with the abolitionists:

> Grievances! For what grievances do these petitioners seek redress? Does slavery in this District interfere with them? ... Has the constitution guaranteed to these people, having neither a general or local interest in the matter, the right to come here and require me to weaken and abolish the very institution which I represent? Am I, acting for three fifths of the slave population of South Carolina, to impugn the very principle upon which I hold my seat? ... Am I to furnish a torch for my own dwelling, a knife for my own throat?
> ... An enemy, savage, remorseless, and indignant, is thundering at our gates[.] ... Our hearths and altars are running with blood and in flames[.] ... The storm is bursting upon us that is to sweep away the bulwarks of our freedom and union, and fill the land with convulsion and anarchy[.] ... Petitioners, the mad instruments for accomplishing this unhallowed work, are thronging here by the thousands; incendiary pamphlets are circulated; incendiary meetings held; insults, threats, and denunciations, are heaped upon us[.]

To hear Preston speak, one would think that it was the slaveowners who were being mobbed in the streets, intimidated in their own meeting halls, tarred and feathered or worse, or whose lives were being threatened with kidnapping and assassination.

Space does not allow a complete examination of the Congressional battles over abolitionism. But the intent is to show both how radical the Southerners were in their denunciations, and how unpopular and friendless the abolitionists were. This leads to the question: Were the abolitionists right to continue forcing the issues? It seems clear that the slaveowners were too dedicated to their system to change or abandon it unless absolutely compelled to do so. While it was indeed unfortunate that the compulsion took the form of a devastating war, what other means could have been found? Slavery was not about to die off on its own if ignored. It seems that those who blame the abolitionists for making things worse are missing the point: It was the slaveowners' refusal to recognize or accept the basic human rights of the blacks that forced the abolitionists to maintain an adversarial pose.

None of the abuse and ridicule heaped upon the slaveowners in abolitionis literature would compare with these words spoken in Congress by Southern politicians. Why then were the Southerners not accused of being the cause of the nation's unrest during the pre–Civil War years?

Could it be that it's easier to accept the conventional notion of the abolitionists as agitators and trouble-makers? If the present book accomplishes anything, one would hope that the reader becomes more aware of, and sympathetic towards, the tensions with which the abolitionists contended.

And unlike the slaveowners, these brave men and women were not standing up to defend their own lives and property. What is most commendable is that these "fanatics" were willing to suffer almost unbearable consequences in behalf of a cause from which they did not personally benefit.

In both houses of Congress, January seemed to be consumed by constant bickering over postal regulations and petitions. On February 1, James Henry Hammond of South Carolina would demonstrate just how far removed the Southern slaveowner was from admitting that slavery was wrong. He argued at length in the House that slavery.

> ... is no evil. On the contrary, I believe it to be the greatest of all the great blessings which a kind Providence has bestowed upon our glorious region.... I do firmly believe that domestic slavery, regulated as ours is, produces the highest toned, the purest, best organization of society that has ever existed on the face of the earth.

This does not sound like a man who will soon be acknowledging the "essential rights of humanity" of the slave. Nor did the representative from South Carolina sound like he was ready to accept blacks as his fellow man when he remarked:

> Although I am perfectly satisfied that no human process can elevate the black man to an equality with the white—admitting that it could be done—are we prepared for the consequence which then must follow? Are the people of the North prepared to ... place [the black's] political power on an equality with their own? Are we prepared to see them mingling in our legislatures? Is any portion of this country prepared to see them enter these halls and take their seats by our sides, in perfect equality with the white representatives of an Anglo-Saxon race ... and see them wield the destinies of this great republic? From such a picture I turn with irrepressible disgust.

He included within his harangue the typical, time-honored Southern threat of disunion.

> ... [T]he moment this House undertakes to legislate upon [slavery], it dissolves the Union. Should it be my fortune to have a seat upon this floor, I will abandon it the instant the first decisive step is taken towards legislation of this subject. I will go home to preach, and if I can, to practice, disunion, and civil war, if needs be. A revolution must ensue, and this republic sink in blood.

Nine • 1836

Where in all the annals of abolitionism is such a bombastic display of posturing and bullying, of threats and innuendo? And these people had the nerve to label Garrison an incendiary?

Hammond finished with the definitive Southern statement upon those who opposed his cherished institution:

> And I warn the abolitionists, ignorant, infatuated, barbarians as they are, that if chance shall throw any of them into our hands he may expect a felon's death. No human law, no human influence, can arrest his fate. The superhuman instinct of self-preservation, the indignant feelings of an outraged people, to whose hearth-stones he is seeking to carry death and desolation, pronounce his doom; and if we failed to accord it to him we would be unworthy of the forms we wear, unworthy of the beings whom it is our duty to protect, and we would merit and expect the indignation of offended Heaven.

In Hammond's mind, the fight against the abolitionist hordes had become one of sacred, divine honor. As a "good" Southerner, he knew that it was his obligation—to himself, to his women, and to his country—to resist the encroachment of anti-slavery regardless of the cost. It was this sort of fierce, selfish dedication to a barbaric system of racial repression that would drive the nation 25 years later into the very civil war Hammond had predicted.

The Senate committee report on "Incendiary Publications" was presented on February 4. No doubt many Southern Senators were disappointed to hear chairman Calhoun announce that while the committee "agree[d] with the President as to the evil [of the papers which have been attempted to be circulated in the South] and its highly dangerous tendency, and the necessity of arresting it, they have not been able to assent to the measure of redress which he recommends[.]" In other words, the committee did not recommend passing legislation that would deny the use of the mail to the abolitionists.

This initially bewildering conclusion makes more sense when it is remembered that Calhoun's entire political career had been dedicated to the independence of the states. If the states were to allow the federal government to dictate which things could not be sent through the mails, then they might be forced into being told what things they must accept through the mails. Such compulsion by the national authorities was anathema to Calhoun.

As expressed in the committee's report:

> Nothing is more clear than that the admission of the right, on the part of Congress, to determine what papers are incendiary, and as such to prohibit their circulation through the mail, necessarily involves the right to determine what are not incendiary, and to enforce their circulation.

> Nor is it less certain that to admit such a right would be virtually to clothe Congress with the power to abolish slavery, by giving it the means of breaking down all the barriers which the slaveholding States have erected for the protection of their lives and property. It would give Congress ... the authority to open the gates to the flood of incendiary publications which are ready to break upon these States, and to punish all who dare resist as criminals.

In the end, the senator from South Carolina decided that it would be better by far to leave such decisions upon "Incendiary Publications" to the discretion of each state individually.

The most interesting aspect of Calhoun's report was its lengthy gratuitous decision to "touch briefly on the movements of the abolitionists, with the view of showing the dangerous consequences to which they must lead if not arrested." How blatantly hypocritical of Southerners to argue for six weeks against receiving anti-slavery petitions on the grounds that it was undesirable to debate the issue in a public forum, but then take advantage of the opportunity provided to launch their criticism at the Abolitionists.

According to the report, it was clear that the primary function of abolitionism was.

> ... to excite ... hatred and abhorrence against the institutions and citizens of the slave-holding States, by addresses, lectures, and pictorial representations abounding in false and exaggerated statements.
>
> ... Never was its character more fully exemplified than in the present instance. Setting out with the abstract principle that slavery is an evil, the fanatical zealots come at once to the conclusion that it is their duty to abolish it, regardless of all the disasters which must follow. Never was conclusion more false or dangerous.
>
> ... [S]lavery, as it exists in the Southern States, ... involves not only the relation of master and slave, but, also, the social and political relations of two races, of nearly equal numbers, from different quarters of the globe, and the most opposite of all others in every particular that distinguishes one race of man from another. *Emancipation would destroy these relations*[.] [Emphasis added.]

One can only imagine Garrison hoping that such relations could be destroyed. For unless or until such prejudices of the whites towards the blacks could be eliminated, slavery could never be abolished with any hope of safety for the slaves.

> ... It is not the intention of the committee to dwell on the pecuniary aspect of this vital subject, the vast amount of property involved, equal at least to $950,000,000; the ruin of families and individuals; the impoverishment and prostration of an entire section of the Union, and the fatal blow that would be given to the productions of the great agricultural sta-

ples[.] ... As great as these disasters would be, they are nothing, compared to what must follow the subversions of the existing relation between the two races[.]...

Under this relation, the two races have long lived in peace and prosperity[.] ... [T]he African race has multiplied, ... accompanied by great improvement, physically and intellectually, and the enjoyment of a degree of comfort with which the laboring class in few countries can compare[.] ... [Does any modern reader believe this claim?]

To destroy the existing relations would be to destroy this prosperity, and to place the two races in a state of conflict, which must end in the expulsion or extirpation of one or the other.... [I]t is impossible for them to exist together in the same community ... under any other relation than that which now exists....

He must be blind, who does not perceive that the subversion of a relation which must be followed with such disastrous consequences can only be effected by convulsions that would devastate the country[.]

Just four days after Calhoun's presentation, Henry L. Pinckney of South Carolina delivered his committee's report on "Slavery in the District of Columbia" to the House of Representatives. As they had in the Senate, Southerners would use the opportunity provided to be openly critical of the abolitionists with no fear of rebuttals or debate. According to the report, the committee had:

> long considered the movement in relation to this matter [of abolishing slavery in Washington] as fraught with incalculable evils, not only to the slaveholding States, but to every portion of our common country. They rejoice, therefore, that the great body of the people of the non-slaveholding States have come forward, as they have done, in the true spirit of American patriotism, to sustain their constitutional obligations to their Southern brethren, and to arrest the disturbance of the public peace.
> ... [The committee] cannot too strongly express their condemnation of the conduct of the abolitionists, and their utter abhorrence of the consequences to which, if persisted in, it must inevitably lead.... [B]y persevering in machinations which threaten to bring the citizens of the different States into collision, and to overthrow the whole system of civil society itself, in the slaveholding portions of the Union ... there can be no doubt that they have done, and are doing, incalculable evil[.]...
> Your committee deem it their duty to say that, in their opinion, the people of the South have been very unjustly censured in reference to slavery.... Your committee cannot too strongly express their unanimous and unqualified disapprobation of all such movements....
> It is all important, therefore, that the spirit of abolition, or, in other words, of illegal and officious interference with the domestic institutions of the South, should be arrested and put down; and men of intelligence and influence at the North should endeavor to produce that sound and rational state of public opinion which is equally due to the South and to the preservation of the Union.

Having had their say, the committee proposed, in an effort to promote peace and harmony, that a select committee be appointed to receive all pending anti-slavery petitions, and the committee be specifically instructed to report that Congress had no authority to interfere with slavery in the states or in the District of Columbia.

Pinckney's report was virtually dismissed by most Southerners as being too mild a remedy for the situation. The debate continued well into the spring.

Much has been written of the "dough-faced" Northerners, those spineless individuals who were willing to comply with the requests (and demands) of the slaveowners to protect them and their institution rather than stand up, as the Abolitionists were doing, for what was right. However, in reading the impassioned speeches of the Southern legislators, it's hard to be terribly critical of the sympathizing Northerners. It's impossible to say for certain whether the advocates of slavery painted such a terrible picture out of a sincere belief that such atrocities would occur, or simply to strengthen their own position and protect their peculiar institution. (And perhaps, in reality, the truth was somewhere between the two extreme positions.) But if one listened long enough to them—and Northerners had been listening to the same arguments for a long, long time—their arguments seemed convincing.

To many otherwise well-intentioned individuals, it may indeed have seemed that the dire results of emancipation would be catastrophic for the entire nation. Who could fault them if they were not willing to be responsible for being the cause of social upheaval? It was one thing to feel compassion for the slaves; it was something altogether different to contemplate plunging the nation into chaos on their behalf. What right-minded individual was willing to take such chances?

Of course, the abolitionists would argue there was no chance that things could be as bad as the slaveowners predicted. They felt confident that emancipation could be safely achieved; if only the slaveowners desired it and were willing to cooperate. Of course, they didn't, and they weren't. Perhaps the Northern sympathizers knew and understood this better than did the abolitionists, which is why they acted the way they did.

The battle of words in Congress would soon be overshadowed by actual battles half a continent away. On March 2, Texas declared its independence. Of course, declaring it and getting it were different matters. It would not come painlessly.

On March 6, a stubborn but unnecessary sacrifice of nearly 200 men, consisting of Texans and allies—that included James Bowie and former congressman Davey Crockett immortalized the Alamo in American folklore. Though of dubious military value, the heroic stand at the besieged mission became a rallying point for the Texans in their struggle against Mexico.

On March 17, while the fight for independence was still being waged, Texas adopted its first constitution. An interesting portion of this was Section 9 under "*General Provision*":

> All persons of color who were slaves for life previous to their emigration to Texas, and who are now held in bondage, shall remain in the like state of servitude: *Provided,* The said slave shall be the *bona-fide* property of the person so holding said slave as aforesaid. Congress shall pass no laws to prohibit emigrants from bringing their slaves into the republic with them, and holding them by the same tenure by which such slaves were held in the United States; nor shall congress have power to emancipate slaves; nor shall any slaveholder be allowed to emancipate his or her slave or slaves without the consent of congress, unless he or she shall send his or her slave or slaves without the limits of the republic. No free person of African descent, either in whole or in part, shall be permitted to reside permanently in the republic without the consent of congress; and the importation or admission of Africans or negroes into this republic, excepting from the United States of America, is forever prohibited, and declared to be piracy.

The establishment of Texas as a pro-slavery republic motivated Southern support for its struggle, while at the same time it reduced Northern sympathies.

Less than five weeks later on April 21 the Texans achieved their independence in the "Battle of San Jacinto." An interesting bit of folklore surrounds this Texan victory. It concerns Emily West, otherwise known as "The Maid of Morgan's Point." Emily was a mulatto who was living in the Texas village of New Washington when it was overrun by Mexican General Santa Anna on April 18. Santa Anna, a bit of a ladies man, was said to be "immediately struck by her beauty."

As the story is told, West, as a loyal Texan, allowed herself to be seized by Santa Anna as a "spoil of war," while a young mulatto boy made his escape to warn Sam Houston of the Mexican general's presence. Supposedly, West was still exercising her charms upon the unsuspecting General as Houston attacked on the afternoon of April 21. West's role was considered by many at the time a "significant contribution" to the victory. (See Appendix 2.)

On April 28, a scene of unbelievable atrocity took place in St. Louis, Missouri. The most complete version of the story was that popularized and circulated by the abolitionists, as published by Theodore Weld in his 1839 expose *American Slavery as It Is*:

A free mulatto named Francis L. McIntosh arrived via boat from Pittsburgh. St. Louis' deputy sheriff, George Hammond, tried to arrest

McIntosh, aided by the city's deputy constable, William Mull. The cause of the arrest is uncertain; some accounts claim that McIntosh had interfered in Hammond's arrest of two unruly sailors, others that McIntosh had been involved in a street fight.

McIntosh resisted arrest and ran off. When the two officers found him, he stabbed both of them with a knife. Hammond died almost instantly from a wound to the neck. Mull survived the attack, though according to some accounts died later. (The most detailed accounts don't mention this, so perhaps Mull's wound did not prove fatal.)

McIntosh was pursued by an angry mob, captured and put into jail. Soon a crowd gathered, stormed the jail and forcibly removed him. He was dragged to a tree, chained to it and wood was piled around him. The crowd watched as he burned to death.

The details of the actual lynching were reported by a number of different sources. Weld's account says that the lynching occurred "in open day ... in the midst of the city." The diary of an unidentified St. Louis physician claims that "McIntosh died very slowly," he wrote, "An alderman threatened to shoot anyone who tried to loosen the chains binding McIntosh to the tree.... As the fire burned through McIntosh's abdomen and his entrails spilt out, someone in the crowd asked the victim if he still felt pain. McIntosh answered that he felt a great deal of pain."

The *St. Louis Observer*, edited by Elijah P. Lovejoy, reported the lynching as described by "reliable" witnesses:

> When McIntosh, chained with his back to the tree, realized that the mob intended to burn him, not whip him, he pleaded to be shot. As he felt the flames on his body, he "commenced singing a hymn and trying to pray." [According to Martineau: "[B]ecause he was heard to pray as his limbs were slowly consuming, he was pronounced by the magistrates to be in league with the abolitionists."] When he grew silent and his head dropped, someone in the crowd speculated that he had died. With most of his facial features destroyed by the fire, McIntosh managed to speak. He still felt the pain, he said. He could hear all that was said around him. Again he pleaded to be shot.

Lovejoy, a transplanted New Englander of only moderate anti-slavery views, saw the lynching as an example of the ruthlessness of Southern life that came from a society half-free and half-slave. Many abolitionists shared this belief.

The only other contemporary account seems to have been the St. Louis *Republican*, which acknowledged the attack but differed in some details of it. According to its report, Hammond had tried to arrest McIntosh around seven o'clock, implying that the burning took place in the early evening, not "in open day" as Weld claimed. The *Republican* also stated that the mob took McIntosh "to the border of town," as if the crime becomes less horrendous by being less centrally located.

John F. Darby, who happened to be mayor of St. Louis at the time of the attack, described the lynching in his memoirs written four decades later. While admitting that he had not been present at the burning, he claimed that the suggestion to burn the captive had come not from a Southerner, but a Connecticut man. Darby also claimed that McIntosh's death was not slow and painful, saying that "the whole business, from the murder of Hammond to the death of McIntosh, had occurred within an hour."

The saddest aspect of this incident is that many, even modern, sources strive to discredit the abolitionist account due to its inconsistencies with the *Republican* and Darby accounts. The question is whether the critical issue is the exact time and place of the event, or the fact that a man was burned in public by a mob and no one intervened to stop it.

After spending nine months in a Washington jail, Dr. Rueben Crandall's case finally came to trial. The prosecution's arguments rested upon the simple fact that there were multiple copies of certain abolitionist newspapers in Crandall's possession. The implication was that these papers were not solely for his own use, but that his intention was to distribute them to others. While admitting the logic of this argument, this does not necessarily suggest that his plan was to give them to slaves in order to incite insurrection. However, this was the conclusion the government attorneys readily reached and argued throughout the trial.

Assuming that his plan was to distribute such material, the next step in the argument was to declare that anyone who was actively circulating such incendiary documents was just as culpable as those who originally printed them. Thus, the charge against Dr. Crandall became "publishing malicious and wicked libels, with the intent to excite sedition and insurrection among the slaves and free colored people of this District."

During the trial, reference was made to portions of the newspapers found within Crandall's possession that were considered particularly obnoxious. Among them were such things as.

> ... [The Abolitionists argued] that the descendants of African parents, born in this country, have as good a claim to a residence in it, as the descendants of English, German, Danish, Scotch, or Irish parents.... [T]hat they have as good right to deport us to Europe, under the pretext that there we shall be prosperous and happy, as we have to deport them to Africa on a similar plea.
> ... [W]e believe that every man has a right to reside in his native country if he chooses, and that every man's native country is the country in which he was born[.]

Another quoted passage declared the intention of the abolitionists to circulate their ideas.

> ... Our plan of emancipation is simply this—to promulgate the doctrine of human rights in high places and low places, and all places where there are human beings—to whisper it in chimney corners, and to proclaim it from the housetops, yea, from the mountain tops—to pour it out like water from the pulpit and the press—to raise it up with all the force of the inner man from infancy to gray hairs—to give line upon line, precept upon precept, till it forms one of the foundation principles and parts indestructible of the public soul.
>
> I [which the prosecution interpreted to mean Crandall] am not unaware that my remarks may be regarded by many as dangerous and exceptionable; that I may be regarded as a fanatic for quoting the language of eternal truth; and denounced as an incendiary for maintaining in the spirit, as well as the letter, the doctrines of American Independence. But if such are the consequences of a simple performance of duty, I shall not regard them.

Perhaps considered the must offensive passage was the following.

> ... [S]o long as slavery is tolerated, no ... peace can exist. Liberty and slavery cannot dwell in harmony together.... No matter under what law or compact their union is attempted, the ordination of Providence has forbidden it—and it cannot stand. Peace! there can be no peace between justice and oppression—between robbery and righteousness—truth and falsehood—freedom and slavery. The slaveholding States are not free. The name of Liberty is there, but the spirit is wanting.... They know, they must know, that the present state of things cannot long continue. Mind is the same everywhere; no matter what may be the complexion of the frame which it animates, there is a love of liberty which the scourge cannot eradicate—a hatred of oppression, which centuries of degradation cannot extinguish. The slave will become conscious, sooner or later, of his strength—his physical superiority—and will exert it. His torch will be at the threshold, and his knife at the throat of the planter. Horrible and indiscriminate will be the vengeance. Where then will be the pride, the beauty, and the chivalry of the South? The smoke of her torment will rise upward, like a thick cloud, visible over the whole earth.

A dire warning, but was it a call to insurrection? And more importantly, could Crandall be held criminally responsible for having made it? Obviously, Francis Scott Key was convinced not only that he could be so held, but that he must be. Here is Key's final argument:

> I consider this one of the most important cases ever tried here[.] ... It is a case to try the question, whether our institutions have any means of legal defence against a set of men of most horrid principles, whose means of attack upon us are insurrection, tumult, and violence. The traverser defends himself by justifying the libels. We are told that they are harm-

less—that they have no tendency to produce the horrid results which we deprecate. We have been told that *this* community has not been endangered.... If such publications [as these within his possession] are justifiable, then are we, indeed, at the tender mercy of the Abolitionist[.] ... What does he propose for the slave? Immediate emancipation. In one instant the chains of the slave must snap asunder. Without delay, and without preparation, he becomes a citizen, a legislator, goes to the polls, and appoints *our* rulers. If this be the plan, then am I ready ... to seek refuge in other parts of the United States. Are you willing, gentlemen [of the jury], to abandon your country; to permit it to be taken from you, and occupied by the Abolitionist, according to whose taste it is to associate and amalgamate with the negro? Or, gentlemen, are there laws in this community to defend you from the immediate Abolitionist, who would open upon you the floodgates of such extensive wickedness and mischief?

Despite Key's impassioned words, the jury dismissed the charges against Crandall. Considering the fury of hatred surrounding the abolitionists, history should commend them for their noble stand. However, while Crandall's exoneration could be considered a small victory for the abolitionists, their triumph had been marred by the fact that the trial took place at all, and the fact that a young man spent close to a year in jail simply for possession of materials that advocated the abolishment of slavery. The message was clear: mobs and violence were not the only threats to the abolitionists. Their own government, which should have been there to protect them, could not always be counted on. That this was indeed the case became even more evident as the year progressed.

On May 16 a grand jury convened in St. Louis to investigate the lynching of Francis McIntosh, presided over by Judge Luke Lawless. Lawless opened his proceedings by observing that "the destruction of the murderer [McIntosh] himself raised the question of what, if any, action of the Grand Jury is called for." There was obviously no need to issue an indictment for the murder of Hammond. However, the method of McIntosh's killing—certainly "cruel and unusual," and, therefore, forbidden by the Constitution—left the question of what to do about "those persons who effected the destruction of the murderer."

"The difficult work which presents itself arises as to the possibility and expediency of visiting on the perpetrators of that act the penalties of the law," Lawless observed.

The judge at first appeared to denounce the act as "an outrageous violation of the Law and Constitution." Anarchy would be the result if people were allowed to disregard the law. However, he then launched upon a rather novel interpretation of what was meant by "the people." That is, "whether the destruction of McIntosh was the act of the 'few' or the act of the 'many.'"

If the act had been committed by "a small number of individuals separate from the mass," then the grand jury ought to "indict them all without a single exception." If, however, as appeared to be the case, the deed had been the will of the general mass of the public "seized upon and impelled by that mysterious, metaphysical, and almost electric phrenzy" by which societies protect themselves in a time of crises, then the judge's recommendation was that the grand jury ought to "act not at all in the matter, the case transcends your jurisdiction, it is beyond the reach of human law." That is, since those involved had acted in the best interests of society, and the inevitable result—McIntosh's death—was the same as it would have been if they had not acted, he felt no need to place any blame upon them.

Lawless felt certain that those people "most actively engaged in this tragic scene, must already regret what they have done." The key, as he saw it, was the fact that had the laws been faithfully executed, McIntosh would still be dead. And instead of being distracted by the atrocities that had been committed upon McIntosh, the people of St. Louis could concentrate instead upon "similar atrocities committed in this and other states by individuals of negro blood against their white brethren."

It seemed apparent to the judge as, he insisted, it must be to his listeners, that the "passions and intellect" of the "wretched McIntosh" had been excited by the fanatic abolitionists! This had been made clear "by the peculiar character of his language and demeanor." Lawless emphasized McIntosh's "rapid denunciations of the white man, his professions of deadly hostility to the whole race, his hymns and his prayers so profanely and frightfully mixed up with those horrid imprecations." (Considering that within hours of his arrival in the city McIntosh was already dead, what record could there have been of his "deadly hostility" to the whites? Lawless seems to be embellishing a bit.)

The inescapable conclusion the judge reached was that the true moral responsibility for Hammond's death and the lynching of McIntosh lay with the abolitionists. They were the ones inciting the blacks to fight the whites; how else could McIntosh have conceived the idea to kill a white man? Lawless read to the jurors from a copy of Lovejoy's *Observer*, noting its lurid, graphic description of the event, followed by its claim that "slavery is a sin and ought to be abandoned."

Another editorial in the same paper lamented the "abandonment of virtue" among the "pro-slavery men of modern times." Therefore, Lawless instructed the jurors to seek methods of silencing the voice of abolitionism.

The grand jury's job was done. No indictments had been issued, yet the public had been clearly alerted to the real danger within their midst.

Lovejoy, not surprisingly, harshly criticized the whole proceeding, deploring the barbarism that slavery promoted.

Lovejoy himself soon felt the barbarism directly. Two attacks were made on his press, convincing him that St. Louis was no longer a safe place for him or his ideals. He decided to relocate to the free state of Illinois.

On May 18, after much debate and bickering, the House of Representatives heard the final, modified report of the Pinckney Committee. Its original position was modified to include the following non-ambiguous resolution concerning slavery in the District of Columbia.

> ... [W]hereas it is extremely important and desirable, that the agitation of this subject should be finally arrested, for the purpose of restoring tranquility to the public mind, your committee respectfully recommend the adoption of the following additional resolution, viz:
>
> All petitions, memorials, resolutions, propositions, or papers, relating in any way, or to any extent whatsoever, to the subject of slavery or the abolition of slavery, shall, without being printed or referred, be laid on the table and that no further action whatever shall be had thereon.

On May 26, through a series of parliamentary maneuvers and the refusal of the Speaker of the House to acknowledge or recognize the critics of it, this proposition passed without debate. When the voting took place, it was the aged veteran John Quincy Adams who raised the only protest against it. When his name was called, he slowly rose from his seat and boldly proclaimed to the listeners around him: "I hold the resolution to be a direct violation of the constitution of the United States, the rules of this House, and the rights of my constituents." He returned to his seat amidst the boos and shouts of his fellow legislators.

Despite Adams's outburst, this so-called Pinckney "gag rule" passed easily by a vote of 117 to 68.

On June 8, the Senate heard Calhoun's final arguments against the proposed legislature on incendiary publications. "Was there any one there," he asked, "who would say, that the States had not the power to pass laws prohibiting ... the circulation of papers, calculated to incite insurrections among their slaves?" As Calhoun saw it, there was no need for the Senate to "pass a law to abridge the freedom of the press, or to prohibit the publication and circulation of any paper whatever—this has been done by the States already."

The proposed bill was rejected by a vote of 25 to 19. This could be seen by some as a triumph of freedom of the press. However, as Calhoun had so aptly pointed out, the states could manage repression of the mails on their own without federal assistance. Southern states would continue to police the mails and prevent the circulation of unwanted materials until the Civil War. Therefore, any victory the abolitionists had gained in the Senate was a hollow one, devoid of any practical impact.

On the night of July 12, a band of 30 or 40 men broke into the Cincinnati, Ohio, premises of Mr. Pugh, the printer of James Birney's *Philanthropist*. They tore up paper, destroyed ink and dismantled the press, carrying away many of its principal parts. According to the detailed report issued later in the year by the Ohio Anti-Slavery Society, the perpetrators of the act were those "who, whilst they have their citizenship in the free states, are desirous of aiding in the perpetuation of slavery in the South[.]" Among these people—generally men of business or worth in the community—there was, according to the society's report, "an alacrity of subservience" to the will of the slavemasters "that is altogether astonishing. In the excess of their fidelity to the interests of the South, they forget that there are any interests of the North."

Had there been any doubt as to the cause of the vandalism, it was made clear by the following notices that appeared throughout the city the succeeding evening:

> The Citizens of Cincinnati, embracing every class, interested in the prosperity of the City, satisfied that the business of the place is receiving a vital stab from the wicked and misguided operations of the abolitionists, are resolved to arrest their course. The destruction of their Press on the night of the 12th instant, may be taken as a warning.... If an attempt is made to re-establish their press, it will be viewed as an act of defiance to an already outraged community, and on their own heads be the results which follow.

The pro-slavery *Evening Post* commented the following day upon the situation:

> A considerable excitement against the Abolitionists has existed in our city for some time past. Murmurs of discontent at their proceedings have been heard on all sides, and there is reason to believe that there is something like a systematized plan on foot to prevent the publication of their Journal in this city. We had entertained a hope that there would be order and quiet after the proceedings of the night of the 12—that the Abolitionists would desist from publishing their paper here, and that those who had undertaken to prevent them, would be satisfied with what had already been done, and the peace of the city preserved. But ... there is a *cause* to fear that unless the arm of the law is strong enough to protect the Abolitionists, some act disgraceful to our city will be performed if they attempt the reestablishment of their press.

The Executive Committee of the Anti-Slavery Society had a meeting with the mayor. In an effort to allay the spirit of discord, it was suggested that the mayor officially offer a reward of $100 for the apprehension of the rioters. The mayor agreed to do so, and the committee deposited the $100 with him.

As good as his word, the mayor's notice appeared on July 15:

> I do ... offer the sum of ONE HUNDRED DOLLARS, for the apprehension and conviction of the person or persons concerned in the transaction [of the night of July 12th.]—And I do hereby forewarn all persons from engaging in acts of a similar nature[.]

Had that been the end of the mayor's notice, it would no doubt have satisfied the Abolitionists. However, he finished with the following notice:

> And I do earnestly entreat those persons whose proceedings, it is alleged, have prompted to the commission of the riot complained of, as they value the quiet of the city, to abstain from the further prosecutions of such measures as may have a tendency to inflame the public mind, and lead to acts of violence and disorder, in contempt of the laws and disgraceful to the city.

In view of this tirade against the abolitionists, the likelihood of the mayor's notice leading to an "apprehension or conviction" seemed remote.

In a blatant mockery of this reward offer, the following handbill, whose tone and wording mimicked typical advertisements for fugitive slaves, began appearing on street corners within a few days:

> FUGITIVE FROM JUSTICE
> $100 REWARD
> The above sum will be paid for the delivery of one James G. Birney, a fugitive from justice, now abiding in the city of Cincinnati. Said Birney in all his associations and feelings is black; although his external appearance is white. The above reward will be paid and no questions asked by
> OLD KENTUCKY.

The Cincinnati Whig of July 21 contained the following article:

> Mr. Editor:—Allow me to ask the people of Cincinnati (I mean those really interested in her prosperity) ... if they do not intend at this time, to give so decided an expression of their sentiments as regards abolition, that those who are injuring the character and prospects of this city, may know and feel that this is not the place for them.
> Will they permit a band of fanatics, led by an English emissary [Thompson], to make this city the theatre of their operations, from whence they may throw fire-brands in the slave States, that will kindle a fire, that will not be quenched till this glorious Union shall be dissolved, and the blood of the innocent—of women and children—cry for vengeance?

Apparently, black women and children were not to be considered innocent.

On the morning of July 21, a public meeting was announced in the *Cincinnati Gazette*.

> A meeting of the citizens is requested on Saturday evening next ... to decide whether they will permit the publication or distribution of Abolition papers in this city.... [It has been] alleged that there is a settled determination existing in an overwhelming majority of the citizens to put down the alleged evil by force if admonitions are found insufficient.

The *Whig* on July 23 proclaimed in an editorial:

> [T]he city will protect herself[.] ... I say to those whom it may concern—to those enemies of the Union, who are now here, by printing and publication, whether from *treasonable* or mistaken views, doing the work of those who would destroy us and our institutions—desist.
>
> ... What has already occurred is "*not a beginning*." Once more then hear the warning voice of one that will not willingly injure you, but who will be obeyed—*desist*—or sure there will be a *beginning*, and when that beginning comes the *ending* is also at hand.

The same paper, in another article, argued:

> Far be it from us to tolerate that murderous and despicable doctrine [abolition] in the slightest degree. We loathe, we utterly abhor it.... [W]e are perfectly justifiable in arresting the hand of the assassin even though in doing so we find it necessary to proceed to the severest extremities. If, then, the Abolitionists place themselves in the position of the assassin, what can they expect?

The aforementioned meeting was held on Saturday, July 23 and attended, it was said, by over 3,000 people. The following preamble and resolutions were unanimously adopted:

> *Whereas*, The citizens of Cincinnati are now laboring under a serious excitement, in consequence of the existence of an Abolition Press in this city, from the influence of which, the most deplorable results may be justly apprehended. *And, whereas,* although we deprecate the existence of slavery as a great evil, yet we hold it to be one for which the present generation is not responsible; and disclaiming all right to interfere with the regulations of our sister states on this subject, we regard the conduct of the abolitionists as justly calculated to excite unfriendly dispositions on their part[.] ... And *whereas*, While we recognize the constitutional right of liberty of speech and of the press, ... we deem it our duty to utter a warning voice to those concerned in the promulgation of abolition doctrines[.]
>
> Resolved, That in the opinion of this meeting nothing short of the

absolute discontinuance of the publication of the said abolition paper in this city, can prevent a resort to violence[.]

Resolved, That a committee ... be appointed ... to wait upon James G. Birney and his associates ... to request them ... to desist from the publication of their paper, and to warn them that if they persist, we cannot hold ourselves responsible for the consequences.

Perhaps, indeed, men like Birney were fanatics to persevere in their thankless task against such sustained intimidation.

Upon being contacted by the citizen's committee formed for that purpose, Birney informed them that it was not his decision alone to publish or not to publish the *Philanthropist*. It was "the organ of the Ohio Anti-Slavery Society, which numbers at this time, perhaps, not less than twelve thousand of our citizens, in different parts of the State." He suggested that they contact the society's executive committee regarding their concerns.

On July 26, the *Whig* reported that "Birney and his Abolition associates still persist in the publication of their villainously misnamed *Philanthropist*." As such, the *Whig* felt that the abolitionists were "to all "intents and purposes *mobocrats*," and moved "that they be arrested by the Police officers as rioters and disturbers of the public peace."

In the meantime, the Ohio Anti-Slavery Society's Executive Committee had contacted the citizen's committee to set up a meeting, which was held on July 28. At this meeting, one of the society's members suggested that he could conduct a public "exposition of anti-slavery principles, and be willing to hear any arguments that might be offered against them. It was at once replied, that such a meeting could not be held in the city, that the people would hear no public discussion on slavery, and that the speaker would lose his life in attempting to discuss it." It was apparent at this meeting that the citizens were not seeking a solution to, or an examination of, the slavery issue. Their desire was nothing less than the "absolute discontinuance" of the *Philanthropist*. In a carefully prepared statement released the next day, the executive committee explained why it "decline[d] complying with" the other group's "request:"

> We decline complying ... because compliance involves a tame surrender of the FREEDOM OF THE PRESS—THE RIGHT TO DISCUSS.
> The *Philanthropist* is the only journal in this city or neighborhood, through which these facts, and arguments, and appeals [concerning slavery] can be fully addressed to the community. It has been conducted with fairness and moderation[.] ... It has invited the slaveholders themselves to the use of its columns for the defence of slavery, and has given up to a republication of their arguments a large share of its space. [No doubt with the clear intention of refuting such arguments; yet this was still more than the slave-owners had ever yielded to the anti-slavery side of the argument.]

> We decline complying—because the demand is virtually the demand of the slave-holders, who, having broken down all the safe-guards of liberty in their own States, in order that slavery may be perpetuated, are now, for the fuller attainment of the same object, making the demand of us to follow their example.
>
> We decline complying—because the attempt is now first made in our case, formally and deliberately, to put down the freedom of speech and of the press. We are, to be sure, the object of the attack—but there is not a freeman in the State whose rights are not invaded, in any assault which may be made on us, for refusing to succumb to an imperious demand to surrender our rights.
>
> We believe, that a large portion of the people of Cincinnati are utterly opposed to the prostration of the liberty of the press—and that there is among us—whatever may be said to the contrary—enough of correct and sober feeling to uphold the laws, if our public officers faithfully discharge their duty.

While this argument was being directed at a specific case at a particular time and place, there can be little doubt that the sentiments articulated here were being considered by many Americans as they watched the persecutions of the abolitionists escalate in frequency and intensity. So far, the voices of the pro-slavery advocates seemed to command more public attention and respect than did those of their opponents. But was this because the bulk of Americans agreed with slavery or because they were intimidated into silence by it? Perhaps it was the role of the abolitionists to stand up to persecution in order to open the eyes of the cautious masses. Once the eyes of "the people" were opened, perhaps they would begin to add their voices to those of the abolitionists in criticism of the cherished Southern institution of bondage.

Only time would tell if there existed a "silent majority" that would ultimately side with the abolitionists in their struggle.

"[I]n discharging their duties," wrote the citizens' committee, referring to themselves in the third person, "they have used all the measures of persuasion and conciliation in their power. That their exertions have not been successful, the above correspondence [from the abolitionists] will show." They washed their hands of the whole situation, remarking in conclusion that they "express their utmost abhorrence of every thing like violence and earnestly ... implore their fellow citizens to abstain therefrom."

The Cincinnati Whig seemed to find the behavior of the abolitionists particularly exasperating. "Are the abolitionists in this city mad?" they asked. "Will they not take counsel of what has occurred? Or will they persist in contemning public sentiment until they bring upon themselves the excited vengeance of the multitude?"

From the published report of the Ohio Anti-Slavery Society:

On Saturday night, July 30, very soon after dark, a concourse of citizens assembled ... and upon a short consultation, broke open the office of the *Philanthropist*, ... scattered the type into the streets, tore down the presses, and completely dismantled the office.... A portion of the press was then dragged down Main Street, broken up and thrown into the river.... An attack was then made on the residence of some blacks, in Church Alley[.] ... [T]he houses were found empty, and their contents destroyed.—It was now about midnight, when the party parading down Main street, was addressed by the Mayor, who had been a silent spectator of the destruction of the printing office.

According to the report of a gentleman who was present, these were the words of the mayor to the crowd: "We have done enough for one night. The abolitionists themselves, must be convinced themselves by this time, what the public sentiment is, and that it will not do any longer to disregard, or set it at naught." The mob quietly melted away, apparently quite satisfied with a good night's work well done.

This outrage was the proverbial last straw. On Tuesday, August 2, the *Gazette* published a notice for a:

> PUBLIC MEETING
> The friends of order, of Law, and the Constitution, having no connection with the Anti-Slavery Society, and who are opposed to the action of this mob, under any possible circumstances, are requested to meet THIS AFTERNOON, (TUESDAY,) at 3 o'clock at the Court House.

The editor of the *Gazette* published his account of the meeting, which he had attended. He began with the customary criticism of the abolitionists:

> We have deplored the efforts of a portion of [our] fellow citizens, who have aimed to bring about a premature abolition of slavery, as calculated by their tone and spirit, to excite hostile feelings between different sections of our common country.
>
> We regard slavery as a domestic institution of the States in which it exists, with which the other states have no right to interfere. But, while we respect the rights of our fellow citizens of the slave-holding States, ... we also respect the rights of our fellow citizens of the non-slaveholding States[.] ... Among these rights—and of all the dearest because it is the bulwark of all the rest—is the right of FREE DISCUSSION—the right of every citizen to write, speak, and print, upon every subject, as he may think proper, being responsible to the laws and the laws ONLY, for the abuse of that liberty. If this right shall perish through the violence of a mob, the grave that entombs it must be the sepulchre of American freedom.... [L]et not the hand of violence be raised against the exercise of this precious right. However obnoxious the exercise may be, let the right itself be acknowledged and respected, Let us not, for the sake of removing some unsightly blemish, pull out the very corner-stone of the great temple of liberty.

The "silent majority" had finally spoken out. Their estimation of the abolitionists was hardly flattering to that group. Yet the fact that they had been willing to speak out at all on their behalf must have been comforting. At that meeting, a number of resolutions were passed. Perhaps the one that most pleased the Anti-Slavery Society was the one that stated:

> *Resolved*, That we are fully of opinion, that while a considerable number of our fellow citizens have been led to approve, or acquiesce in the action of a mob, *the greater majority of the voters in the city, and the almost unanimous voice of the freemen of the country*, [emphasis added] concur in the sentiment, that there are no times and no circumstances, in this land of universal suffrage, of equal right, and equal law, which can justify or excuse a resort to the violence of mob force, or a submission to the employment of such force[.]

One can argue that this simple resolution, though obscure and seldom read today, is one of the most significant statements of the pre–Civil War era. It belies the popular misconception that the North supported the pro-slavery persecution of the abolitionists. The record of these years—full of insults, violence, and terror as it is—has led to the pro-slavery myth that the abolitionists did more to hurt the cause of the blacks than to aid it, that perhaps they were even wrong in agitating the issues as they did. This conclusion is only valid if one accepts that these incidents, perpetrated by a minority in the Northern population (albeit a vocal and dangerous minority), were a valid indicator of the will of the Northern majority. This group of Cincinnati citizens obviously did not believe that to be the case.

No other nation in history has attempted to blend together as many diverse elements within its borders as has the United States. Admittedly, this very diversity occasionally has lead to internal conflicts and acts of intolerance. There are events in the historical record of which Americans are ashamed, such as the treatment of blacks or the Native Americans. But the strength and beauty of America is that, given time, its citizens can come to recognize these flaws within the body politic, admit the errors, and rectify them over time.

This process of repair is not always straightforward, nor is it painless. It may advance with jumps and gaps. Sometimes when caught within its midst, we fail to see that progress is being made—but we must believe that it will be. If it can't be, then the great "experiment of liberty" has failed. There have been times in American history that it may have seemed democracy was doomed, times when our critics have pronounced it a failure. At these times, it may be the role of some small group to remind citizens of what the ideals and beliefs of the United States really are. Americans can disagree with or disapprove of one another, but can

Nine • 1836

do so without being repressive or oppressive. And sometimes, there must be a willingness to fight to protect these rights, even though there may be disagreement over rights and beliefs.

The first step to losing one's freedom is to deny freedom to someone else. History provides many examples of this. The day that Americans refuse to fight for the rights of those with whom they disagree is the day that we have failed as a nation.

This is what the story of the abolitionists is about. These dedicated men and women were willing to fight, seemingly alone and unaided, for the rights of the blacks. And eventually the great "silent majority" of the nation came to realize that they, likewise, were obligated to fight for the rights of the abolitionists.

The citizens of Cincinnati had learned this important lesson, as indicated in their last two resolutions:

> *Resolved*, That ... it is the imperious duty of every peace officer, and of every good citizen, upon the first hint or threat of mobbish violence, to assume a stern and undaunted front in support of a due observation of the laws, and for the maintenance of the public peace; and we take to ourselves the shame and reproach of having failed to adopt this course in the case that has just occurred.
>
> *Resolved*, That we pledge ourselves, one to another, forthwith to organize an efficient Committee of safety, so to act in concert, and in sufficient numbers, to crush any future attempt by mobbish violence, in night time or in day time, to subvert the laws, and jeopardize the security of life, liberty, or property.

This group's clearly articulated feelings of moral outrage and dedication to duty could be seen as an expression of why the North was willing to go to war 25 years later.

There appear to be no more incidents of intimidation or violence directed towards Birney and the *Philanthropist* after this. Cincinnati quieted down after its period of unrest. However, a similar incident would occur in another city the following summer with even more devastating results.

The story was not, however, completely over. On August 1, a curious document appeared, purportedly the result of a meeting of the Cincinnati Union Society. Within the document, this group of black freemen stated.

> ... We have, for the last ten months, witnessed the efforts [made] by a few misguided and fanatical men amongst us, styled abolitionists, and headed by one Birney, and whereas, we have become convinced, that the means they are using have [a] direct tendency to injure the interest of the colored population of the free states by exciting the passions of the

white inhabitants, and we believe, to rivet more firmly, the chains of the slave.

Therefore, be it *resolved*, That we disclaim, in the most positive manner, all connection with the abolitionists, and hold in horror and contempt, their amalgamation doctrine in principle, as, degrading, both to the white and colored population.

Resolved, That the publication of the *Philanthropist* and other abolition papers and tracts in this city, have had, and, we believe, will continue to have an injurious and prejudicial effect on the interests of the colored population.

Resolved, That if Mr. Birney and his associates have ... the well being of the colored race at heart, they will cease their misguided efforts here[.] ...

Resolved, That we consider the future publication of abolition papers in this city, as an attempt to excite against us, angry feelings and the personal violence of anti-abolitionists.

Resolved, That we have nothing to do with either colonizing or abolition societies.

The above declaration was followed by the signatures of 35 members of the Cincinnati Union Society.

This is a totally unexpected and extraordinary document. To judge by these statements, one would be forced to believe that the pro-slavery arguers were correct that blacks were satisfied with their conditions. The abolitionists were not simply interfering where they had no place to do so; their interference was not desired or appreciated by those in whose behalf they claimed to be toiling. What, then, is one to make of this?

Apparently, not too much. A few days afterwards, a disclaimer was published to the above statement:

> We, the undersigned, members of the Cincinnati Union Society of colored persons, having seen, with regret, our names affixed to a publication, purporting to be the proceedings of [our meeting], do hereby declare that our names were used ... without our knowledge or consent.

This was signed by 28 of the 35 "signers" of the "original" document. This appears to have marked the end of the conflict in this Ohio city.

Mention has been made previously of the role of Southern spiritual leaders in supporting slavery. Not much, however, has been said about the Northern side of the story simply because the record is too inadequate to say much about it authoritatively.

The early writings of the abolitionists often allude to the apathy of the church. The implication is that Northern ministers may not have been actively supporting slavery as were their Southern counterparts. Yet neither were they speaking out in public against it. This changed somewhat with the emergence of the Lane Seminary students after the 1834 debates, many of whom went on to be ordained and used their positions to preach the gospel of anti-slavery. (The other notable exception being the anti-slavery, albeit also anti-abolitionist, writings of William Ellery Channing.)

By 1836 the churches of the North began to take active notice of the increasing anti-slavery arguments. That summer, conservative church leaders issued a call to stop such protests. Congregational ministers in Connecticut and Massachusetts were instructed to exclude any speakers whose "erroneous or questionable views" were deemed "dangerous to the influence of the pastoral office and fatal to the peace and good order of the churches."

Speaking at the Presbyterian General Assembly in Pittsburgh, Lyman Beecher—former head of the Lane Seminary and father to Harriet—counseled against any discussion whatsoever of slavery within the church. He praised the "silken ties" that bound Christians in the North and South, and that made the church a national bulwark against the fanaticism of abolitionism.

Throughout that summer, the pens of two Philadelphia Quakers had been busily scribbling their impressions of the abolition conflict. The South could not have been prepared for Angelina Grimké's *Appeal to the Christian Women of the South*, which was published by the New York Anti-Slavery Society. Grimké brought to the abolition arguments not only the unique perspective of a woman, but that of a woman who had been born and raised in a slave-holding family. Her appeal was concise, emotional and well-reasoned. It was also written in a deeply personal tone intended to soften hearts long-hardened to slavery:

> RESPECTED FRIENDS,
> It is because I feel a deep and tender interest in your present and eternal welfare that I am willing thus publicly to address you.... Be not afraid ... to read my appeal; it is not written in the heat of passion or prejudice, but in that solemn calmness which is the result of conviction and duty. It is true, I am going to tell you unwelcome truths, but I mean to speak those truths in love.... I do not believe the time has yet come when Christian women "will not endure sound doctrine," even on the subject of Slavery, if it is spoken to them in tenderness and love, therefore I now address you.
> ... All the excuses and palliations of [the slave] system must inevitably be swept away, just as other "refuges of lies" have been, by the irresistible torrent of a rectified public opinion.... It will be ... clearly perceived and fully acknowledged by all ... that in principle it is as sinful to hold a human being in bondage who has been born in Carolina, as one who has been born in Africa.
> ... We must come back to the ... doctrine of our forefathers who declared to the world, "this self-evident truth that all men are created equal, and that they have certain inalienable rights among which are life, liberty, and the pursuit of happiness." It is even a greater absurdity to

suppose a man can be legally born a slave under our free Republican Government, than under the petty despotisms of barbarous Africa. If then, we have no right to enslave an African, surely we can have none to enslave an American; if it is a self evident truth that all men, every where and of every color are born equal, and have an inalienable right to liberty, then it is equally true that no man can be born a slave, and no man can ever rightfully be reduced to involuntary bondage and held as a slave, however fair may be the claim of his master or mistress through wills and title-deeds.

... [M]an, who was created in the image of his Maker, never can properly be termed a thing, though the laws of slave states do call him "a chatttel personal."

Grimké devoted a considerable portion of her document to examining the biblical and historical basis of slavery. According to her reasoning, slavery as practiced in the South was not defensible by any historical or biblical precedents.

Nor did she limit her criticism to the South. She blasted the North for its docile and cowardly acquiescence to the fugitive slave laws by quoting scripture:

"Thou shalt not deliver unto his master the servant that is escaped from his master unto thee. He shall dwell with thee, even among you, in that place which he shall choose, in one of thy gates where it liketh him best: thou shalt not oppress him." Deut. xxiii, 15,16.

Here, then, we see that by this ... law, the door of Freedom was opened wide to every servant who had any cause whatever for complaint; if he was unhappy with his master, all he had to do was to leave him, and no man had a right to deliver him back to him again, ... the absconded servant was to choose where he should live, and no Jew was permitted to oppress him.... Is it so at the South? Is the poor runaway slave protected by law from the violence of that master whose oppression and cruelty has driven him from his plantation or his house? No! no! Even the free states of the North are compelled to deliver unto his master the servant that is escaped from his master unto them.... In the wide domain even of our free states, there is not one city or refuge for the poor runaway fugitive; not one spot upon which he can stand and say, I am a free man— I am protected in my rights as a man, by the strong arm of the law; no! not one. How long the North will thus shake hands with the South in sin, I know not.... [B]ut one thing I do know, the guilt of the North is increasing in a tremendous ratio as light is pouring in upon her on the subject and the sin of slavery.... [W]e will assuredly be condemned and punished for obeying Man rather than God, if we do not speedily repent and bring forth fruits meet for repentance.

Grimké next presented a long list of ways in which the laws and practices of the South deprived the slave of his basic human rights, and by their cumulative effect, reduced him to something less than a man.

> The Code Noir of the South robs the slave of all his rights as a man, reduces him to a chattel personal, [Chattel is a piece of personal property other than real estate for which the owner can be taxed.] and defends the master, in the exercise of the most unnatural and unwarrantable power over his slave.... Truly it was wise in the slaveholders of the South to declare [the slaves] to be "chattels personal;" for before they could be robbed of wages, wives, children, and friends, it was absolutely necessary to deny they were human beings. It is wise in them, to keep them in abject ignorance, for the strong man armed must be bound down with the iron chains of nescience before we can rob him of his rights as a man; we must reduce him to a thing before we can claim the right to set our feet upon his neck[.]
> ... [S]ome slaveholders have said [that] slaves are accustomed to it, their backs are fitted to the burden.... I am willing to admit that you who have lived in freedom would find slavery even more oppressive than the poor slave does, but then you may try this question in another form— Am I willing to reduce my little child to slavery? You know that if it is brought up a slave it will never know any contrast, between freedom and bondage, its back will become fitted to the burden just as the negro child's does[.] ... It has been justly remarked that "God never made a slave," ... the man must be crushed within him, before his back can be fitted to the burden of perpetual slavery; and that his back is not fitted to it is manifest by the insurrections that so often disturb the peace and security of slaveholding countries. Who ever heard of a rebellion of the beasts of the field; and why not? simply because they were all placed under the feet of man, it was originally designed that they should serve him[.] ... [N]ot so with man, intellectual, immortal man! I appeal to you, my friends, as mothers; Are you willing to enslave your children? You start back with horror and indignation at such a question. But why, if slavery is no wrong to those upon whom it is imposed? why, if as has often been said, slaves are happier than their masters, free from the cares and perplexities of providing for themselves and their families? why not place your children in the way of being supported without your having the trouble to provide for them[?]

She criticized the South's hypocrisy towards the slave dealer who was generally despised "as much as anyone can" be and who was "never admitted into genteel or respectable society."

> But why hold slavedealers as despicable, if their trade is lawful and virtuous? and why despise them more than the gentlemen of fortune and standing who employ them as their agents? Why more than the professors of religion who barter their fellow professors to them for gold or silver? We do not despise the land agent, or the physician, or the merchant, and why? Simply because their professions are virtuous and honorable; and if the trade of men-jobbers was honorable, you would not despise them either. There is no difference in principle in Christian ethics, between the despised slavedealer and the Christian who buys slaves from, or sells slaves to him; indeed, if slaves were not wanted by the respectable, the wealthy, and the religious in a community, there would be no slaves

in that community, and of course no slavedealers. It is then the Christians and the honorable men and women of the South, who are the main pillars of this grand temple built to Mammon and Moloch. It is the most enlightened in every country who are the most to blame when any public sin is supported by public opinion....

She ultimately reached the point of explaining just why the *Appeal* had been addressed to Southern women:

> But perhaps you will be ready to query, why appeal to women on this subject? We do not make the laws which perpetuate slavery.... [W]e can do nothing to overthrow this system[.] ... To this I reply, ... that you are the wives and mothers, the sisters and daughters of those who do; and if you really suppose you can do nothing to overthrow slavery, you are greatly mistaken....
> ... Speak then to your relatives, your friends, your acquaintances on the subject of slavery; be not afraid if you are conscientiously convinced it is sinful, to say so openly[.] ... Above all, try to persuade your husband, father, brothers, and sons, that slavery is a crime against God and man, and that it is a great sin to keep human beings in such abject ignorance[.] ...
> ... Some of you own slaves yourselves. If you believe slavery is sinful, set them at liberty[.] ... [T]each them, and have them taught the common branches of an English education[.] ...
> But some of you will say, we can neither free our slaves nor teach them to read, for the laws of our state forbid it. Be not surprised when I say such wicked laws ought to be no barrier in the way of your duty[.] ...
> But some of you will say, if we do free our slaves, they will be taken up and sold, therefore there will be no use in doing it. Peter and John might just as well have said, we will not preach the gospel, for if we do, we shall be taken up and put in prison, therefore there will be no use in our preaching. Consequences, my friends, belong no more to you, than they did to these apostles. Duty is ours and events are God's....
> I know this doctrine of obeying God, rather than man, will be considered as dangerous[.] [B]ut I would not be understood to advocate resistance to any law however oppressive, if in obeying it, I was not obliged to commit sin. If for instance, there was a law, which imposed imprisonment or a fine upon me if I manumitted a slave, I would on no account resist that law, I would set the slave free, and then go to prison or pay the fine....
> But perhaps you will say, such a course of conduct would inevitably expose us to great suffering. Yes! ... I believe it would, but this will not excuse you or anyone else for the neglect of duty.

It seems likely that these words were read by a young man who at the time was a student at Harvard. Thirteen years later, this same man, Henry David Thoreau, would expostulate very similar ideals in his landmark work, *Civil Disobedience*.

Grimké also paid homage to the crusading work of the Women's

Anti-Slavery Societies of the North, but was quick to point out that they could not accomplish much working alone:

> Northern women may labor to produce a correct public opinion at the North, but if Southern women sit down in listless indifference and criminal idleness, public opinion cannot be rectified and purified at the South. It is manifest to every reflecting mind, that slavery must be abolished[.] ... Now there are two ways in which [slavery] can be effected, by moral power or physical force, and it is for you to choose which you prefer. Slavery always has, and always will produce insurrections, wherever it exists, because it is a violation of the natural order of things, and no human power can much longer perpetuate it.

She warned her Southern sisters that unless "moral power" had its way, their region "must be visited with divine vengeance soon. Abolitionists believe ... that this must inevitably be the case if you do not repent, and they are not willing to leave you to perish without entreating you, to save yourselves from destruction."

> Heard you not the thunders of Divine anger, as the distant roar of the cannon came rolling onwards, from the Texian country, where Protestant American Rebels are fighting with Mexican Republicans—for what? For the re-establishment of slavery; yes! of American slavery in the bosom of a Catholic Republic, where that system of robbery, violence, and wrong, had been legally abolished for twelve years. Yes! citizens of the United States, after plundering Mexico of her land, are now engaged in deadly combat, for the privilege of fastening chains, and collars, and manacles ... upon native born American Republican citizens[.]

Next she launched into a fervent, personal plea on behalf of the much-maligned abolitionists.

> Doubtless you have all heard Anti-Slavery societies denounced as insurrectionary and mischievous, fanatical and dangerous. It has been said they publish the most abominable untruths, and that they are endeavoring to excite rebellions at the South. Have you believed these reports, my friends? Have you also been deceived by these false assertions? Listen to me, whilst I endeavor to wipe from the fair character of Abolitionism such unfounded accusations. You know that I am a Southerner; you know that my dearest relatives are now in a slave State. Can you for a moment believe I would prove so recreant to the feelings of a daughter and a sister, as to join a society which was seeking to overthrow slavery by falsehood, bloodshed, and murder? ... [B]efore I would join an Anti-Slavery Society, I took the precaution of becoming acquainted with some of the leading Abolitionists, of reading their publications and attending their meetings[;] ... and it was not until I was fully convinced that their principles were entirely pacific, and their efforts only moral, that I gave my name as a member[.] ... I never have seen a single insurrectionary para-

graph, and never read any account of cruelty which I could not believe. Southerners [and, apparently, some modern historians] may deny the truth of these accounts, but why do they not prove them to be false. Their violent expressions of horror at such accounts being believed, may deceive some, but they cannot deceive me, for I lived too long in the midst of slavery, not to know what slavery is. When I speak of this system, "I speak that I do know," and I am not at all afraid to assert, that Anti-Slavery publications have not overdrawn the monstrous features of slavery at all. And many a Southerner knows this as well as I do. A lady in North Carolina remarked to a friend of mine, about eighteen months since, "Northerners know nothing at all about slavery; they think it is perpetual bondage only; but of the depth of degradation that word involves, they have no conception; if they had, they would never cease their efforts until so horrible a system was overthrown."

Next, she discussed why Abolitionism was so unpopular in the North:

> The Northern merchants and manufacturers are making their fortunes out of the produce of slave labor; the grocer is selling your rice and sugar; how then can these men bear a testimony against slavery without condemning themselves? But there is another reason, the North is most dreadfully afraid of Amalgamation. She is alarmed at the very idea of a thing so monstrous, as she thinks. And lest this consequence might flow from emancipation, she is determined to resist all efforts at emancipation without expatriation. It is not because she approves of slavery, or believes it to be the "cornerstone of our republic," for she is as much anti-slavery as we are; but amalgamation is too horrible to think of.... I will leave you to judge whether the fear of amalgamation ought to induce men to oppose anti-slavery efforts, when they believe slavery to be sinful. Prejudice against color is the most powerful enemy we have to fight with at the North.

She continued with her discussion on the criticism of the abolitionists:

> Great fault has been found with the prints which have been employed to expose slavery at the North, but my friends, how could this be done so effectually in any other way? Until the pictures of the slave's sufferings were drawn and held up to public gaze, no Northerner had any idea of the cruelty of the system, it never entered their minds that such abominations could exist in Christian Republican America; they never suspected that many of the gentlemen and ladies who came from the South to spend the summer months in traveling among them, were petty tyrants at home....
> We know that the papers of which the Charleston mail was robbed were not insurrectionary, and that they were not sent to the colored people as was reported. We know that Amos Dresser was no insurrectionist though he was accused of being so, and on this false accusation was pub-

licly whipped in Nashville in the midst of a crowd of infuriated slaveholders.

Grimké completed her work with a final argument against the danger of freeing the slaves:

> Perhaps you have feared the consequences of immediate Emancipation, and been frightened by all those dreadful prophecies of rebellion, bloodshed, and murder, which have been uttered.... Slavery may produce these horrible scenes if it is continued, ... but Emancipation will not.
> ... In St. Domingo in 1793 six hundred thousand slaves were set free in a white population of forty-two thousand ... and the negroes all continued quietly to work on the different plantations, until in 1802, France determined to reduce these liberated slaves again to bondage. It was at this time that all those dreadful scenes of cruelty occurred, which we so often unjustly hear spoken of, as the effects of Abolition. They were occasioned not by Emancipation, but by the base attempt to fasten the chains of slavery on the limbs of liberated slaves.

She cited the example of Great Britain in legislating immediate emancipation. (In the second edition of her appeal, published the same year, Lydia Marie Child added some notes about the effects of this legislation. According to Child: "The slaves are now emancipated in every British colony; and in effecting this happy change, not one drop of blood has been spilt.")

In common with the other abolitionists, Grimké could see no danger in immediate emancipation:

> And why not try it in the Southern States, if it never has occasioned rebellion; if not a drop of blood has ever been shed in consequence of it, ... why should we suppose it would produce such disastrous consequences now? ... There is nothing to fear from immediate Emancipation, but every thing from the consequences of slavery.
> Sisters in Christ, I have done.... Count me not your "enemy because I have told you the truth," but believe me in unfeigned affection,
> Your Sympathizing Friend,
> ANGELINA E. GRIMKE

It seems clear that Grimké wrote with every effort to avoid conflict with the South. However, if she believed that she had accomplished her goal, she was sadly mistaken.

The work was banned throughout the slave states. Her gender did not protect her from abuse as severe as any Garrison had ever received. The authorities in Charleston, where her mother and most of her family still resided, informed her family that she must not attempt to visit them. The authorities warned they could not guarantee their ability to protect her from the wrath of those whom she had offended.

As a result, she and her sister, Sarah, would never return to the state of their births.

On Monday, December 5, the second of two sessions of the Twenty-Fourth Congress began. Things seemed to be going much more smoothly than at the previous sessions, which meant there were no antislavery petitions being presented to disrupt the proceedings. Such a state of affairs was not to last long.

On December 26, former president John Quincy Adams rose to present a petition calling for the abolishment of the slave trade in the District of Columbia. Immediately the gag rule from the previous session was invoked against him. Adams argued that the rule had expired with the session in which it had been passed. Speaker of the House Polk ruled, one assumes reluctantly, that Adams was correct. As if it was a replay of the beginning of the previous session, members presented motions to table this petition. Motions were granted, but Adams responded with more petitions.

As the year ended, the struggle promised to dominate the new year unless something was done about it.

Former president James Madison died on June 28, at the age of 85. Madison was the last surviving signer of the United States Constitution. With his death, the generation often referred to as the Founding Fathers the signers of the Declaration of Independence and of the Constitution—became extinct. The young nation was now an orphan of sorts.

As if to emphasize the nation's break with its beginnings, Martin Van Buren was elected as the nation's eighth president. He became the first president elected who had been born after the signing of the Declaration of Independence.

Arkansas was admitted into the Union as the twenty-fifth state on June 15,; temporarily giving the slave states a majority over the free states. Michigan would even the balance again if it came in as a free State as expected. However, its entry was delayed in the aftermath of the "Toledo War." Despite Michigan's legitimate claim to the disputed territory, Congress sided with Ohio. The reality was that Ohio had more political influence than did the territory of Michigan, particularly in an election year.

To mollify Michigan, Congress offered to add the western three-quarters of the Upper Peninsula to the state's borders in exchange for relinquishing its claims on the disputed lands to Ohio. Though this was an increase of 9,000 square miles, the region was virtually unknown, and it was not immediately apparent whether what was being gained would be worth what was lost. Initially reluctant to even consider the offer, the Washington lawmakers made Michigan's entry into the union conditional upon acceptance.

Bowing to the pressure, Michigan conceded on December 14, though it would not be formally admitted as the twenty-sixth state until January 26, 1837.

Twenty years later, Harriet Martineau would claim this unusual solution was made at the particular insistence of Southern legislators. The land in the Upper Peninsula had been considered part of the Wisconsin Territory prior to its annexation to Michigan. By diminishing Wisconsin's area in this manner, the pro-slavery element in Congress felt certain that there would not be enough land left to allow the formation of more than one free state when it was Wisconsin's turn to enter the Union. Therefore, so the argument goes, this manipulation of territories helped reduce the threat of Northern superiority in the Senate.

There apparently exists no documentation that supports Martineau's claim. Presumably she heard the story from someone, or perhaps this was simply an example of abolitionist paranoia on her part. However, the simple fact that such a belief could exist and be expressed at the time goes to show how little the South was trusted by many who were against slavery.

After three years of complaining to his superiors about conditions at Fort Armstrong, Dr. John Emerson was transferred. Not, however, as he had hoped, back to St. Louis, but five hundred miles in the other direction. His new post was Fort Snelling in the Upper Louisiana Territory. Again he took his slave—apparently now going by the more familiar name of Dred Scott—with him. Again he neglected to tell the black man that they would be living on free soil.

While living at Fort Snelling, Dr. Emerson purchased from a slaveowner named Lawrence Taliaferro a young black woman of fifteen or sixteen named Harriet Robinson. Apparently Harriett formed an attachment to Dred, even though he was many years her senior. (The best guess as to his birth seems to be around 1795.) Dr. Emerson allowed his two slaves to be married some time that year.

On July 1, the government of the United States finally decided to accept the bequest of James Smithson. However, British pounds were not legal tender in America, and arrangements had to be made to somehow transfer the money over the Atlantic Ocean.

In August, Richard Rush was chosen by the United States government to travel to England for Smithson's treasure. The fifty-six-year-old Rush, whose father Benjamin had been one of the signers of the Declaration of Independence, was one of the most accomplished diplomats in the country. Having served as the American minister in London from 1817 to 1825, Rush was a natural choice for the job.

In a letter written from Troy, New York, Theodore Weld described for a friend the rigors of speaking as an anti-slavery orator.

> Since my last [letter ?] we have been mobbed again in the daytime. The mayor and the city officers were with a few exceptions totally inefficient and pursued such a course as to embolden rather than to intimidate the mob. One of the city officers was openly a leader of the mob. Twice a rush was made up the aisles to drag me from the pulpit. Stones, pieces of bricks, eggs, cents, sticks, etc. were thrown at me while speaking [.] ... I was a target for all sorts of missles—was hit by two stones, tho' not hurt seriously. The mob made desperate attempts to get me into their clutches but were kept at bay by our friends, though often with extreme difficulty. Anti-abolition fury ... is breaking out anew, and with deadlier hate than ever.

Nor were physical attacks the only method used to intimidate abolitionists. Lewis Tappan received a box in the mail that contained the severed ear of a black. A note recommended that he add the grisly piece to his "collection of natural curiosities."

Just over the Maryland state line from Washington, D.C., was the city of Bladensburg. Traveling down a dirt road, one came to a small bridge that crossed a stream that had come to be nicknamed "Blood Run." Crossing the bridge, one entered the "Dueling Grounds,"—where many prominent men had been settling scores for close to a generation. Though dueling was technically illegal in Maryland, the practice was too deeply ingrained to be dispensed with. Stephen Decatur, naval hero of the War of 1812, had been killed there on March 18, 1820. Records indicate that 50 or more duels took place there over the years. However, public opinion would soon turn dramatically against the practice, due in part to a couple of high-profile duels.

The first of these took place in June 1836. It caused the death of 20 year-old Daniel Key, a son of Francis Scott Key. Though all would agree that the death of a man so young was tragic, it seemed particularly senseless in the case of Key. While returning home from an ocean voyage, Key apparently argued with John Sherborne, a good friend, about, of all things, the speed of two steamships. Apparently tempers rose so high that, upon arriving in Washington, they headed to the dueling grounds to finish the argument. It was settled with the death of Key.

A loud outcry arose, but it would take another prominent death two years later before the public really called for legislation to halt the brutal practice.

On May 23, the Senate ratified the Treaty of New Echoata, thus validating the federal government's plan to forcibly remove the Cherokee Indians from Georgia. The Treaty was passed by a bare one-vote margin. Plans were begun for the relocation of the Indians to reservations west of the Mississippi River. Many in the North saw this as just another example of Southern aggression and expansion.

Ten

1837

John Quincy Adams continued to stir up trouble in the House of Representatives by presenting unwanted anti-slavery petitions until, in exasperation, a motion was made by Albert G. Hawes of Kentucky to reinstate the gag rule of the previous session. On January 18, this new motion passed by a vote of 115 to 57.

Yet even this was not enough to deter the feisty old man. As each new petition day arrived, Adams was ready to offer petitions that he knew would not be received. It soon became a regular part of the routine of the House of Representatives to turn down his petitions. That, however, was about to change.

On February 6, Adams changed his tactics, and in so doing brought a torrent of abuse down upon himself. One can picture the dignified old man quietly standing and delivering his statement with well-feigned innocence:

> MR. ADAMS said he held in his hand a paper on which, before it was presented, he desired to have the decision of the speaker. It was a petition from twenty-two persons, declaring themselves to be slaves. He wished to know whether the speaker considered such a petition as coming within the order of the House. Now he, (Mr. A) wished to do nothing except in submission to the rules of the House. This paper purported to come from slaves, and it was one of those petitions which it had occurred to his mind as not being what it purported to be.... [T]he petition declared itself to be from slaves; and he was requested to present it. He would send it to the Chair.

The Congressional Record literally seethes with the mounting anger of the pro-slavery delegates. John Lawler of Alabama objected to the paper even being sent to the chair and insisted upon the record noting his disapproval. Charles E. Haynes of Georgia made a speech saying that he was speechless. His "astonishment reached a height which he felt it impossible to express." He insisted that if Adams did not withdraw the petition, it should be immediately rejected.

Dixon Lewis of Alabama requested that Haynes withdraw his motion, as being entirely inadequate to the situation. Lewis insisted that the "outraged feelings" of the slaveholders present could only be satisfied by the summary punishment of the perpetrator of such a foul act. "If this is not done," insisted Lewis, "every member from the slave States should immediately, in a body, quit the House, and go home to their constituents. We have no longer any business here."

Seaton Grantland of Georgia enthusiastically responded to Lewis's motion. "I will second the motion for punishment, and go all lengths for it," he exclaimed.

This proposal was supported by cries of "Expel him" from the room. Julius Alford of Georgia observed that "as an act of justice to the South" the offending petition should "be taken from the House and burnt. The moment any man should disgrace the government under which he lived, by presenting a petition from slaves praying for emancipation, he hoped the petition would, by order of the House, be committed to the flames."

What a striking picture this presents with members of the Federal government calling for the ritual burning of a petition.

Meanwhile, Waddy Thompson of South Carolina had his own suggestion to make. In his estimation, Adams deserved to be censured for "gross disrespect of the House." The culprit should be "instantly brought to the bar to receive the severe censure of the Speaker."

One can only imagine the elder statesman's thoughts and feelings as the hot-headed Southerners surrounded him with their threats. How galling it must have been to the proud old man that a bunch of insolent pups would suggest that he be reprimanded by the Speaker. And for what offense? For trying to present a petition that had been entrusted to him, a petition that was his moral duty and legal obligation to present.

One wonders who present in that group recalled the words of the immortal Declaration of Independence: "In every stage of these Oppressions We have Petitioned for Redress in the most humble terms: Our repeated Petitions have been answered only be repeated injury."

Certainly Adams did. However, if he felt himself threatened or intimidated by the flood of invective surrounding him, he gave no indication.

The motions and proposals finally took form in the following resolution:

Ten • 1837

> Resolved, that J. Q. Adams, a member from the State of Massachusetts, by his attempt to introduce into this House a petition of slaves for the abolition of slavery in the District of Columbia, committed an outrage on the rights and feelings of a large portion of the people of this Union, a flagrant contempt on the dignity of this House; and by extending to slaves a privilege only belonging to freemen, directly incites the slave population to insurrection; and that the said member be forthwith called to the bar of the House, and censured by the Speaker.

Having sat silent for so long, Adams at last rose; presumably to offer a statement in his own behalf. Apologetically he explained that he had refrained from speaking for so long because he felt it his duty to do so, but that he could no longer allow the House to continue upon its course. The resolution upon which they were about to vote was based upon an erroneous statement or two that he felt obligated to correct before the vote took place.

In the first place, he reminded his esteemed colleagues that he had not attempted to present the petition; he had simply asked the Speaker to give a ruling upon its status. And in the second place, the gentlemen of the House had jumped to an incorrect conclusion about the content of the petition. In point of fact, it did not request the abolition of slavery.

Instead, the slave signers of the document supposedly were "imploring the members from the North to cease offering petitions for their emancipation which could have no other tendency than to aggravate the burden of their servitude." This was a common pro-slavery argument against the abolitionists: that by stirring up trouble, they had magnified the burdens upon the slaves. Adams would later admit that he "had suspicions that [the petition] came really from the hand of a master, who had prevailed upon his slaves to sign it." Presumably it had been sent to Adams as some kind of prank, or in an attempt to embarrass or discomfort him.

The petition in Adams's hand went even further than just asking for an end to anti-slavery petitions. It also recommended "that the Northern members who should persist in presenting them should be expelled."

A new offense was now leveled against Adams:

> Resolved, That the member from Massachusetts ... by creating the impression, and leaving the House under such impression, that said petition was for the abolition of slavery when he knew it was not, has trifled with the House.

This was a daring and exciting new charge. Nobody had ever deigned to "trifle with the House" before. Which raises the question of why Adams was doing this.

Adams is not a very well-known historical figure. His generally unsuccessful presidency was stained by allegations of having "fixed" his election by working out a deal with opposing candidate Henry Clay. This claim originated with, and is still supported by, advocates of Andrew Jackson. While Jackson received the highest number of popular votes in the election of 1824—153,544 to 108,740 for Adams—as well as the larger number of electoral votes—99 to 84—neither candidate had a necessary majority, and the verdict was left to the House of Representatives to decide. Eventually, fourth-place candidate Clay, who was no longer in the running, threw the influence of his support behind Adams, who ultimately won in the House.

Adams probably demonstrated incredible political ineptness by later "rewarding" Clay with the position of Secretary of State, though there is no proof that any "corrupt bargain" had been made. However, the shadow of corruptness would darken his presidency. His term was also marked (some might say marred) by his fierce spirit of independence. Adams was never one to court political favors from others, even when doing so would work to his own advantage. Relatively ineffective as a president for these reasons, his greatest service to the country came while serving in the House after his retirement as chief executive.

While not strictly a member of the "Founding Fathers" generation, Adams grew up with a strong attachment to the Revolutionary era. He was only nine when the Declaration of Independence was written. During most of his early childhood, his father was absent serving the fledgling nation, and both his mother and the seldom-present father instilled within him early in his life a strong sense of duty and responsibility to the country. He was never one to avoid a confrontation if he felt the fight was worth the effort. In his eight-year struggle against the gag rule in Congress he found the perfect arena for his unique abilities.

Adams had very strong anti-slavery opinions, though he never considered himself an abolitionist. He has been severely criticized by many historians for the unsympathetic role he played as Secretary of State towards the Africans of the *Antelope*. However, his struggles during the 1830s on the behalf of the blacks (both in the House and a few years later in the celebrated *Amistad* case) would do much for the battle against slavery.

To Adams, the petition, despite its dubious origin, had "opened to my examination and enquiry a new question ... namely, Whether the right to petition Congress, could in any case be exercised by slaves?" The presentation of this belief was but his first step in a personal battle against the gag rule. He was determined to wage this battle—alone if need be—despite any personal criticism his behavior might draw down upon him. And there would be plenty of that.

Sixteen Southerners spoke out against Adams over the course of the next four days. His behavior was variously described as "wanton," "absurd and offensive," "odious and indefensible," "unquestionably reprehensible," or "disgraceful and unpardonable." He had committed "an outrage upon the genius and spirit of the Constitution," and had "aimed a deadly blow" at the slaveholding states.

In the views of most of the Southern delegates, the most serious aspect of his actions was his contention that slaves might have the right to petition. (At one point, a resolution was made condemning Adams for "giving color to the idea" that slaves had such a right; but this had to be rephrased after it elicited a few puns and some mockery.) J. F. H. Claiborne of Mississippi described any such idea as "an outrage that has no parallel in parliamentary history."

"With a parricidal and sacrilegious hand," said the outraged Hopkins Hosley of Georgia, "he has attempted to sap the foundation of the temple raised by our ancestors as the adobe of fraternal peace and the guarantee of international liberty.... The people whom I represent will deny it with the sword in one hand and the constitution in the other.... He has concentrated in his bureau all the combustible elements of the republic, and week after week presented them to this House, under circumstances so marked and aggravated, as to leave no room to mistake his intentions."

Claiborne finished the arguments against Adams by describing him as one who "rejoiced in the alarm and excitement he occasions, like the midnight incendiary who fires the dwelling of his enemy, and listens with pleasure to the screams of his burning victims."

Not all members, however, were willing to go so far as to censure his behavior. John Robertson of Virginia called the notion of allowing slaves the right to petition "preposterous," and the application of it "wanton," yet he would defend Adams's idiocy in doing so. William J. Graves of Kentucky disapproved most heartily of what Adams was doing, but would not go so far as to endanger the liberty of speech in the House by a vote for censure.

The only wholehearted support Adams received was from his fellow state representatives. In the words of Levi Lincoln:

> [I]t has fallen to the lot of my venerable colleague to have been charged with more of these petitions than all of his associates in the delegation together. His age, his characters, the stations he has held, and his standing before the world, have brought upon him responsibilities which others might not have borne. The people have thrown upon the shoulders of Ajax the weight which no common man might have sustained. They trusted his talents, his learning, and his great experience, to secure to him the deference of respect due to these qualifications in the duties he was

called upon to discharge.... [W]hether I stand alone or whether I am supported, I can never consent that my venerable colleague shall be brought to your bar, to be censured for a conscientious discharge of duty. What he has done he has manfully, rightfully, nobly done, in defense of the inestimable right of petition and the freedom of speech in this House.

Caleb Cushing also spoke on the behalf of Adams:

[T]o no resolution of censure, ... to no rebuke, express or implied, to no action of the House that shall touch that individual [Adams] with so much as the uttermost edge of the shadow of indignity, will I give my assent. If, in the present contingency, any thing had transpired of itself tending to justify the resolution of censure, I could not fail to remember that he, who is the object of it, has presided over the destinies of my country; that he is at this moment a representative, in common with myself, of the State of Massachusetts; that eminent as he is by reason of his long public service, and the exalted stations he has held, he is yet more eminent for his intellectual superiority; that his character no longer belongs to his State or his country, but to the history of civilizations and of liberty, and I would have members ponder well the case, before they proceed, whether to gratify friends or appease foes, to record their votes in censure of such a man.

While the tempest raged around Adams in the House, Calhoun was stirring up his own storm in the Senate. That august body had also been tormented by the presentation of anti-slavery petitions. On February 6, the senator from South Carolina could no longer sit silently through these proceedings.

I do not belong, said Mr. C, to the school which holds that aggression is to be met by concession. [My creed] teaches that encroachments must be met at the beginning, and that those who act on the opposite principle are prepared to become slaves. In this case, ... I hold concession or compromise to be fatal.... Consent to receive these insulting petitions, and the next demand will be that they be referred to a committee in order that they may be deliberated and acted upon.... The most unquestioned right may be rendered doubtful, if once admitted to be a subject of controversy[.] ... The subject [at hand] is beyond the jurisdiction of Congress—they have no right to touch it in any shape or form, or to make it the subject of deliberation or discussion.

Calhoun admitted that the "incendiary Spirit" of abolitionism had spread, but was convinced that it "has not yet infected this body, or the great mass of the intelligent and business portion of the North." However, he warned that "unless it be speedily stopped, it will" continue to "spread and work upwards till it brings the two great sections of the Union into deadly conflict."

He discussed how the spirit of abolitionism had started when a "large

Ten • 1837

portion of the Northern States believed slavery to be a sin." It had commenced with the "fanatical portion of society," and fed its incendiary doctrine upon "the ignorant, the weak, the young, and the thoughtless." He lamented that "the spirit now abroad in the North ... will continue to rise and spread, unless prompt and efficient measures to stay its progress be adopted."

> However sound the great body of the non-slaveholding States are at present, in the course of a few years they will be succeeded by those who will have been taught to hate the people and institutions of nearly one-half of this Union[.] ... By the necessary course of events ... we must become, finally, two people.... *Abolition and the Union cannot coexist.* [Emphasis added.]

Calhoun was speaking for the South, and no doubt many of his compatriots applauded his sentiments. How ironic that the South would be so critical years later of Abraham Lincoln when he but echoed Calhoun by declaring that "a House divided against itself can not stand."

> We of the South will not, cannot, surrender our institutions. To maintain the existing relations between the two races, inhabiting that section of the Union, is indispensable to the peace and happiness of both. It cannot be subverted without drenching the country in blood, and extirpating one or the other of the races. Be it good or bad, it has grown up with our society and institutions, and is so interwoven with them that to destroy it would be to destroy us as a people. But let me not be understood as admitting, even by implication, that the existing relations between the two races in the slaveholding States is an evil—far otherwise. I hold it to be a good, as it has thus far proved itself to be, to both, and will continue to prove so if not disturbed by the fell spirit of abolition.... Never before has the black race ... attained a condition so civilized, and so improved, not only physically, but morally and intellectually.... But I take higher ground. I hold that in the present state of civilization, where two races of different origin, and distinguished by color, and other physical differences, as well as intellectual, are brought together, the relation now existing in the slaveholding States between the two, is, instead of an evil, a good—a positive good.... I may say with truth, that in few countries so much is left to the share of the laborer, and so little exacted from him, or where there is more kind attention paid to him in sickness or infirmities of age.... [L]ook at the sick, and the old and infirm slave, ... in the midst of his family and friends, under the kind superintending care of his master and mistress[.] ... I fearlessly assert that the existing relation between the two races in the South ... forms the most solid and durable foundation on which to rear free and stable political institutions.

He ended his "positive good" speech by a plea for the soutthern states to wake up to the danger facing them:

> If we do not defend ourselves, none will defend us; if we yield, we will be more and more pressed as we recede; and if we submit, we will be trampled under foot. Be assured that emancipation itself would not satisfy these fanatics—that gained, the next step would be to raise the negroes to a social and political equality with the whites; and that being effected, we would soon find the present condition of the two races reversed. They and their Northern allies would be the masters, and we the slaves[.]

There are fewer stronger expositions of the pro-slavery view than this speech. Calhoun has clearly articulated what Virginia discovered after the slave debates of 1831–1832: it is impossible to protect slavery unless you also defend it as a positive good. As editorialized in the *New Orleans True American*:

> If the principle be once acknowledged, that slavery is an evil, the success of the fanatics is certain. We are with Mr. Calhoun on this point. He insists that slavery is a *positive good* in our present social relations—that no power in the Union can touch the construction of Southern society, without actual violation of all guaranteed and unalienated rights. This is the threshold of our liberties. If once passed, the tower must fall.

The same paradox would plague the Confederacy during the Civil War. To defend slavery, one had to confess that it was a good thing. If you did not so confess, then you had no arguments to use against its detractors. However, most of the nations of the civilized world had long since agreed that it was not and were unlikely to support a new nation based upon the foundation of slavery. Therefore, the South was forced to pretend that it no longer believed slavery was good. To do so, Southerners shifted their arguments from a defense of slavery to one of states rights. It is to the credit of England and France at the time that both nations recognized the hypocrisy of the slaveholders and, as a result, refused them recognition.

John Quincy Adams was still doing everything within his power to contribute to the collapse of the tower of slavery. Having quietly listened to days of abuse with little said in his defense, he finally had the opportunity to speak on his own behalf on February 9:

> How long will it be before the gentleman from South Carolina himself [he meant Representative Waddy Thompson of that State, but he could just as well have been addressing Calhoun in the Senate] ... will have to answer ... for words spoken here[?] ... Let that gentleman, let every member of this House, ask his own heart with what confidence, with what boldness, with what freedom, with what firmness, he would give utterance to his opinion on this floor if, for every word, for a mere question asked of the Speaker, involving a question belonging to human freedom, to the rights of man, he was liable to [censure before the chair.]

Ten • 1837

When the vote to censure at last came, only 22 members of those present were willing to cast their lot against Adams. His position, while not secure, was at least safe for the time being.

Having failed in their rebuke of Adams, the Southern members then turned to the issue of slave petitions in general. Waddy Thompson declared:

> Slaves have no right to petition. They are property, not persons; they have no political rights, and even their civil rights must be claimed through their masters. Having no political rights, Congress has no power in relation to them, and therefore no right to receive their petition. They are property, not persons, under the Constitution. The Constitution is the paramount rule of the House; and any attempt, however made, to present petitions from them is a violation of that Constitution and a flagrant disrespect and insult to a portion of its members.
>
> ... Does any man dare to claim that the House of which I am a member is a tribunal to which appeals from my slaves are to be addressed, and in which their denunciations of me are to be received? This is a question I will not argue.

Henry L. Pinckney, also of South Carolina, elaborated further on the same point, stating that he:

> would just as soon have supposed that the gentleman from Massachusetts would have offered a memorial from a cow or a horse—for he might as well be the organ of one species of property as another. Slaves were property.... Who ever dreamt that any member of this House would so far forget its dignity as to attempt ... to introduce a memorial from Negroes!

John Robertson of Virginia hoped that Adams was "too intelligent to assert, in his calmer moments the preposterous position, that those who under the Constitution are recognized as property, who constitute no part of the body politic, can exercise political rights."

Nor were such arguments limited to just Southerners. Aaron Vanderpoel of New York was just as appalled as were the representatives from South Carolina. "The idea that slaves had a right to petition the American Congress," said the New Yorker, "is indeed too monstrous to justify any labored attempt at refutation. Had anyone, before today, ever dreamed that the appellation of the people embraced slaves?"

Obviously the House had to take a stand on this issue, and did so on February 12. On that day, by a vote of 162 to 18, it passed the following:

> Resolved, That slaves do not possess the right of petition secured to the people of the United States by the Constitution.

It seemed that, at least for the time being, the voice of abolition had once again been silenced in the House of Representatives.

Events were quietly going on in rural Pennsylvania that would ultimately assume National importance. Edward Prigg, a professional slave catcher, presented himself before Thomas Henderson, Esquire, who was a justice of the peace in the county of York. Prigg was the "duly and legally constituted and appointed" agent of Margaret Ashmore, of Maryland. On her behalf, Prigg had come to "seize and arrest" Margaret Morgan, who was the property of Ashmore, "as a fugitive from labour." Morgan had been living in Pennsylvania since her escape in 1832, and she was no doubt surprised that the authorities had finally caught up to her.

Prigg, either alone or with the help of unnamed others, apprehended Morgan and her children and took them before judge Henderson. However, Henderson refused to authorize Prigg to remove them from the state, citing an 1826 act of the Commonwealth of Pennsylvania that protected fugitives from labour and free people of color. Prigg then took the entire family out of the state against the judge's orders, in effect kidnapping them and delivering them "into the custody and possession of" Margaret Ashmore in Maryland.

Most grievous in the eyes of Pennsylvania was that one of Morgan's children had been conceived and born during Morgan's residence in the commonwealth: thereby, by state law, that child was free by birth. Prigg claimed that he took the ostensibly free child along with its slave mother as an act of kindness; otherwise he would have had to separate the mother and child.

The simple fact that the Commonwealth of Pennsylvania charged Prigg with kidnapping on the behalf of Morgan and her child indicates that, contrary to popular opinion, blacks were not without rights in at least some Northern states. However, no documentation regarding the progress of the case as it made its way to the courts can be found.

Apparently, after lengthy negotiations, Maryland allowed Prigg to be extradited to Pennsylvania to stand trial. In return, Pennsylvania agreed to rush the proceedings through so that it could quickly make its way to the Supreme Court. Both states—and, presumably, the entire nation—were anxious to have the court's ruling on legislation protecting fugitive slaves.

The state of Pennsylvania completed its case in May 1839. The Supreme Court's ruling was passed down in January 1842. The high court's ruling declared laws such as the Pennsylvania act of 1826 to be unconstitutional. According to the Taney court, Prigg was entirely within his constitutional rights to seize Ashmore's property and return it to her. As a result of this ruling, many Northern states passed personal liberty laws to protect blacks living within their borders. These Northern antislavery laws would ultimately lead to the passing of more rigorous fugitive slave laws in 1850.

On March 3, the last official act of the Jackson administration was the official recognition of the independent country of Texas. It appeared to be only a matter of time before the newly formed slave nation formally offered to annex itself to the United States. Pro-slavery citizens of the South were elated at the prospect. Many others soberly reflected upon the effects such a course of action would have upon the peace of the nation.

On March 4, President-elect Martin Van Buren delivered his inaugural address. The first president from New York, he was only the third president who was not a slaveowner. However, that fact alone proved to be of no comfort to the opponents of the peculiar institution. In his inaugural, Van Buren identified "the institution of slavery" as "perhaps the greatest ... source of discord and disaster" in the nation. He made it clear that it would not be a problem if it wasn't for the fanatics who dared to interfere with the established traditions of the nation. He called upon his fellow citizens to be deaf to the dictates of the abolitionists:

> I must go into the presidential chair the inflexible and uncompromising opponent of every attempt, on the part of Congress, to abolish slavery in the District of Columbia, against the wishes of the slaveholding States; and also with a determination equally decided to resist the slightest interference with it in the States where it exist.

In early May, the country was gripped by a financial panic, precipitated at least in part by Jackson's removal of funds from the national bank. By the middle of the year, the country was in the midst of a severe depression. The mercantile house of Arthur Tappan was one of those hit, as it failed to make good on its debt of $1.2 million. It seemed, at least for a while, that financial news would take precedence over the abolition controversy.

That was until Sarah and Angelina Grimké accepted a speaking invitation from the New England Anti-Slavery Society. Starting in late May, the two young women from South Carolina traveled across New England, adding their personal touch to the plea against slavery. Initially, they found themselves restricted to small parlor meetings of interested women. However, as their notoriety increased, they found themselves presenting to ever larger crowds, often now including men and women. Usually churches provided the sites for these presentations.

That same month, the New York Anti-Slavery Society made its decision to focus its energy upon petitioning the federal government. The mail campaign of 1835 had proved to be more of an embarrassment than an aid in the fight against slavery. Undoubtedly, the image of the citizens of Charleston burning federal mail had enraged some Northerners, with perhaps a few of these even joining the abolitionist camp as a result. Yet an increase in the number of Northern supporters of the cause would not of itself advance emancipation. Something more needed to be done.

As the record plainly proves, abolition and anti-slavery petitions were nothing new to the U.S. Congress. Now, however, the anti-slavery societies consciously decided to intensify their efforts. Despite the congressional gag rule forbidding the introduction of such memorials, a movement was initiated to flood the halls of Congress with petitions concerning the subject of slavery.

Lane alumnus Theodore Weld was one of those most instrumental in the movement. He established what was, in effect, a training course for itinerant abolitionists. He provided them with practical instructions on how to face down a mob, tips on how to establish anti-slavery societies in new communities, and practical reference materials with which to refute pro-slavery arguments. Soon well-organized and methodically-prepared abolitionists were combing the countryside, spreading the word of freedom and distributing petitions that would eventually end up in Washington.

Much of the actual burden of gathering signatures for anti-slavery memorials was taken up by social-minded females. Denied any actual voice in running the government, many women saw the distribution of petitions as their only real opportunity to contribute. The petitions that began to make their way into Congress—first a trickle, then a stream and, at last, a flood—were overwhelmingly dominated by the signatures of the nation's fairer sex.

On July 6, in Alton, Illinois, a mob destroyed the printing press belonging to anti-slavery editor Elijah Lovejoy. Lovejoy, it will be recalled, had fled to the free state of Illinois to escape the harassments he had experienced in St. Louis.

Recognizing the fact that anti-slavery sentiments were being expressed in New England churches despite the previous summer's call against doing so, a group of Northern church leaders drafted an even stronger plea. Released on July 28, it was entitled a Pastoral Letter of the General Association of Massachusetts to the Congregational Churches under their care." It deplored the "perplexed and agitating subjects" that were spreading across the country, and specifically enjoined the churches not to permit "strangers to preach on subjects [which] the ministers do not agree with." Though never naming the Grimké sisters, it appeared to be directed at them when it warned of "the dangers which at present seem to threaten the female character with widespread and permanent injury." In no uncertain terms, the statement denounced women "who so far forget themselves as to itinerate in the character of public lecturers and teachers." But when she assumes the place and tone of man as a public reformer, our care and protection of her seem unnecessary ... and her character becomes unnatural."

This pastoral letter was a failure in its goal to keep abolition sentiment out of New England churches. It did, however, produce two distinct results.

First, it displayed to the country at large how ineffective the church leaders of the North were in curbing their ministers' support of the antislavery cause. As has been previously discussed, the Southern churches, either by inclination or in self-preservation, were by now fully committed to the defense of slavery. By the summer of 1837, the Southern members of the Presbyterian Church could no longer feel secure in their connection with the North. The result was a schism within the church along purely regional lines. Though there were other issues involved, it seems inarguable that, as it was in the political arena, slavery was the one issue that could not be settled.

The Methodists would have a similar division over the issue of slavery in 1844, as would the Baptists in 1845. As a result, by the time of the Civil War, any claim that the North and South shared a common faith would be a romanticized notion with little veracity to it.

The other result of the pastoral letter was due to its emphasis on the role of women in America. Angelina and Sarah Grimké had not set out to challenge the masculine rule of society. But in the condescending role of women as defined in the pastoral letter, they rightfully recognized the issue of women's rights. Soon, the sisters were arguing that women in America were just as oppressed as the blacks. While we can look upon this from a current viewpoint and acknowledge the correctness of their complaint, many of their contemporaries were less willing to do so. Unfortunately, the emerging issue of "women's rights" would soon become a devisive element within the abolition community.

For the time being, the Grimkes continued to be popular speakers, drawing ever larger and more attentive crowds as their summer tour progressed. During July, they spoke to audiences totaling 12,000 people at 19 appearances in 14 separate towns.

On August 4, the Republic of Texas presented its formal offer to annex itself to the United States. The ever-increasing flood of anti-slavery petitions pouring into the U.S. Congress would soon be supplemented by petitions calling for or against the prospect of annexing additional slave territory to the nation. Though many historians have tried to picture the struggle against receiving Texas as a Northern ploy to sap the political strength of the South, such criticism seems unwarranted.

It can be conceded that the hopes of Northern political superiority might have been viewed by some as a legitimate reason for the refusal to accept Texas into the Union. But perhaps it was time that the numerically superior North began to have more influence in the affairs of the nation.

More important is the fact that thousands and tens of thousands of American citizens deplored the annexation of Texas for humanitarian reasons. After years of struggling to contain slavery, the voluntary addition of a huge slaveholding territory seemed to many a giant step backwards. Over time, their protests would shake the halls of the federal government.

On August 21, Elijah Lovejoy had a second printing press destroyed by a pro-slavery mob. Undaunted, he soon ordered a replacement.

Tiring from their tour, Angelina and Sarah Grimké slowed down their engagements for the month of August, but made up for the lapse by renewed appearances in September. In that month alone, they gave twenty-eight lectures in 23 towns to more than 13,000 people. As their 27-week tour came to an end, they had every reason to be pleased with their accomplishments. They had made 88 presentations in 67 towns and cities, carrying their message to an estimated 40,000 listeners. Many of these listeners joined the growing ranks of abolitionists as a tribute to the strength of that message. The Grimké's left behind them a trail of newly formed Women's Anti-Slavery Societies and a rising generation of women who felt themselves empowered to speak out against oppression.

On the September 21, during Elijah Lovejoy's absence from Alton, his third printing press was delivered to the city. According to a later report written by Horace Greeley:

> [That night] ten or twenty ruffians ... broke into the [warehouse where it was stored,] rolled the press across the street to the riverbank, broke it into pieces, and threw it in. Before they had finished the job, the Mayor was on hand, and ordered them to disperse. They replied, that they would, so soon as they got through, and were as good as their word. The Mayor declared that he had never witnessed a more quiet and gentlemanly mob!

Upon his return a few days later, Lovejoy "was mobbed at the house of his mother-in-law." According to Greeley, "the mob attempted ... to drag him from the house, but were defeated, mainly though the courageous efforts of his wife and one or two friends."

Undaunted or self-destructive, Lovejoy ordered yet a fourth press. It arrived in St. Louis on November 5. Arrangements were made to have it delivered to Alton in the early hours of the morning of November 7, in the hopes that it could be brought in without arousing a disturbance. However, word circulated about town regarding its imminent arrival.

Ten • 1837

According to Greeley, Lovejoy contacted the mayor's office to request the services of special constables for the protection of his property. His plea was ignored. Contrary to this report, many sources claim that, while unable (or unwilling) to provide police constables, the mayor authorized Lovejoy and his companions to protect their press.

Upon its arrival in the city, the printing press was safely delivered to a warehouse owned by a Mr. Gilman. The dangerous part was going to be transferring the equipment from the warehouse to the offices of Lovejoy's *Observer*. In the absence of official assistance, Lovejoy and a few friends decided to protect the press themselves by occupying the warehouse until the transfer could be effected. Greeley continues the saga:

> About ten o'clock, some thirty persons, as if by preconcert, suddenly emerged from a neighboring grog-shop—a few of them with arms, but the majority with only stones in their hands—formed a line at the south end of the store, next the river, knocked and hailed. Mr. Gilman, from the garret door, asked what they wanted. Their leader replied: "The press." Mr. Gilman assured them that it would not be given up; adding: "We have no ill feelings towards any of you, and should much regret to do you any injury; but we are authorized by the Mayor to defend our property, and shall do so with our lives." The leader replied that they were resolved to have the press at any sacrifice, and presented a pistol, whereupon Mr. Gilman retired into the building. The mob then passed around to the opposite end of the warehouse and commenced throwing stones, which soon demolished several of the windows. No resistance was offered, the inmates having agreed not to fire unless their lives were in danger.
>
> The warehouse being of stone, and solidly built, no further impression was made on it by this assault. Finding their missiles ineffectual, the mob fired two or three guns into the building, by which no one was hit. The fire was then returned, and several of the rioters wounded, one of them mortally. Hereupon, the mob recoiled, carrying off their wounded. But they soon returned with ladders, and other preparations for firing the roof of the warehouse, cursing and shouting, "Burn them out! burn them out!" They kept carefully on the side of the building where there were no windows, so that they could not be injured or repelled by its defenders. The Mayor and a justice were now deputed by the mob to bear a message to the inmates of the building, proposing that, on condition the press were given up, no one should be further molested, and no more property destroyed. The proposition was quietly declined....
>
> The mob now raised their ladders against the building, mounted to the roof, and kindled a fire there, which burned rather slowly. Five of the defenders hereupon volunteered to sally out and drive them away. They left by the south door, passed around the corner to the east side of the building, and fired upon the man who guarded the foot of the ladder, drove him off, and dispersed his immediate comrades, returning to the store to reload. Mr. Lovejoy and two others stepped again to the door, and stood looking around just without the building—Mr. Lovejoy in advance of the others. Several of the rioters were concealed from their

view behind a pile of lumber a few rods in their front. One of these had a two-barreled gun, which he fired. Mr. Lovejoy received five balls, three of them in his breast, probably each mortal. He turned quickly, ran into the store, and up a flight of stairs into the counting-room, where he fell, exclaiming, "Oh God, I am shot! I am shot!" and almost instantly expired.... Those remaining alive in the building now held a consultation, and concluded to surrender. One of their number went up to the scuttle and appraised the mob that Mr. Lovejoy was dead, and that the press would now be given up. A yell of exultation was sent up by the rioters [who] then rushed into the building, threw the press out of the window, broke it up, and pitched the pieces into the river. They destroyed no other property, save a few guns.... At two o'clock, they had dispersed and all was quiet again.

Lovejoy's body lay all night where it had fallen. In the morning, his remains were borne away and secretly buried in an unmarked grave for fear that they would be disturbed. It was November 9th; his 35th birthday.

In 1864, when Lovejoy's body was reinterred, a free Black stone cutter named Johnston was the only one who knew where the original grave site was. Since that year, an annual memorial service has been held at noon on November 9th in Lovejoy's honor.

A monument was dedicated to his memory in 1897, on the sixtieth anniversary of his death. It consists of a 93 foot granite column topped by a 17 foot statue of Winged Victory. This is flanked by two 30-foot granite columns topped by bronze eagles.

Incredibly, in the aftermath of the tragedy, a grand jury indicted Gilman and 10 others for inciting a riot. Arguing that the use of force was justified in self-defense but not in the defense of personal property, the court charged the defenders with responsibility of the disturbance. Ultimately they were exonerated of the charges, but so were the members of the mob when they were similarly charged.

Although Lovejoy's death had occurred in a free state at the hands of Northerners, opinion throughout the nation seemed to be fairly universal that the underlying cause was slavery. However, there was widespread disagreement over which party involved was more reprehensible. Not surprisingly, the abolitionists blamed the attacking mob, whose behavior they viewed as just another attack on freedom of speech and the press by the pro-slavery hordes. Conversely, those sympathetic towards slavery, or perhaps just naturally conservative, saw the actions of Lovejoy and his fellow defenders as another example of anti-slavery fanaticism disturbing the peace of the community.

The Massachusetts Anti-Slavery Society defended Lovejoy's conduct as justified by "the example of our revolutionary fathers," equating it with the "patriotic sacrifices" that earlier generation had made in the fight for freedom.

Garrison, the pacifist, was "shocked" that Lovejoy had taken up arms to defend his rights. He agreed that Lovejoy "was certainly a martyr—[but] strictly speaking—he was not ... a Christian martyr" due to his resort to violence. However, "In destroying [Lovejoy's] press," Garrison wrote in the *Liberator*, "the enemies of freedom have compelled a thousand to speak out in his stead."

And speak out they soon did.

Many in the North who had tried to ignore the issues of slavery and abolitionism felt themselves no longer able to do so. Cities across the nation staged demonstrations in response to the tragedy in Alton. The largest of these was the one held on December 8, 1837, in Boston, where 5,000 people jammed Faneuil Hall. Garrison was cautioned by friends to limit his remarks to a defense of free speech, as being more likely to gain public support than to "mix up the meeting with Abolition."

One of the first speakers of the evening was Massachusetts State Attorney General James T. Austin who denounced Lovejoy and other abolitionists for frightening slaveholders specifically and the public in general with their wild schemes of turning hordes of blacks loose on the nation. Who could fault any community that rose up against them in what they considered their own self-defense? In Austin's words, Lovejoy "died as the fool dieth," and any recriminations drawn from the situation should be against the fanatic incendiaries themselves. He went so far as to commend the Alton "mob" for their virtuous stand against those who would disrupt the peace of the nation, likening their assault upon Lovejoy's press to the Revolutionary patriots who had dumped British tea into Boston Harbor.

Undoubtedly there were many listening to his words who agreed with Austin. There was, however, one who most certainly did not.

Wendell Phillips had been a mute witness to Garrison's mobbing the previous year; but now found himself unable to remain silent any longer. Gaining the floor, he assailed Austin's position and the crowd's response to it:

> I hope I shall be permitted to express my surprise at the sentiments of the last speaker,—surprise not only at such sentiments from such a man, but at the applause they have received within these walls. A comparison has been drawn between the events of the Revolution and the tragedy at Alton.... [W]e have heard the mob at Alton, the drunken murderers of Lovejoy, compared to those patriot fathers who threw the tea overboard! [Great applause.] Fellow-citizens, is this Faneuil Hall doctrine? ["no, no."] The mob at Alton were met to wrest from a citizen his just rights,— met to resist the laws.... [The difference is,] Our fathers resisted, not the King's prerogative, but the King's usurpation.... To draw the conduct of our ancestors into a precedent for mobs, for a right to resist laws we ourselves have enacted, is an insult to their memory.... [T]he men of that

day went for the right, as secured by the laws.... The rioters of our day go for their own wills, right or wrong. Sir, when I heard the gentleman lay down principles which place the murderers of Alton side by side with Otis and Hancock, with Quincy and Adams, I thought those pictured lips [pointing to the portraits in the Hall] would have broken into voice to rebuke the recreant American—the slanderer of the dead. [Great applause and counter applause.]

Apparently Austin had not been the only speaker who had denounced Lovejoy's role in the tragedy. Phillips referred to "a reverend clergyman of the city" who had told the crowd "that no citizen has a right to publish opinions disagreeable to the community! If any mob follows such publication, on him rests its guilt!" Phillips ridiculed such "clerical absurdity" that accepted "as a check for the abuses of the press, not the law, but the dread of a mob."

This impassioned defense of Lovejoy brought Phillips instant fame among the nation's abolitionists. Some sources refer to him as the most impassioned of all anti-slavery speakers. Unfortunately, the fire of his convictions would add fuel to the approaching controversy among the nation's reformers.

For almost a decade, the name of Garrison had been almost synonymous with abolitionism. For many years it had seemed like the editor was fighting a one-man battle against the behemoth slavery. Yet there was only so much one man could do; the battle needed more troops. By the late 1830s, the reinforcements had arrived to add numbers to the ranks. Paradoxically, as the number of people involved in the fight against slavery increased, Garrison's grip on the movement's direction weakened. When followers were few, his way was the way. Now, there were many other people involved who had their own ideas of how the struggle should be continued.

Despite all the criticism Garrison has received over the years, it seems clear that he never condoned the use of force or violence. Phillips, on the other hand, commended Lovejoy for his strong, manly stand against his oppressors. "[F]rom the bottom of my heart," he told the crowd in Faneuil Hall that night, "I thank that brave little band at Alton for resisting." Lovejoy was lionized as the first warrior of the abolition ranks.

Few realized in 1837 just how big a gap separated Garrison from many of the "new-breed" of more-militant abolitionists. Garrison never expected, or desired, to have people literally fighting for abolitionism. By the time Kansas began to bleed, Garrison's ideals of passive resistance seemed to many to be totally inadequate to the actual situation at hand.

Garrison also disagreed with his long-time benefactors, the Tappans, concerning the political direction of the movement. Unwilling to make any covenant with a government that condoned slavery, Garrison abhorred any political activity. Yet there were many abolitionists—some as dedicated in their own ways as was Garrison—who believed that change could only be produced by working within the political framework as it existed. It would not be long before such conflicting opinions upset the unity of the abolitionists.

Yet another issue had been raised by the triumphant progress of the Grimké sisters along their New England tour. In delivering the message of black emancipation, the two women sowed the seeds of emancipation for the fairer sex as well. As they talked about the oppression of Blacks, they began to more fully appreciate their own inferior position in society. Soon they would be speaking out for women's rights as well. In fact, many historians consider the Grimkes to be the founders of the women's movement in America.

Garrison, always willing to take on a new reform no matter how unpopular, quickly jumped on the bandwagon that demanded equal rights for women. Many of his fellow abolitionists, while struggling wholeheartedly for the rights of the slaves, were unwilling to make the same concession to women.

These three issues—the use of force, political activism and women's rights—would soon cause a split within the anti-slavery societies.

As the Second Session of the twenty-fifth Congress convened, it fell upon former president John Quincy Adams to initiate the presentation of anti-slavery petitions in the House of Representatives. On Tuesday, December 12, he presented "a petition praying for the abolition of slavery and the slave trade in the District of Columbia." Commenting that this petition, combined with those received in previous sessions, embraced "upwards of 50,000 signers," he respectfully asked that it "be referred to the Committee" for said District, "with instructions to consider and report thereon." This petition was immediately tabled on the motion of Henry Wise of Virginia.

Adams followed this with "several other petitions from Massachusetts, Pennsylvania, etc., on the same subject." These were also laid on the table at Wise's suggestion. "Mr. ADAMS then presented another of the same tenor," which was also tabled. And so, it seems, it would continue.

On Monday, December 18, John C. Calhoun once again spoke up in the Senate against the "spirit of fanaticism, which was daily increasing" in the nation. "It was particularly our duty," he declared, "to keep the matter" of slavery "out of the Senate, out of the Halls of the National Legislature. [H]e hoped every man from the South would stand by him to put down this growing evil. There was but one question that would ever destroy this Union, and that was involved in this principle" of interfering with the South's domestic institution.

Benjamin Swift of Vermont assured the speaker that "the petitioners were not the miserable fanatics which the Senator from South Carolina supposed; they were among the most intelligent and respectable of the community; and the Legislature of Vermont had adopted resolutions on this subject" as well.

John Roane of Virginia was appalled by Swift's words. The senator from Vermont presumed too much if he were to claim the citizens of his state had the right "peaceably to assemble and petition—for what? To take away my right to enjoy life, liberty, and the pursuit of happiness." No sir[!]"

To the argument that the people of Vermont were united in their goal of abolition, Roane responded:

> Sir, let me inform that Senator, and the whole North, that the entire country south of the Potomac, without any regard whatever to party, or any thing else, is as firmly united as can possibly be the people of Vermont, and will boldly face and defy the storm of abolition, come when and whence it may.

William C. Preston of South Carolina went even further, declaring "that if Congress does not protect the South, it will be obliged to protect itself.... [H]e was disposed to do it quietly if possible; but, if not, he would say, with great emphasis, 'we will protect ourselves.'"

On Wednesday, December 20, William Slade of Vermont added his support to Adams in the House with the presentation of a memorial signed by "upward of five hundred" citizens of his state. He had prepared a full-fledged anti-slavery speech for the occasion. A speech which, owing to the protests of his Southern colleagues, he never got to fully deliver. According to one account, "Slade was obliged to sit down without having completed [his] interrupted sentence."

Henry Wise of Virginia, whose sensibilities were no doubt enraged by Slade's boldness, called upon his fellow state delegates "to retire with him from the hall."

> Mr. [Hopkins] HOLSEY made the same request to his colleagues from Georgia, and expressed a hope that the whole Southern delegation would retire.
> Mr. [Seaton] GRANTLAND [of Georgia] also joined in the same wish.

While the chairman of the House was admonishing Slade of Vermont for speaking out of order, 50 or 60 Southern members left the hall in what could be described as the first act of Southern secession.

A North Carolina member moved to adjourn. But in the absence of the missing delegates, the number of members remaining was insufficient to conduct even the business of adjournment. The offended members were prevailed upon to return so that the meeting could be adjourned.

As the day's business concluded, Robert Barnwell Rhett of South Carolina called upon "the whole Southern delegation" to meet with him in a committee room.

In a report he subsequently circulated to his constituents, John Quincy Adams described the events of that meeting:

> This meeting, in which no member from a non-slaveholding State was admitted to participate, but in which members of the slave representation in the Senate took part in common with those of the House, prepared and adopted a gag-resolution, in substance the same with that of the two preceding annual sessions; and they appointed Mr. [John] Patton ... to present it to the House[.] ... It was accordingly presented ... the next day ... and carried by yeas and nays, 122 to 74; of which majority 51 members were from non-slaveholding States, who received and voted for this resolution, as dictated by the Southern conventicle of Senators and Representatives, without having been permitted to share in the deliberations of the meeting by which it had been prescribed.

Patton's resolution, as accepted by the House on Tuesday, December 21, proclaimed:

> That all petitions, memorials, and papers, touching the abolition of slavery, or the buying, selling, or transporting of slaves, in any State, District, or Territory, of the United States, be laid on the table, without being debated, printed, read, or received, and that no further action whatever shall be had thereon.

And thus died the constitutionally protected right of petition. Though not without one final protest.

> When the name of Mr. ADAMS was called [to cast his vote], that gentleman rose, and said: "I hold the resolution to be a violation of the Constitution of the United States." [Loud cries of "Order!" "order!" from every part of the Hall.]

While James Birney's press in Cincinnati was secure, events were transpiring to create more problems for him. It appears that at some time during the year Birney hired a housekeeper named Matilda. Matilda, it turned out, was not white as Birney had assumed her to be but actually a light-skinned mulatto.

This wouldn't have been a problem if she hadn't also been a fugitive slave. Matilda was the daughter (and lawful property) of Larkin Lawrence, a resident of St. Louis. Birney pleaded that he had been ignorant of her status, which indeed he may have been. However, in view of his abolitionist beliefs, it is quite likely that he might have hired her even if he'd been fully aware of the circumstances.

It is also within the realm of possibility that the charges against him were motivated by pro-slavery citizens frustrated by their earlier efforts to discourage Birney. In any event, he was charged with harboring a fugitive slave, a direct violation of an Ohio statute of 1804. His case came to trial in December, where he was represented by a young transplanted New England lawyer named Salmon Chase.

Chase argued eloquently that Birney could not be charged with harboring a fugitive when he had been unaware that she was one. More importantly, he challenged the constitutionality of the Ohio statute as a violation of the Northwest Ordinance of 1787.

Judge D. K. Este was unimpressed. Birney was found guilty as charged and fined $50. Matilda was returned to her original owner in St. Louis. Two days later, Lawrence sent her to New Orleans where she was sold at public auction.

The year 1837 was a time of change in American industry. The introduction of the factory system in the textiles industry had dramatically increased productivity in New England mills. Where total production just 20 years earlier had been only four million yards, the production for the year 1837 was 308 million yards. Unfortunately, with the industry's rising output came an increased dependence on the South's staple slave-crop of cotton.

In international news, June 20, 1837, was an important day for Great Britain. A young girl (just a month past her 18th birthday) who had spent most of her childhood alone and in seclusion was suddenly thrust into prominence upon the death of her uncle, William IV. The young woman had been born Princess Alexandria Victoria, but on that day she ascended the throne as Queen Victoria.

One of those present at the queen's first ceremonial sessions was actress Fanny Kemble, who was revisiting the country of her birth both to see friends and family, and to separate herself from her husband, Pierce Butler. Marriage so far had not been a happy state for Kemble. She chafed under her husband's dictatorial rule. During her summer apart from him, however, she came to realize that the fault was not all his. In a letter to him, she remarked that their time apart had allowed her "to reflect upon some passages of our intercourse with self-condemnation, and a desire to discharge my duty to you more faith-fully." She wanted to be a dutiful wife.

However, she couldn't help reminding him that she valued her independence, and resented his control. She expressed "regret" for the "manner" of her resistance, but "not the fact itself."

"There is no justice in the theory," she continued "that one rational creature is to be subservient to another."

That fall, Butler journeyed to England to retrieve his wife. They returned to their home in Philadelphia where, presumably much to Butler's chagrin, many of Kemble's friends and associates were Quakers and/or abolitionists.

Eleven

1838

Attorney Salmon Chase appealed James Birney's conviction of harboring a fugitive slave to the Ohio State Supreme Court, which heard the case in January. Besides his earlier arguments, Chase now introduced the fact that on at least one occasion, previous to her escape, Matilda's master had voluntarily conducted her into the free state of Ohio. As such, she had ceased to be a slave according to the constitution of that state.

The court chose the politically expedient course of ignoring Chase's new arguments and declaring simply that, under the circumstances, there was no way that Birney could have been aware that his housekeeper was a fugitive. They dismissed the charges against Birney without ever having addressed the constitutional issues that had been raised.

Even as a child, Reuben Crandall's constitution had been a fragile one. His nine-month stay in the unhealthy atmosphere of the Georgetown jail had left him frail and weakened. He passed away in January, at the age of 32.

On Wednesday, February 21, Angelina Grimké was invited to address a committee of the legislature of the state of Massachusetts in Boston. It was the first time in the nation's history that a woman would speak before any legislative body. The subject, naturally, was abolitionism. But she took the opportunity to also argue the role of women in America; appropriately so, since, as she must have been well aware, there were many before her who questioned the legitimacy of her appearance there that day:

> I stand before you as a citizen, on behalf of the 20,000 women of Massachusetts whose names are enrolled on petitions which have been submitted to the Legislature.... These petitions relate to the great and solemn subject of slavery.... And because it is a political subject, it has often

tauntingly been said, that women had nothing to do with it. Are we aliens, because we are women? Are we bereft of citizenship because we are mothers, wives and daughters of a mighty people? Have women *no* country, *no* interests staked in public weal—no liabilities in common peril—no partnership in a nation's guilt and shame?

She answered her own rhetorical questions by arguing that women had every right "inasmuch as we are citizens of the public, and as such our honor, happiness and well-being are bound up in its politics, government and laws." She emphasized her personal involvement in the issue of slavery:

> I stand before you as a Southerner, exiled from the land of my birth by the sound of the lash and the piteous cry of the slave. I stand before you as a repentant slaveholder. I stand before you as a moral being and as a moral being I feel that I owe it to the suffering slave and to the deluded master, to my country and to the world to do all that I can to overturn a system of complicated crimes, built upon the broken hearts and prostrate bodies of my countrymen in chains and cemented by the blood, sweat and tears of my sisters in bonds.

She continued her address the following day, at which time she spoke upon "the Dangers of Slavery, the Safety of Emancipation, Gradualism, and Character of the Free people of Color, [and] the cruel treatment they were subjected to thro' the influence of prejudice—this prejudice always accompanied gradual emancipation."

By many accounts, Grimké's presentation was a stunning success. However, most such accounts were written by individuals who were predisposed to agree with her arguments. Conversely, she was highly criticized by some for over stepping the bounds of women in society, though it might also be related that many of these criticisms came from those who were prejudiced against her message.

In the grand scheme of things, it would be hard to judge the impact of her presentation. Grimké and her sister had certainly created a great deal of interest in themselves. Yet their overall contribution to the abolition struggle seems to have come to an end. By compounding the issue with the concept of rights for women, they negated much of the good they might otherwise have accomplished. As events would soon show, their role as leading abolitionist speakers was about to end.

On February 24, the nation was shocked to hear of the shooting death of 35-year-old congressmen Jonathan Cilley of Maine on the notorious Bladensburg dueling ground. His opponent was another congressman, William Graves of Kentucky. Cilley had charged a New York newspaperman, James W. Webb, with influence peddling. Webb had requested Graves to deliver a challenge to Cilley. When Cilley refused to acknowledge the challenge, Graves challenged the Maine congressman on his own behalf.

It is unclear just why Cilley accepted the challenge from Graves.

On the first exchange, Cilley's gun discharged into the ground, and Graves missed. On the second exchange, it was Graves's shot that entered the ground, and Cilley was the one that missed. This should have been enough to satisfy anyone's honor and settle the issue. It seems that Graves's second, Congressman Henry Wise of Virginia, encouraged Graves to demand one more exchange. On the third shot, Cilley was hit in the leg. His femoral artery was severed, and he quickly bled to death.

The public outcry in the nation's capital was swift and loud. The two Southern congressmen involved were publicly castigated for their dedication to an ancient and barbaric ritual. Though the issue had nothing to do with slavery, it was seen by many as typical Southern bullying and violence. A Maine newspaper, *The Argus*, editorialized the violence as just another example of the prevalent Southern attitude "that those who can't be intimidated must be silenced." If nothing else, the duel seemed to highlight the differences between the two sections of the country. Where Northerners were appalled, Southerners were contrite but not particularly concerned.

In the aftermath of the tragedy, lawmakers passed legislation outlawing dueling. As a result, dueling became more secretive and those involved more circumspect in their proceedings. Yet the practice continued—almost exclusively among or between Southerners—until the time of the Civil War.

As the spring progressed, petitions continued to pour into Congress. Knowing that the Patton gag would prevent the reception of Abolition petitions per se, the anti-slavery societies shifted their emphasis to the fight against the annexation of Texas. The ploy fooled no one, least of all pro-slavery Southerners who wished to avoid the issue. However, it soon became apparent that if the House ignored petitions against annexing Texas, it also would have to ignore those in favor of so doing.

There seemed no way out but to submit the entire lot to a special committee appointed by Speaker of the House James K. Polk. Of the nine committee members, five were from slaveholding states. At least six of the nine were supporters of President Van Buren, who had already spoken out against the abolitionists. It was not an auspicious mix for the future.

Monday, May 14th, promised to be one of celebration for the anti-slavery community of Philadelphia. The day opened with the official dedication of Pennsylvania Hall, which was located within walking distance of Independence Hall. The three-story building, built at a cost of $40,000, had been completely financed by the sale of $20 shares to 2000 associates. Pennsylvania Hall was the realization of long years of dreams by the abolitionists. No longer would they have to scrounge and beg for public meeting halls to rent for their gatherings. Located on the first floor were committee rooms and stores, while a huge hall and gallery occupied the second and third floors. Here would be a citadel dedicated not just to abolition, but to free-thinking for everyone. Many saw the opening of Pennsylvania Hall as a bright new day for free speech and free assembly.

Many others, unfortunately, did not.

Many of the same abolitionists who had happily attended the opening ceremonies earlier in the day of Pennsylvania Hall gathered that night to witness the marriage of Theodore Weld and Angelina Grimké. Having been brought together by their efforts on behalf of the anti-slavery movement, and sharing the same passions and desires for the cause, theirs seemed like a perfect match.

Their joy in the occasion would soon be overshadowed; for that night dangerous forces were at work. The next morning, notices began to appear throughout the city, warning the people of Philadelphia that:

> A convention to effect the immediate emancipation of the slaves throughout the country is in session in this city, and it is the duty of citizens who entertain a proper respect for the Constitution of the Union and the right of property to interfere.

The notice called for an assembly the following day (Wednesday) to demand the dispersal of the abolitionists from the newly opened hall they had helped to finance.

As Wednesday night arrived, a crowd estimated at over 3,000 jammed into the second-floor "grand saloon" of Pennsylvania Hall. But before the meeting could get underway, a mob broke into the downstairs lobby. Amid the shouting from below and outside, Angelina Grimké was called upon to say a few words. She spoke out bravely above the noise and confusion.

> Those voices without ought to awaken and call out our warmest sympathies. Deluded beings! "They know not what they do." ... Do you ask, "what has the North to do with slavery?" Hear it—hear it. Those voices without tell us that the spirit of slavery is here, and has been roused to wrath by our abolition speeches and conventions: for surely liberty would not foam and tear herself with rage.... This opposition shows that slavery has done its deadliest work in the hearts of our citizens.... [C]ast out ... the spirit of slavery from your own hearts, and then lend your aid to convert the South.... The great men of this country will not do this work; the church will never do it. A desire to please the world, to keep the favor of all parties and of all conditions, makes them dumb on this and every

other unpopular subject. They have become worldly-wise, and therefore God, in his wisdom, employs them not to carry on his plans of reformation and salvation. He hath chosen the foolish things of the world to confound the wise, and the weak to overcome the mighty.

As a Southerner I feel that it is my duty to stand up here to-night and bear testimony against slavery. I have seen it—I have seen it. I know it has horrors that can never be described. I was brought up under its wing: I witnessed for many years its demoralizing influences, and its destructiveness to human happiness. It is admitted by some that the slave is not happy under the worst forms of slavery. But I have never seen a happy slave. I have seen him dance in his chains, it is true; but he was not happy. There is a wide difference between happiness and mirth. Man cannot enjoy the former while his manhood is destroyed, and that part of the being which is necessary to the making, and the enjoyment of happiness, is completely blotted out. The slaves, however, may be, and sometimes are, mirthful. When hope is extinguished, they say, "let us eat and drink for to-morrow we die." (Just then stones were thrown at the windows,—a great noise without, and commotion within.)

What is a mob? What would the breaking of every window be? What would the levelling of this Hall be? Any evidence that we are wrong, or that slavery is a good and wholesome institution? What if the mob should now burst in upon us, break up our meeting and commit violence upon our persons—would this be anything compared with what the slaves endure? ...

Many persons go to the South for a season, and are hospitably entertained in the parlor and at the table of the slave-holder. They never enter the huts of the slaves; they know nothing of the dark side of the picture, and they return home with praises on their lips of the generous characters of those with whom they tarried. Or if they have witnessed the cruelties of slavery, by remaining silent spectators they have naturally become callous—an insensibility has ensued which prepares them to apologize for barbarity. Nothing but the corrupting influence of slavery on the hearts of the Northern people can induce them to apologize for it; and much will have been done for the destruction of Southern slavery when we have so reformed the North that no one here will be willing to risk his reputation by advocating or even excusing the holding of men as property.... (Another outbreak of mobocratic spirit, and some confusion in the house.)

... I feel that all this disturbance is but an evidence that our efforts are the best that could have been adopted, or else the friends of slavery would not care for what we say and do.... Many times have I wept in the land of my birth, over the system of slavery....

Grimké was particularly harsh towards those of the North who refused to cooperate in the struggle. "[O]n this subject," she argued, "there is no such thing as neutral ground. If you are on what you suppose to be neutral ground, the South look upon you as on the side of the oppressor."

Again she was interrupted, as the sound of stones being thrown against the windows filled the room. "There is nothing to be feared," she claimed, "by those who would stop our mouths, but they themselves should fear and tremble." She interpreted the actions of the mob outside as proof that the abolitionists had "caused the Bastille of slavery to totter".

She called upon the women in the audience to "especially let me urge you to petition." She readily admitted that "men who hold the rod over slaves, rule in the councils of the nation; and they deny our right to petition and to remonstrate."

Yet she insisted that the sending of petitions to Congress, even though they be ignored, was not a futile effort. "The fact that the South looks with jealousy upon our measures shows that they are effectual," she said.

Finally, after speaking for over an hour, the noise of the mob outside seemed to have somewhat subsided, and the decision was made to end the meeting. Yet the memories of Garrison's mobbing in Boston and Lovejoy's murder in Alton must have been in the minds of many of those present as they prepared to leave the hall in the face of the angry men outside. Slowly, they exited, mercifully unmolested by the remnants of the throng that had raged against their meeting.

The next morning, the abolitionists returned amid rumors that the hall would be torched. When the mayor arrived to assess the situation, he convinced those assembled to adjourn and disperse for the sake of public tranquility. They quietly complied with his wishes.

Within minutes of their departure, the mob rushed the hall, breaking open the doors with axes. They ran wildly through the building, smashing furniture and overturning files and records. The gas lines were cut, and a torch was applied to the temple of free speech. The zinc roof of the hall burned with a hot blue flame, easily seen throughout most of the city, the same city that had not far from that very spot witnessed the signing of both the Declaration of Independence and the Constitution.

Local firemen soon arrived, pouring water upon neighboring buildings to prevent the spread of the flames. The roof caved in within an hour, and by midnight only blackened walls remained.

Could there be a more pathetic image than the senseless destruction of Pennsylvania Hall? While this action, like so many other incidents within this narrative, cannot be directly contributed to slaveholders, it seemed clear to most Northerners that the mob had been excited by visions of negro amalgamation and the fear of black equality. This sense of racial paranoia would continue to be one of the South's strongest weapons in its fight against anti-slavery.

And also, as in so many other cases, this blatant disregard of the rights of the abolitionists tended to rebound to their benefit as more and more people took the time to consider their arguments and beliefs.

Many people in the nation considered the subject of Texas to be one of the most momentous issues of the times. Literally thousands of petitions were flowing in to Congress imploring the federal government not to annex the newly independent nation. Memorials from Northern legislatures echoed this prayer, while Southern state governments were calling just as frantically to gather Texas to the nation's bosom. It was with feverish excitement that the House awaited the committee's report. Many Northerners were concerned that the pro-slavery majority of the committee would sway things towards annexation, though few could have suspected the committee's ultimate response to the situation.

On Wednesday, June 13, George Dromgoole of Virginia presented the report on Texas to the House of Representatives. The suggestion was that the members of the committee be "discharged from the further consideration of the whole subject, and that all the papers relating thereto, and to them referred, be laid on the table."

That was it. End of discussion, before it had barely begun.

In the expressed opinion of the committee, since the subject of Texas had never officially been opened upon the floor, there was no need to waste time with it. Adams pointedly "propounded an inquiry of Mr. Dromgoole whether the committee had [even] read the petitions." The Virginia delegate, with haughty dignity, denied Adams's right to pose such a question.

In the eyes of many Southerners—and, apparently, this committee—it would be dangerous to open the floor to a discussion on Texas. Such a discussion would, inevitably, lead to the taboo subject of slavery, which was the last thing they wanted.

Unfortunately for them, and for the exact same reasons, this was exactly what Adams desired. Adams's hope was that with "the Texas question once opened, the gag upon the slavery topics could no longer be effectively maintained."

By the rules of the House, the afternoon hours were reserved for business. The morning hour was given to delegates to speak. By parliamentary procedure, once a delegate "had the floor," he was not required to relinquish it until he was done having his say. Within a few years, this practice would become common in the Senate, where speakers would drone on and on interminably to obstruct congressional business. We now refer to such a practice as a filibuster.

In Adams's case, his intention was two-fold: he wished to forestall any possible action on annexing Texas, and he hoped to circumvent the gag rule.

On June 16, he again questioned whether Dromgoole had ever read the documents that had been entrusted to his attention. In a dig at the other committee members, Adams explained that he "had intended to propound the same inquiry to each individual member of the committee, but he would abstain from doing so, as some of the members ... might find it difficult to decide between their obligations to duty and party considerations."

Eventually Hugh Legare, a committee member from South Carolina, boldly responded to Adams:

> Mr. Legare: For myself, I have not read the papers, or looked into them, nor was I bound to.
> Mr. Adams: I understand the gentleman from South Carolina now formally to admit that he has never looked into the documents referred to the committee on the subject of Texas at all.
> Mr. Legare: Not one of them.
> Mr. Adams: Into not one of them?
> Mr. Legare: Not one.

Having established to his own satisfaction that the committee had not seriously studied or considered the situation, Adams set out to do what he could to rectify their omission. He lectured the House on the history of slavery, on the gag rule, on the annexation of Texas, on anything remotely associated with the issue just so that he could fill his hour and not relinquish the floor.

From the *Congressional Globe*:

> Wednesday, June 20th: Mr. ADAMS resumed his remarks on the report of the Committee on Foreign Affairs, on the subject of the annexation of Texas.... Mr. A. had not concluded when the orders of the day were called for.
> Thursday, June 21st: Mr. ADAMS resumed his remarks in opposition to the report of the Committee on Foreign Affairs on the annexation of Texas[.] ... Mr. A. again gave way, without concluding, to the orders of the day.
> Friday, June 22nd: Mr. ADAMS continued his remarks in opposition to the report of the Committee on Foreign Affairs on the subject of the annexation of Texas[.] ... In the course of his remarks, Mr. A. has given a detailed account of the proceedings of the House in relation to their actions upon the subject of petitions regarding slavery, and the annexation of Texas, as incidental to that subject. He has given, in order, the different times when petitions and resolutions of State Legislatures have been presented to the House, and has stated the action of the House thereon. He has also read and commented upon many of the memorials and resolutions, with arguments to show that the actions of the House had not been correct in principle, nor in accordance with the wishes of a large portion of the people. Mr. A. then gave way for the orders.
> Saturday, June 23rd: Mr. ADAMS proceeded in his remarks on the report of the Committee on Foreign Affairs, in relation to the annexation of Texas, and was referring to the right of slaves to petition, and the proceedings in the House last Congress upon his tendering a petition of that character[.]

> ... Mr. A. was proceeding in this line of remarks, when
> The SPEAKER called him to order, saying that the remarks were irrelevant to the subject under consideration.
> Mr. ADAMS said he was putting an extreme case, by way of illustration, which was in order.
> Mr. LEGARE rose, and said he felt compelled to call the gentleman from Massachusetts to order; and cries of order were heard in various parts of the House.
> [After some futile arguments in his own behalf] the decision of the CHAIR was sustained by the House, and Mr. ADAMS thus declared to be out of order. [He did, however, still maintain the floor at the end of the day.]

By Friday, July 6, the *Congressional Globe* felt the need to remind its readers that "Mr. ADAMS had taken the floor [on June 13th], and has kept possession of it for the morning hour ever since, ... and has it still, not having concluded this morning."

Saturday, July 7, was the last scheduled day of that session of Congress. "Mr. [Samuel] INGHAM entreated Mr. ADAMS to give way this morning[.]"

"Mr. ADAMS, however, declined, and went on with his remarks." Significantly, "Mr. A. had not concluded when the orders of the day were called for." This meant that when the next session on Congress convened in December, Adams would still have the floor, to continue his remarks upon Texas if he so desired.

While the Southern delegates were no doubt enraged by Adams's behavior, he accomplished at least some of what he had set out to do. That is, he held up any serious consideration of annexing Texas. In doing so, he made it a matter of public record that many in the nation were against such an action.

So thorough was he that on October 12 Texas officially withdrew its offer of annexation due to the lack of action in Congress on the proposition. It seemed that at least for the time being the spread of slavery had been curtailed.

On November 27 and 28, Dr. Erasmus Hudson and Rev. Nathaniel Colver presented anti-slavery lectures at the Baptist Church of Georgetown, (Redding) Connecticut. Both meetings were disrupted by the hecklings of anti-abolitionist mobs. According to a local resident, inhabitants of the town were awakened about two o'clock the following morning "by a tremendous report and rumbling noise, which jarred the houses and broke the windows in the immediate neighborhood" of the church. Someone, it seems, had exploded a keg of gunpowder under the church in protest of the meetings that had been held there. "The pulpit was demolished, the front of the building displaced several feet, the windows broken out, and the walls destroyed."

Despite such intimidation, Hudson and Colver managed to organize an anti-slavery society in Georgetown the following month that was one of the first in the State.

When the House of Representatives reconvened on December 3, one of its new members was 43-year-old Joshua Reed Giddings of Ohio. Giddings was the first self-avowed abolitionist to be elected to Congress. He would soon join the ranks of John Quincy Adams and William Slade in trying to argue against slavery before the House.

[In March of 1842, Giddings would make such strong statements in the House concerning the rights of slaves in the "Creole" case that he was formally censured for his comments. Afterwards, he resigned in order to appeal to his constituents, who immediately reelected him by a strong majority.]

A scant eight days after the session opened, and before Adams, Slade, or newcomer Giddings could present any petitions, a motion was made for a new gag rule. This new rule—the fourth one in as many years—would differ from the preceding three in two significant ways.

First, there would be no waiting for the issue to be introduced. It was, so to speak, a preemptive strike against the abolitionist fanatics. The rule would be in place before the need for it arose.

The second, and perhaps more startling difference, was that this gag rule was introduced by a Northerner, Charles G. Atherton of New Hampshire. Atherton's motion consisted of five separate resolutions that would be debated and voted upon over the course of two days.

The first resolution was clearly a declaration of states' rights:

> *Resolved*, That this government is a Government of limited powers, and that, by the Constitution of the United States, Congress has no jurisdiction whatever over the institution of slavery in the several States of the Confederacy.

This resolution, which echoed the time-honored belief that the Northern states could not interfere with slavery in the states where it already existed, passed easily by a vote of 198 to 6 on the first day of deliberations.

The second resolution quite accurately described the true reason behind the flood of petitions:

> *Resolved*, That petitions for the abolition of slavery in the District of Columbia and the Territories of the United States, and against the removal of slaves from one State to another [that is, the inter-state slave trade], are a part of a plan of operations set on foot to affect the institution of slavery in the several States, and thus indirectly to destroy that institution within their limits.

This resolution passed on December 12 by a vote of 136 to 65. The third resolution was:

> *Resolved*, That Congress has no right to do that indirectly which it cannot do directly; and that the agitation of the subject of slavery in the District of Columbia or the Territories, as a means, and with the view, of disturbing or overthrowing that institution in the several States, is against the true spirit and meaning of the Constitution, an infringement of the rights of the States affected, and a breach of the public faith upon which they entered into the Confederacy.

Certain members insisted upon breaking this up into two branches. The passage that ended with "directly" passed by a vote of 173 to 30. The remaining branch, on a separate vote, passed 164 to 40.

> *Resolved*, That the Constitution rests on the broad principle of equality among the members of this Confederacy, and that Congress, in the exercise of its acknowledged powers, has no right to discriminate between the institutions of one portion of the States and another with a view of abolishing the one and promoting the other.

The initial branch of this resolution, ending at "Confederacy," passed by a vote of 180-26, with the rest of this resolution passing 174 to 24. It was the fifth and final resolution that actually encompassed this session's "gag rule."

> *Resolved*, Therefore, That all attempts on the part of Congress to abolish slavery in the District of Columbia or the Territories, or to prohibit the removal of slaves from State to State, or to discriminate between the institutions of one portion of the Confederacy and another, with the view aforesaid, are in violation of the Constitution, destructive of the fundamental principle on which the Union of these States rests, and beyond the jurisdiction of Congress and that every petition, memorial, resolution, proposition, or paper, touching or relating in any way, or to any extent whatever, to slavery as aforesaid, or the abolition thereof, shall, on the presentation thereof, without any further action thereon, be laid upon the table, without being debated, printed, or referred.

This resolution, like the two before it, was also voted on in two separate branches. The first section, up to and including the second time the word "Congress" appears, passed by a vote of 146 to 52. The final portion, which effectively prohibited the introduction or discussion of any slavery, related topics, passed 126 to 78.

With the passing of the Atherton Resolutions and the withdrawal of the Texas offer of annexation, there was no need for John Quincy Adams to continue his filibuster of the previous session, so he relinquished the floor. However, it would not be long before he, Slade and Giddings were again embroiled in controversy with the rest of the House.

It was during the fall of 1838 that American emissary Richard Rush returned onboard the ship *Mediator* from his trip to England to secure the legacy of James Smithson. He presented to the United 104,960 gold sovereigns (plus 8 shillings and sevenpence) stuffed into 105 sacks. Each sack held 1,000 gold sovereigns (except the last, which held only 960). The sacks were packed into 11 boxes (ten of which held 10 sacks, the final only 5), each box (but the last) weighing 187 pounds.

Once delivered to the treasury, all but two of the coins—which are now part of the Smithsonian Institution's collection—were melted down and reminted into $10 U.S. gold pieces. The total worth of the gift was $508,318.46. (About $50 million today.) Congress was still undecided what to do with the money. Over the course of the next few years, John Quincy Adams would be instrumental in establishing the Smithsonian as a national organization for the diffusion of scientific knowledge.

On February 6, 1938, during a brief sojourn in St. Louis, Dr. John Emerson married Irene Sanford. His return trip to Fort Snelling with his wife and Dred and Harriett Scott was made aboard the steamboat *Gypsey*. Somewhere along the way, but certainly well above the northern boundary of the state of Missouri, Harriett gave birth to a child named Eliza. This child, born of slave parents but in a free territory, was legally free. However, neither of her parents were aware of that fact, and Emerson was certainly not going to tell them.

Anti-slavery petitions continued to make their way into Congress. It has been said that they filled a room 20 by 30 by 14-feet, packed to the ceiling. James Birney, who was now the secretary for the American Anti-Slavery Society, estimated the total number of signatures on petitions against slavery to Congress that year alone had been one-half million. Scholars disagree about the numbers, some citing figures as high as two million (or more) for the combined total of the peak petition-writing years. It's hard to arrive at a totally accurate count, but it seems certain that the number was significant, particularly when one considers that the upcoming (1840) census would enumerate a total population for the Northern (free) states of just 9,698,014.

Historian Dwight Dumond made a particular study of the third session of the 25th Congress (the one that had begun with the Atherton resolutions of December 1838 and ended in March of 1839). According to Dumond, there were 1,496 antislavery petitions presented during this single session of Congress, bearing a total of 163,845 signatures. New York State supplied the largest number of petitions with 362, followed by Massachusetts with 346, Vermont with 177, Ohio with 171, and Pennsylvania and Maine each sending more than 100. All of which seems to belie the Southern claim that such petitions were the work of a few fanatics.

Not surprisingly, it was John Quincy Adams who presented the largest number of these, being personally responsible for 693. (It was not necessary for a petition to be presented by a representative from the state in which it originated. Many petition senders specifically requested Adams to do the honor of their memorials.) William Slade was second at 430, and newcomer Giddings was third with 42. One can only imagine Southern representatives cringing each time one of these three began to speak.

[As recently as the 1930s, historian Gilbert Barnes claimed that "truckloads" of these petitions were still being "stored here and there about the Capitol." Barnes also described finding "a caretaker in the Capitol keeping his stove hot with bundles of antislavery petitions. There were so many of them, the caretaker said, that those he used would never be missed."]

So while it may be impossible to say with any certainty how much support the abolitionists had in the North, it seems clear that they had more than the conventional histories would credit to them. Nor were their numbers as feeble as many authors suggest. It has been said that by the end of 1838, there were as many as 1,350 antislavery societies in the United States, with close to 250,000 members among them.

In May 1838, Federal troops were sent to Georgia to begin the 1,000-mile evacuation of the Cherokee to their new western reservations. The army officer in charge of the relocation operation was General Winfield Scott. Scott and his troops moved the Indians under deplorable conditions. They arrived in Oklahoma in the late fall, facing one of the most brutal winters on record. Many of the Indians succumbed to exposure or disease along the way.

The removal was not completed until the following spring, by which time over 4,000 members of the tribe had died. This journey has become known in Cherokee legend as "Nunna daul Tsuny," literally "The Trail Where They Cried" or "The Trail of Tears."

Canals in the Northwest were contributing to the rapid development of cities along the Great Lakes, diverting much of the Mississippi River trade. By 1838, more grain and flour was shipped through Buffalo than through New Orleans. By the year 1840, canal mileage in the nation totaled 3,326. The newly developing railroad was not far behind, with an total of 2,818 miles. Pennsylvania led the nation in both, with 954 miles of canals and 576 miles of railroads.

Railroads were about to outstrip the waterways: By 1850, there were 3,698 miles of canals, but railroads now totaled 9,021 miles. Pennsylvania still led the nation that year with 954 miles of canals, but New York commanded in railroad mileage with 1,361, which was more than the total miles of both canals and railroads for the entire country just 20 years earlier.

On June 28, Great Britain celebrated the coronation of Queen Victoria with festivals and celebrations. As a reigning monarch for over 60 years, she would come to symbolize both her nation and her era.

A French painter and physicist named Louis-Jacques Mandé Daguerre had nearly completed the development of his procedure for capturing an image by exposing a plate sensitized with chemicals to light. He would publicly reveal his technique the following year, and it would be hailed as a stunning scientific achievement. The process would become known as the "daguerreotype." This fledgling art of photography would come of age during the Civil War, allowing men such as Matthew Brady, Alexander Gardner and many others to bring the harsh realities of the conflict home to the American public with a vividness never before experienced by noncombatants.

On September 3, Frederick Douglass escaped from slavery in Maryland. He would soon become one of the most celebrated abolitionist orators in the nation. In 1845 he published his autobiography. This work, coupled with his presence as a powerful and emotional speaker, would bring the vivid reality of Southern slavery to many Northerners for the first time.

During the summer of 1838, the United States launched its most ambitious voyage of scientific study since the Lewis & Clark Corps of Discovery over a quarter of a century earlier. Labeled the "U.S. Exploring Expedition," it consisted of six vessels with 82 officers, 342 sailors, and nine naturalists and artists. The goal of the "ExEx," as it was called, was to extensively research and map the South Pacific, primarily as an aid to American foreign commerce, but also, as expressed in the official orders, "to extend the bounds of science and to promote knowledge." The flagship of the small fleet was the *Vincennes*, the same ship that had completed a celebrated circumnavigation of the globe just a few years earlier. The captain of the *Vincennes* and commander of the mission was 40-year-old Charles Wilkes. (In 1861 it would be Wilkes who would be responsible for the seizure of Confederate ambassadors James Mason and John Slidell from the British mail-steamer *Trent*, thereby precipitating an international incident that almost brought Great Britain into war against the union.)

For four years, Fanny Kemble and Pierce Butler had been married. Except for the time she spent apart from him while she visited in England, they had lived together in Philadelphia. She knew that her husband's status and income was based upon slavery, but she had not yet seen a slave plantation firsthand. While her feelings tended towards sympathy for the slaves in a general, philosophical way, she had never encountered the harsh realities of the system. That was about to change.

Butler had spent too many years away from his plantations, too many years allowing his affairs to be managed by others while he was absent. In an effort to bolster his fortunes, he returned to Georgia in the fall of 1838. It is not clear why he permitted his wife to accompany him. Some historians have suggested that he hoped to wean her of her emerging abolitionist tendencies by allowing her to see slavery firsthand. He considered himself an "enlightened" slave-owner, and apparently was niavely convinced that his wife would accept the peculiar institution as readily as he did. In this he was mistaken.

Fanny Kemble's experiences are important to consider. Many Europeans—such as Martineau and de Tocqueville—had opportunities to observe slavery while visiting America as outsiders. But none were ever drawn so fully into the life of a Southern slave plantation in quite the manner as was Kemble. That part of her life, however, will have to be told somewhere else.

Unnoticed at the time was an event that would ultimately prove to be of great significance to the nation. On May 10, on a little farm in Bel Air, Maryland, just 25 miles south of the Mason-Dixon line, was born a child who would grow up to alter the course of history in a way that few others ever had. He was given the name John Wilkes Booth.

Epilogue

The story of the abolitionists and their struggles against slavery does not end in 1838 as this study does. When I commenced this project, I decided to limit the discussion to the 10-year period that has now come to a close. This is not meant to suggest that there were no abolitionist activities after 1838. The rest of their story must be told at another time, in another place.

In closing, it may be appropriate to summarize the accomplishments of these 10 years. The record has shown there were always individuals in America who spoke out against slavery, but it wasn't until this period that their numbers increased from just a few solitary voices to become a large and dedicated community. During this time, they were often the target of both verbal and physical abuse. While consistently critical of slavery and its proponents, at no time have we seen them directing similar abuse towards the slaveowners, despite the fact that the conventional picture of them paints them as insurrectionists and firebrands. That they spoke boldly and forthrightly cannot be denied. That they were the heralds of a message many in the nation wished not to hear is just as certain.

What is perhaps not as clear is whether, in the long run, they helped or hindered their cause with their agitation. Again, much of the conventional wisdom would suggest that they caused as much harm as good. Clearly they enraged the pro-slavery element of the South, with the consequent loss of "good feeling" between the two sections.

It has often been stated in the years since the Civil War—as it was claimed by many slaveowners prior to the war—that the abolitionists' agitations were responsible for the stricter slave laws and black codes that were enacted throughout the South in the 30 years prior to the war. However, to place such blame upon them seems at least a little disingenuous. The abolitionists were not responsible for the South's commitment to slavery, nor for the slaveowners' increased vigilance on its behalf when it came under systematic attack. It was the slavery-dependent South that refused to abandon its antiquated labor system that was at fault.

The abolitionists universally acknowledged that it would not be easy or painless for the country to give up slavery. History proved them correct. Yet there is absolutely no evidence to support the belief that emancipation would have been accomplished either sooner or less destructively without their contributions. Undoubtedly, slaveowners would have continued to own their chattel as long as there was no overpowering reason for them not to. If the abolitionists had not provided such a reason by forcing the nation to consider and address the issue of slavery, who would have?

Each reader is, of course, welcome to disagree with these conclusions about the importance of the abolitionists. Yet I hope all will agree that this fascinating decade of American history deserves to be more carefully considered and more fully appreciated.

Whether one agrees or disagrees with the policies of the abolitionists, I for one would like to think that we can all admire their courage and strength in standing up as they did for the rights of others. Their story deserves to be told and remembered.

APPENDIX 1

Influence of Slaveholding States on the Federal Government

Introduction

I have tried to demonstrate in the accompanying charts that in the years prior to the American Civil War the slave states wielded an influence in the federal government far superior to that which their numbers alone would have warranted. While not directly related to the issue of abolitionism, this information demonstrates why it was often so hard for antislavery sentiment to have any impact upon the national government. It may be overstating the facts to say that the South dominated the government of the United States during these years; but it is an unarguable mathematical fact that the slave states, with only about one-third of the total white population throughout most of the pre-war period, controlled the majority of the important government positions during this time. The only place where such control was not obvious was in the Senate, but only because the number of slave and free states—and, therefore, the number of senators from each region—was approximately equal throughout this period.

The numbers represented in the chart on the following page indicate the number of representatives for which each region was eligible in any given period during the 72 years prior to the Civil War. The number was determined by adding to the total white population three fifths of the slave population. Of course, the actual number of representatives physically present at any one time would vary from day to day, due to such factors as travel delays, illness, death, conflicting business, etc.

House of Representatives - Actual Numbers

Therefore, the numbers given on these pages should not be considered as a strict accounting of the population of the House at any particular moment as much as a relative comparison of the potential numbers present.

It should not be assumed that every representative from a slave state was a slaveowner (or even, necessarily, pro-slavery) However, the delegates from the slave states did tend to be relatively united in their defense of the "peculiar institution" that they tended to view, not without some degree of justification, as essential to their way of life. So it may be fair to consider these numbers as the number of slave representatives.

Likewise, it cannot be assumed that all free state representatives held anti-slavery sentiments. In fact, many of them shared the South's view that the wellbeing of the nation was dependent on slavery. So even though the number of free Representatives surpassed the number of slave representatives every year after 1804, it would probably be wrong to conclude that the majority of the members of the House were, at any time, personally against slavery.

The 1st Congress convened in New York City on March 4, 1789. The number of representatives apportioned to each state had been based upon estimates provided by delegates to the Constitutional Convention. At this time only five (5) of the original 13 states had already abolished slavery (Rhode Island in 1774, Pennsylvania in 1780, Massachusetts in 1781, New Hampshire in 1781 and Connecticut in 1784). The remaining two (2) that would ultimately be considered free states would join their ranks in 1799 (New York) and 1804 (New Jersey). As these remaining two original slave states became free states, the numbers of the former would be reduced, and the numbers of the latter would be correspondingly increased.

The first federal census was conducted in 1790, and the number of representatives for which each state was eligible was recalculated based upon these new numbers (again counting each slave as three fifths of a white man). Of course, these numbers were not immediately available, and there were delays before elections could be held and the newly elected officers actually made their appearances in Congress. No attempt has been made while compiling this chart to adjust for these individual differences.

Subsequent to the first Census, a new population count has been conducted at every 10-year interval. As the populations of the states increased, the number of representatives for which each state was eligible also increased. As in the time following the original census, these numbers were not immediately available, nor were these new positions always filled in a consistently timely manner. Therefore, there would have been an ever-increasing number of new representatives arriving in Washington during the year or two directly following each new census until the maximum allotment was reached. Again, no effort has been made here to reflect these transition periods within this chart. Instead, the numbers for each census year are indicated simply as those which would have been used once all the dust had settled.

A third factor that affected the number of representatives from each region was the occasional introduction of new states into the Union. Normally, new states tried to send their representatives to Washington as soon as authorized to do so by Congress though when that would be during the congressional session would vary in the case of each newly entering state. On these charts, the increase in delegates due to such an addition has been indicated according to the year of the state's entry into the Union, and in individual cases may not precisely reflect when that state's delegate(s) actually arrived.

Despite such limitations, I feel that there is some value in this chart. It clearly shows that the free state representation surpassed the slave state representation practically since the formation of the Union. It is significant to note, however, that despite their simple majority, the free states never had the two third majority that would have been necessary to pass legislation concerning the existence of (or even the extension of) slavery.

It is also interesting to consider the situation of the Speaker of the House. At the beginning of each session of Congress, the representatives elect one of their members to preside over their deliberations. The speaker can often be very influential in controlling the business of the House. Judging by the number of representatives from each region, one would expect the free States to have controlled this coveted position due to their majority, but in fact they seldom did.

In the 1st through 36th Congresses—the years 1789–1861—Congress met for 79 sessions totaling 11,275 days. During this time, the coveted speaker position was held by a representative of a slave state during 53 sessions, for a total aggregate of 7,562 hours (just over two-thirds of the time). A free state representative was speaker of the House for just 26 sessions totaling 3,713 hours. Though it wasn't always easy for the South to capture this position, and on at least 10 major occasions between 1809 and 1859 there were heated disputes over selection of a speaker. Four of these—one each in 1839, 1849, 1855 and 1859—held up the business of the House for weeks or months at a time. Most of these disputes arose over the issue of slavery, or, more precisely, on the opinions of the various candidates for the position of speaker upon slavery.

While this chart adequately demonstrates the numerical superiority that the free states held throughout most of the years prior to the Civil War, the next chart is, if anything, even more revealing.

Appendix 1

The numbers represented in the chart on the following page indicate the number of Representatives that each region would have been eligible for in any given year if the apportionment had been based solely on white population (that is, if each slave had not counted as three-fifths of a white man). In other words, this chart is more nearly a representation of the relative white populations of the two regions than the previous chart was.

All the limitations discussed with the first chart hold equally true with this chart. That is, at any given time the actual number of representatives appearing in the House could have been slightly different than the total indicated here. However, I think comparison of this chart with the first one makes it strikingly clear just how politically beneficial the three-fifths rule was to the slave states. In every Congress after the First, the number of slave representatives was increased by anywhere from 17 to 24 members by virtue of the three-fifths rule. And bear in mind that most of the important legislation that was passed, or rejected, by the House during these years was decided by a margin of less than these additional "slave" representatives.

It seems certain that the American public never had this information presented to it during these years in quite this form. However, it seems equally likely that those individuals who were politically knowledgeable about the workings of the government had the same intuitive feel for the political iniquities that the three-fifths rule introduced that this chart should make obvious.

For example, on October 16, 1854, Abraham Lincoln made a speech at Peoria, Illinois. Within this speech, he referred to this precise political inequality when he said:

> [T]here are constitutional relations between the slave and free States which are degrading to the latter.... [I]n the control of the government—the management of the partnership affairs—they have greatly the advantage of us.... [I]n ascertaining the number of ... [representatives], five slaves are counted as being equal to three whites. The slaves do not vote; they are only counted and so used to swell the influence of the white people's votes. The practical effect of this is more aptly shown by a comparison of the States of South Carolina and Maine. South Carolina has six representatives, and so has Maine[.] ...This is precise equality so far; and of course they are equal in senators, each having two. Thus in the control of the government the two States are equals precisely. But how are they in the number of their white people? Maine has 581, 813, while South Carolina has 274,567; Maine has twice as many as South Carolina, and 32,679 over. Thus, each white man in South Carolina is more than the double of any man in Maine. This is all because South Carolina, besides her free people, has 384,984 slaves. The South Carolinian has precisely the same advantage over the white man in every other free State as well as in Maine. He is more than the double of any one of us in this

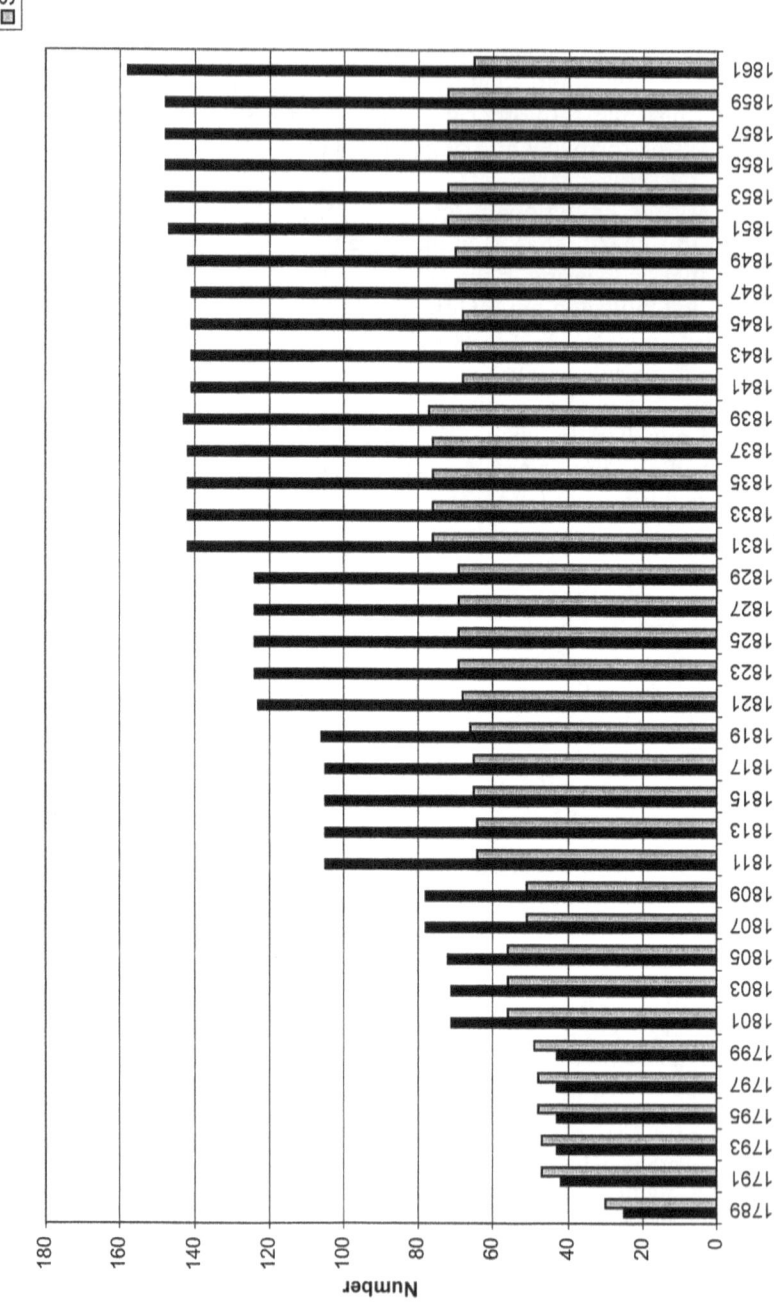

crowd. The same advantage, but not to the same extent, is held by all the citizens of the slave States over those of the free; and it is an absolute truth, without an exception, that there is no voter in any slave State, but who has more legal power in the government than any voter in any free State. There is no instance of exact equality; and the disadvantage is against us the whole chapter through.

Speeches such as this have given rise to the oft-repeated claim that abolitionism was politically motivated. If the South was no longer able to count each of its slaves as three fifths of a white, then the classic Southern argument goes, the North would "take over" the government, and the South would no longer be in control of its own destiny. While this line of reasoning sounds attractive to many, it rings less than true when one considers the following points.

To begin with, there is no evidence in the period 1789–1860 that Northern legislators ever attempted to tamper with, or repeal, the three-fifths rule. That many Northerners recognized the iniquities in the political situation is obvious as shown in the words of Lincoln. But directly following the passage above, Lincoln said:

> Now all of this is manifestly unfair; yet I do not mention it to complain of it, in so far as it is already settled. It is in the Constitution, and I do not for that cause, or any other cause, propose to destroy, or alter, or disregard the Constitution. I stand to it, fairly, fully, and firmly.

If the "true" aim of abolitionism had been a political one the Northern legislators would have been assailing the three-fifths rule directly, which seems never to have taken place.

Another point this political argument misses is why the South should be so much more entitled to be in control of its own destiny than the North. If a democracy is to be run based upon the will of the majority, than the North *should* have been in control of the government after its population had surpassed that of the slave states in 1800. The North was not trying to usurp the South's control, but simply struggling to exert its own fair share.

The numbers represented in the chart on the following page indicate the number of senators for which each region was eligible. In the Senate, each state was allotted two members, thereby the numbers were not affected by the three-fifths rule as had been the case in the House. In the earlier sessions of Congress the slave states outnumbered the free by virtue of the fact that, as explained earlier, not all of the states that would ultimately be considered free had yet abolished slavery. Through most of the early nineteenth century the numbers were fairly equitable, finally achieving precise parity in 1814. With the passage of the Missouri

United States Senate

Compromise in 1820 the idea of keeping the two regions politically balanced seemed to have received the sanction of the federal government.

Surprisingly, even today many people actually believe that the 1820 Compromise stipulated that states, by decree, must enter the Union evenly balanced free-for-slave. This was never the case, though in practice it seemed to happen that way for the next two dozen years. Ultimately, however, there was more free territory available than slave, and, by the eve of the Civil War, the number of delegates from the free Region outstripped the slave.

The presiding officer of the Senate is the President Pro Tempore. Since the number of senators from each region was practically equal throughout this period, one might expect this office to have been equally shared between the free and slave state members. However, this was not the case. Slave state members presided over 59 of the 79 sessions of Congress, their aggregate total of 8,685 hours being more than three times that of the free state members. (Just 20 sessions and 2,590 days).

This timeline on the following page indicates the state of origin of the head of the nation. Within the first 72 years of the country, there were six presidents who hailed from free states, and nine from slave states. Yet even this is deceiving because, with the possible exception of the two Adams, the free state presidents tended to be either pro-slavery or, at the least, not anti-slavery. Perhaps more striking is the fact that no incumbent from a free state was ever reelected, while the first five 5 slave state presidents—all of whom were personally slave owners—served two terms each.

If one takes the time to do the arithmetic it can be seen that the presidency was filled by a free state candidate for a total of just over 22 years, or approximately 31.5 percent of the pre–Civil War period. The slave state presidents accumulated an aggregate of just over 49 years, or 68.5 percent of the period, better than twice that of their Northern counterparts.

As disparate as these numbers seem, it was even worse when one considers the position of Chief Justice of the Supreme Court.

The timeline on page 252 gives the state of origin of the Chief Justice of the Supreme Court. Roger Taney, who presided over the court during the Civil War, was only the fifth person to hold this position. (John Rutledge was never officially appointed chief justice, but he did serve in that capacity for a brief four-month period.)

John Jay, the first chief justice, was from the state of New York. At the time during which he served, it was still a slave state, so I have included his term in office in the total of the slave region. (In fairness to Mr. Jay, it needs to be mentioned that he was personally very anti-slavery. After retiring from the court, he served as the governor of New York.

Presidents of the United States

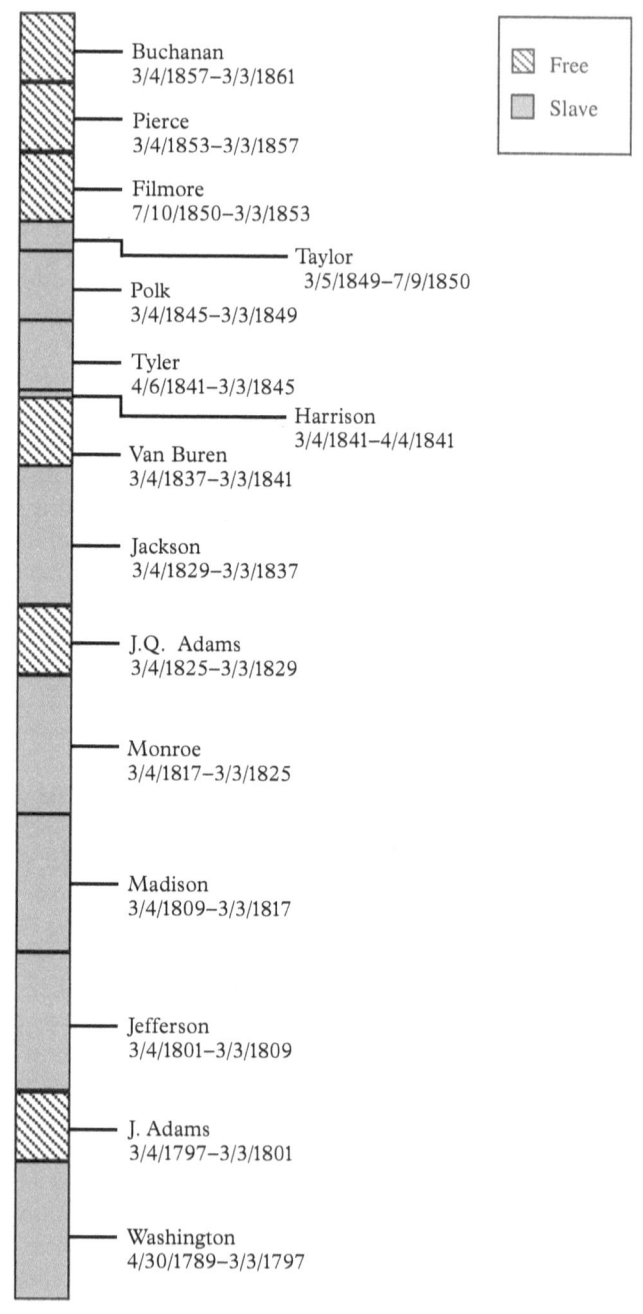

It was he who signed the legislation that abolished slavery in the Empire State.)

The only non-slave state Chief Justice was Oliver Ellsworth of Connecticut, who served for less than five years.

John Marshall of Virginia was one of the most influential justices in the history of the court, serving as chief justice for over 34 years. The available historical evidence makes it clear that Marshall was at one time a slaveowner himself, though I have been unable to determine whether he owned slaves while serving in the court.

Roger Taney of Maryland was also at one time a slaveowner. Taney's biographers state that he freed his own slaves, though it is unclear whether he did so before or during his tenure as chief justice. Taney would make very clear upon the eve of the Civil War just how pro-slavery he was with his majority opinion in the Dred Scott case.

Even including Justice Jay's term along with Ellsworth's, the aggregate total that the chief justice was from a free state was just under 10 years, or barely 14 percent of the total. In the case of the associate justices, there were 30 other men who served on the Supreme Court during the pre–Civil War era, exactly half of whom were from free states. Again, as in the case of the president, many of the justices from the free states might as well have been from the slave states, as the majority of the decisions affecting slavery handed down by the court over the years was sympathetic to, and supportive of, the institution.

So why was it that the slave minority was able to wield such a numerical superiority in so many aspects of the federal government? The good Jeffersonian would say it was because of the "natural aristocracy" of the Southern gentlemen. A cynic might point out that perhaps members of the plantation society, who were used to forcing their wills upon others through bullying and posturing, were more adept at political control than were their Northern counterparts.

I believe that the true strength of the South came from its single-minded devotion to slavery. Northerners might disagree among themselves over tariffs, banking, interstate commerce, internal improvements or any of a myriad of other issues. The result was that it was often impossible to reach, or identify, a Northern consensus on many issues. But you could always count on the Southern politicians to stick together when their "domestic institution" came under attack. It was this common ground that enabled them to maintain their overwhelming presence in the nation's deliberations despite their minority. This powerful pro-slavery element in the federal government certainly made the task of the abolitionists an even more difficult one.

Note: The data for these charts came from *The Historical Statistics of the United States*. The numbers on the chart of the House of Repre-

Chief Justices of the Supreme Court

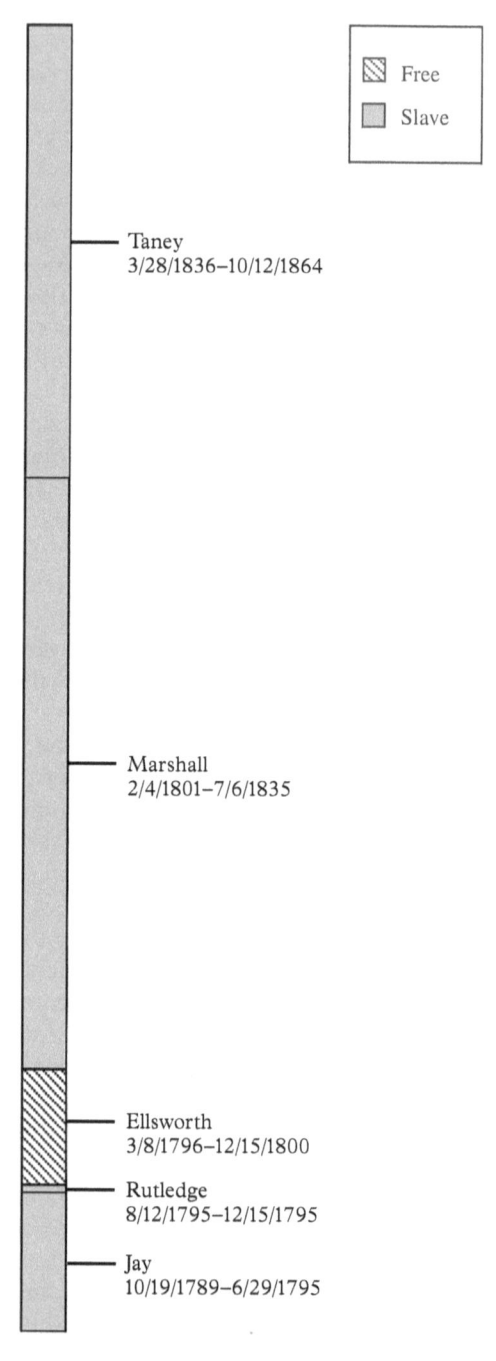

sentives—Without 3/5 Rule were calculated based upon the actual number of Representatives from each state and the relative population of whites to slaves for each. The basic design and format of these charts is my own, though I would like to thank Nick Kulesza, John Gloystein and Ralph Ford for their valuable input during the development stage.

APPENDIX 2

Emily West: The Yellow Rose of Texas

To fully appreciate the story of Emily West (see p. 175) and her unique contribution to Southern history, we need to begin with a bit of linguistic history. By the 1830s "nigger" was common slang for "Negro" and "yellow" was a common vernacular expression for "mulatto" throughout the South. Therefore, when someone was called "yellow" in the antebellum South, they were not being called cowardly. "Yellow" was a racial slur; to call a white person "yellow" was a Southern insult.

In the case of a mulatto, the appellation "yellow" was considered by Southern whites to be no more or less derogatory than the oft-used "nigger" or "darky."

Shortly after Sam Houston's defeat of Santa Anna, the attributes of the comely Emily West were immortalized by some anonymous bard. The earliest copy of this appears to be an unsigned, handwritten manuscript composed contemporaneously with the battle. In it, a "darky" pays homage to his beautiful "yellow" rose. The original lyrics went something like this:

> There's a yellow rose in Texas, that I am going to see
> No other darky knows her, no darky only me
> She cryed so when I left her it like to broke my heart,
> And if I ever find her, we nevermore will part.
>
> (Chorus)
>
> She's the sweetest rose of color this darky ever knew,
> Her eyes are bright as diamonds, they sparkle like the dew;
> You may talk about your Dearest May, and sing of Rosa Lee,
> But the Yellow Rose of Texas beats the belles of Tennessee.

When the Rio Grande is flowing, the starry skies are bright
She walks along the river in the quiet summer night;
She thinks if I remember, when we parted long ago,
I promised to come back again, and not to leave her so.

(Repeat Chorus)

Oh now I'm going to find her, for my heart is full of woe,
And we'll sing the songs together, that we sang so long ago
We'll play the bango gaily, and we'll sing the songs of yore,
And the Yellow Rose of Texas shall be mine forevermore.

It's curious to note that by the time of the Civil War, the song had been popularized to remove its Negro illusions. "Darky" became "soldier," and "She's the sweetest rose of color" had become the more commonly known "She's the sweetest little flower." In 1864, when General John B. Hood's retreating Confederate army added a fourth verse, they probably didn't even realize that they were singing a tribute to a mulatto woman:

And now I'm going southward, for my heart is full of woe,
I'm going back to Georgia, to see my Uncle Joe.
You may talk about your Beauregard, and sing of General Lee,
But the gallant Hood of Texas played hell in Tennessee.

Select Bibliography

America. Various volumes. Chicago: Americanization Department, Veterans of Foreign Wars of the United States, 1925.

Berlin, Ira. *Many Thousands Gone: The First Two Centuries of Slavery in North America*. Cambridge, MA: Belknap Harvard University Press, 1998.

Burleigh, Nina. *The Stranger and the Statesman: James Smithson, John Quincy Adams, and the Making of America's Greatest Museum: The Smithsonian*. New York: William Morrow, 2003.

A Century of Lawmaking for a New Nation: U.S. Congressional Documents and Debates, 1774–1875. Various volumes. Washington, DC: Library of Congress (online).

Child, Lydia Maria. *An Appeal in Favor of That class of Americans Called Africans*. Ed. Carolyn L. Karcher. Amherst: University of Massachusetts Press, 1996.

Clinton, Catherine. *Fanny Kemble's Civil Wars*. New York: Oxford University Press, 2000.

Coclanis, Peter A. *The Shadow of a Dream: Economic Life and Death in the South Carolina Low Country*. New York: Oxford University Press, 1989.

Cooper, William J., Jr. *Liberty and Slavery: Southern Politics to 1860*. New York: Alfred A. Knopf, 1983.

Douglass, Frederick. *Autobiographies*. New York: Library of America, 1994.

Franklin, John Hope, and Schweninger, Loren. *Runaway Slaves: Rebels on the Plantation*. New York: Oxford University Press, 1999.

Freehling, William W. *The Road to Disunion: Secessionists at Bay, 1776–1854*. Oxford: Oxford University Press, 1990.

Garrison, William Lloyd. "A Brief Sketch of the Trial of William Lloyd Garrison, for an Alleged Libel on Francis Todd, of Newburyport, Mass." Boston: Garrison and Knapp, 1831.

Goodman, Paul. *Of One Blood: Abolitionism and the Origins of Racial Equality* Berkeley: University of California Press, 1998.

Gray, Thomas R. *The Confessions of Nat Turner*. Baltimore: Thomas R. Gray, 1831.

Grun, Bernard. *The Timetables of History*. New York: Simon & Schuster, 1975.

Hall, Kermit L., ed. *The Oxford Companion to the Supreme Court*. New York: Oxford University Press, 1992.

Helper, Hinton Rowan. *The Impending Crisis of the South: How to Avoid It.* New York: Burdick Brothers, 1857.
Higginbotham, A. Leon, Jr. *In the Matter of Color: Race and the American Legal Process.* New York: Oxford University Press, 1978.
Historical Statistics of the United States: Colonial Time to 1970. 2 Volumes. Washington, DC: U.S. Department of Commerce, Bureau of the Census, 1975.
History of Pennsylvania Hall Which Was Destroyed by a Mob on the 17th of May, 1838. New York: Negro Universities Press, 1969.
Horton, James Oliver, and Lois E. Horton. *In Hope of Liberty: Culture, Community and Protest Among Northern Free Blacks, 1700-1860.* New York: Oxford University Press, 1997
Jefferson, Thomas. *Writings.* (Ed. by Merrill D. Peterson.) New York: Library of America, 1984.
Kaufman, Kenneth C. *Dred Scott's Advocate: A Biography of Roswell M. Field.* Columbia: University of Missouri, 1996.
Konefsky, Alfred S., and Andrew J. King, eds. *The Papers of Daniel Webster: Legal Papers, Volume 2.* Hanover, NH: University Press of New England, 1983.
Lerner, Gerda: *The Grimké Sisters from South Carolina.* New York: Oxford University Press, 1998.
Malone, Dumas. *Jefferson and His Time.* (6 vols.). Boston: Little, Brown, 1948-1981.
Martineau, Harriet. *Writings on Slavery and the American Civil War.* Ed. Deborah Anna Logan. DeKalb: Northern Illinois University Press, 2002.
Mayer, Henry. *All on Fire.* New York: St. Martin's, 1998.
Mellen, G. W. F.: *An Argument on the Unconstitutionality of Slavery 1841*; reprint, New York: AMS Press, 1973.
Messages and Papers of the Presidents. Various vols. Washington, DC: Bureau of National Literature And Art, 1904.
Miller, William Lee. *Arguing about Slavery.* New York: Alfred A. Knopf, 1996.
_____. *The Business of May Next: James Madison and the Founding.* Charlottesville: University Press of Virginia, 1992.
Nicolay, John G., and John Hay. *Complete Works of Abraham Lincoln.* Various vols. Tennessee: Lincoln Memorial University, no date.
Noonan, John T., Jr. *The Antelope.* Berkeley: University of California Press 1977.
Philbrick, Nathaniel. *Sea of Glory: America's Voyage of Discovery, the U.S. Exploring Expedition, 1838-1842.* New York: Viking, 2003.
Smith, Page. *The Nation Comes of Age.* New York: McGraw-Hill, 1981.
Snay, Mitchell. *Gospel of Disunion.* Chapel Hill: University of North Carolina Press, 1993.
Solberg, Winton U. *The Constitutional Convention and the Formation of the Union.* 2nd ed. Urbana: University of Illinois Press, 1990.
Spears, John R. *The American Slave Trade.* New York: Ballantine, 1960.
Thomas, Hugh. *The Slave Trade.* New York: Simon & Schuster, 1997.
The Trial of Reuben Crandall, M.D., Charged with Publishing Seditious Libels, by Circulating the Publications of the American Anti-Slavery Society, before the Circuit Court for the District of Columbia, Held at Washington, in April, 1836, Occupying the Court the Period of Ten Days." New York: H. R. Piercy, 1836.
"Walker's, David Appeal, in Four Articles: Together with a Preamble to the Coloured Citizens of the World, But in Particular, and Very Expressly, to Those of the United

States of America." Rev. ed. with an Introduction by Sean Wilentz. New York: Hill and Wang, 1995.
Weinstein, Allen, and Frank Otto Gatell, eds. *American Negro Slavery.* New York: Oxford University Press, 1968.
Weld, Theodore Dwight. *American Slavery as It Is: Testimony of Thousand Witnesses.* New York: American Anti-Slavery Society, 1839.
Wilson, Carol. *Freedom at Risk: The Kidnapping of Free Blacks in America.* Lexington: University Press of Kentucky, 1994.

Index

AAS *see* American Anti-Slavery Society
Abraham (biblical) 89
ACS *see* American Colonization Society
Adams, John 33, 218
Adams, John Quincy 27–28, 33, 36, 68, 181, 198, 201–209, 219–221, 230–236
African (Methodist) Church of Charleston 30
Alabama 17, 37, 103, 201–202
Alamo (Texas) 174
Alford, Julius 202
Alien and Sedition Acts 12
Alton (Illinois) 212, 214, 217–218, 229
"America" (song) 84
American Anti-Slavery Society 121–124, 132, 137–138, 144, 155, 235
American Colonization Society 18–19, 31, 155
American Slavery as It Is (book) 175
The Amistad (ship) 74, 204
The Antelope (ship) 29, 31, 204
Anti-Slavery Society 19–120; *see also* American Anti-Slavery Society; Boston Female Anti-Slavery Society; Massachusetts Anti-Slavery Society; New England Anti-Slavery Society; Ohio Anti-Slavery Society; Philadelphia Female Anti-Slavery Society
An Appeal in Favor of That Class of Americans Called Africans (book) 110–120
Appeal to the Christian Women of the South (pamphlet) 191–198

Aptheker, Herbert 30–31
Argus (newspaper) 226
Arkansas 198
Articles of Confederation 4
Ashmore, Margaret 102, 210
Atherton, Charles G. 233
Atherton Gag Rule 231–235
Atlantic Ocean 124, 199
Auburn (New York) 6
Auld, Hugh 81
Auld, Sophia 81
Austin, James T. 217, 218
Austin, Stephen 31
Autobiography of Frederick Douglass (book) 81

B & O Railroad 102
Baldwin, Roger Sherman 74
Baltimore (Maryland) 47, 64, 65, 68, 102
Bank of the United States 125
Baptist 109, 130, 213
Baptist Church of Georgetown (Redding) 232
Barbour, Philip P. (of Virginia) 4–25
Barnes, Gilbert 236
Barton, Clara 37
Battle of New Orleans 33
Battle of San Jacinto 175
Beaumont, Gustave de 85, 103
Beauregard, P.G.T. 256
Beecher, Catherine 37
Beecher, Harriett *see* Stowe, Harriett Beecher
Beecher, Lyman 191

262 Index

Bel Air (Maryland) 238
Benson, George W. 106
Bible 89–90, 139
Biddle, Nicholas 125
Birney, James Gillespie 103, 132, 165, 182–183, 185, 189–190, 221–224, 235
Black Hawk (Sac chief) 102–103
Black Hawk's War 102–103
Black Rock (New York) 136
"Black Seaman's Laws" 163
Blackburn, Lucie 84, 109
Blackburn, Thornton 84, 109
Blackburn Riots 109, 136
Bladensburg Dueling Ground (Maryland) 200, 225
Bleecker Street Presbyterian Church 153
Blood Run (Maryland) 200
Blow, Peter 36, 125
Bonaparte, Napoleon see Napoleon
Boone, Daniel 102
Booth, John Wilkes 238
Boston (Massachusetts) 26, 39, 43, 56, 64, 66, 72, 73, 75, 77, 103–104, 140, 144, 151, 153, 217, 224, 229
Boston Advertiser Press (newspaper) 108
Boston Female Anti-Slavery Society 149, 155
Boston Harbor (Massachusetts) 217
Bowie, James 174
Bradley, James 127–128
Brady, Mathew 37, 237
Brewer (Maine) 38
Brice, Nicholas 65
Britain/British 1, 2, 4, 5, 26, 28, 44, 47, 53, 58, 66, 78, 103, 121, 124, 131–133, 151, 177, 183, 197, 199, 208, 217, 222–223, 235, 237
British West Indies see West Indies
Brougham, Lord 113
Brown, John (abolitionist) 36, 72, 155
Brown, John (of Virginia) 9
Brown, Susan 109
Buchanan, James 105
Buffalo (New York) 136, 236
Bunker Hill (Massachusetts) 72
Burke, Edanus 9
Burke, Edmond 58–59
Butler, Pierce 124, 132, 222–223, 237–238

Calhoun, John C. 19, 27–28, 33, 67, 94, 99, 101, 160, 167, 171–173, 181, 206–208, 219
Campbell, John Reid 151–152
Canaan (New Hampshire) 136, 143
Canada 53, 84, 109, 124, 136
Canot, Captain Theodore 32
Canterbury (Connecticut) 85, 95, 104, 106, 108–109, 120, 131, 136
Carolinas 1, 59; see also North Carolina; South Carolina
Carroll, Charles 102
Catholic 195
Channing, William Ellery 161–163, 191
Charleston (South Carolina) 11, 16, 30, 68, 117, 133, 137, 138, 143–145, 196, 212
Charleston Patriot (newspaper) 145
Chase, Salmon 36, 222, 224
Chatham Street Chapel 129
Cherokee Indians 53, 67, 84, 97, 102, 164, 200, 236
"Cherokee Nation vs. Georgia" 84
The Cherokee Phoenix (newspaper) 53
Cherry Street (Philadelphia) 136
Chestnut, Mary 16
Child, David Lee 83
Child, Lydia Maria 54, 83–84, 110–120, 197
Christ 4, 80, 90
Church Alley (Cincinnati) 187
Cilley, Jonathan 225–226
Cincinnati (Ohio) 37, 52, 126, 140, 165, 181–186, 188–189, 221
Cincinnati Gazette (newspaper) 184, 187
Cincinnati Union Society 189–190
Cincinnati Whig (newspaper) 140, 184–186
City Hall (Boston) 152
Civil Disobedience (book) 194
Civil War (American) 5, 6, 15, 18, 20, 30, 34–36, 53, 97, 114, 118, 120, 141, 163, 169, 181, 188, 208, 213, 226, 237, 239, 241, 244, 249, 251
Claiborne, John F. H. 205
Clarksburg (Virginia) 37
Clay, Henry 18, 21, 25, 47–52, 94, 105–106, 204
Clemens, Samuel Langhorne 131
College of William and Mary 87
Colonization Society 1, 94, 103, 112, 118–119, 126–128, 142; see also American Colonization Society; Kentucky Colonization Society
Columbia (South Carolina) 76
Columbus, Christopher 13

Index

Colver, the Rev. Nathaniel 232–233
Committee of Vigilance (Nashville) 139
Confederation, Articles of *see* Articles of Confederation
Confessions of Nat Turner (book) 79–83
Congregational 11, 16
The Congressional Globe (periodical) 231–232
Connecticut 36–37, 73, 75, 85, 106, 109, 120, 131, 149, 160, 177, 191, 232, 243, 251
Connecticut Supreme Court 120, 130
Constitution of the United States 6, 7, 20, 23, 28, 42, 77, 96, 98–100, 110, 123, 156–157, 162, 179, 198, 206, 227, 233, 247
Constitutional Convention 4, 243
Continental Congress 4, 8–9
Cooley, Buff 152
Cooley, Daniel 152
Cooper, Peter 68
Cooper, William C. 35
Cramer, John 157
Crandall, Prudence 86, 95, 104, 106–110, 120–121, 130–131, 136
Crandall, Reuben 141–142, 177–179, 224
The Creole (ship) 233
Crockett, Davey 174
Cuba 17, 32
Cushing, Caleb 206

Daggett, Judge David 120
Daguerre, Louis Jacques 237
Dailey Commercial Advertiser (newspaper) 136
The Dallas (ship) 29
Darby, John F. 177
David Walker's Appeal, in Four Articles: Together with a Preamble to the Coloured Citizens of the World, but in Particular, and Very Expressly, to Those of the United States of America (pamphlet) *see Walker's Appeal* (pamphlet)
Davids, Tice 84
Davis, Jefferson 37, 103
Davis, John 160
Debates of the Constitutional Convention *see* Constitutional Convention
Decatur, Stephen 200
Declaration of Independence 1, 40, 46, 72, 102, 198–199, 202, 204, 229

"Declaration of Sentiments" (document) 121–124
"Declaration of the Rights of Man" (document) 13–14
"Declaration of the Sentiments of the People of Hartford Regarding the Measures of the Abolitionists" (political statement) 149–150
Delaware (Maryland) 23
Demarara (novel) 131
Democracy in America (book) 165–166
Denmark/Dane 117
Detroit (Michigan) 53, 84, 109, 136
Detroit River 109
Dew, Professor Thomas R. 87–93
Diffusionism 25, 32
District of Columbia 76, 157, 158, 167, 169, 173–174, 198, 203, 211, 219, 233, 234
Donaghe, James 74
Dorchester (Maryland) 37
Douglas, Stephen A. 37
Douglass, Frederick 81, 237
Dresser, Amos 139–141, 196
Dromgoole, George 230
Duane, William J. 125
Dumond, Dwight 235
Dutch 1

Early, Peter 35
Ellicott Mills (Maryland) 68
Ellsworth, Oliver 251
Emancipation Day 129
Emerson, Dr. John 36, 125, 199, 235
Ericcson, John 54
Este, D. K. 222
Euclid 3
Europe 177
Evening Post (New York newspaper) 129, 134, 142, 182
Everett, Edward 67
Ewing, Thomas and Maria 37
ExEx *see* U.S. Exploring Expedition

Fairfield, John 157–158
Faneuil Hall 44, 149, 217–218
Farmington (Connecticut) 160
Federal Fugitive Slave Act 109
Finley, the Rev. Robert 18
Florida 29, 32, 164
Force Bill 105–106
Forrest, Nathan Bedford 37
Fort Armstrong (Illinois) 125, 199

Index

Fort Snelling (Louisiana Territory) 199, 235
Fort Sumter (South Carolina) 4, 11
La Fortuna (ship) 32
Foster, Stephen 37
Fourth of July 1, 39, 129
France/French 13–14, 84–85, 103, 197, 208, 237
Francis (ship) 47
Frankfort (Kentucky) 47
Franklin, Benjamin 8
Franklin, John Hope 30
Franklin College (Georgia) 37
The Frugal Housewife (book) 54

Gardner, Alexander 237
Garrison, William Lloyd 39–43, 46–47, 60, 64–66, 69–73, 75–77, 79, 83–84, 87, 94–95, 104, 108, 114, 118–119, 121, 124, 134, 137, 144–145, 148–149, 151–154, 172, 197, 217–219, 229
Gazette see *Cincinnati Gazette* (newspaper)
General Assembly (of Connecticut) 131
The Genius of Universal Emancipation (newspaper) 46–47, 64–66
George, King 2
Georgetown (Connecticut) 232–233
Georgetown (District of Columbia) 76, 141–142, 224
Georgetown (Ohio) 37
Georgia 5, 9, 11, 35, 37, 53, 64, 67, 76, 95, 97, 102, 124, 138, 160, 164, 200, 202, 250, 217, 220, 236, 238, 256
Germany/German 177
Gettysburg (film) 37
Gettysburg (Pennsylvania) 6
Gettysburg Address (speech) 6
Gholson, Mr. 88
Giddings, Joshua Reed 233, 235–235
Gilman, Mr. 215–216
Goodell, William 135–136
Gordon, Captain Nathaniel 17
Grant, Hiram Ulysses (Simpson) 36
Grantland, Seaton 202, 220
Graves, William J. 205, 225–226
Gray, Thomas R. 79
Great Britain see Britain/British
Great Lakes 236
Greece/Greek 44, 93
Greeley, Horace 214–216
Greenville (Tennessee) 37
Grimké, Angelina 68, 136, 144–145, 191–198, 211–214, 218–219, 224–225, 227–229
Grimké, John Faucheraud 68, 160
Grimké, Sarah 68, 136, 160, 198, 211–214, 218–219
Grimké-Weld, Angelina see Grimké, Angelina
The Gypsey (ship) 235

Haiti 14–15, 71, 78; see also Saint-Domingue
Hamburg (New York) 136
Hamilton, Alexander 102
Hammond, Eliza 10
Hammond, George 175–177, 179–180
Hammond, James Henry 143–144, 158–159, 170
Hancock, John 218
Harris, Sarah 95
Hartford (Connecticut) 149–151
Hartley, Thomas 9
Harvard College 37, 194
Havana (Cuba) 17, 32
Hawes, Albert G. 201
Hayne, Robert Y. 33, 55–64, 88, 101, 133, 137
Hayne-Webster Debates 55–64
Haynes, Charles E. 202
Hemmings, Betty 116
Hemmings, Sally 115–116
Henderson, Thomas 210
Henry, Patrick 26–27
Hispaniola 13
Holsey, Hopkins 205, 220
Hone, Philip 148
Hood, John B. 256
Houston, Sam 175, 255
Hudson, Dr. Erasmus 232–233
Huger, Alfred 137
Hungerford, Henry James 53, 164
Hunt, Hiram P. 159
Huntsville (Alabama) 37, 103

Illinois 102, 115, 125, 212, 245
"Incendiary Publications" (report) 171–172
Independence Day see Fourth of July
Independence Hall (Philadelphia) 226
Indian Removal Act 67, 164
Indiana 32, 164
Ingham, Mr. 232
Ireland/Irish 133, 137
Isaac (biblical) 89
Isabella see Truth, Sojourner

Index

Jackson, Andrew 33, 36, 97–105, 125, 131, 137, 156–157, 164, 204, 211
Jackson, James 9
Jackson, Thomas Jonathan 37
Jackson, William 158
Jay, John 54, 249, 251
Jefferson, Thomas 1–4, 7, 10, 12–15, 29–30, 32–33, 43–44, 53, 70–72, 114–116, 251
Jefferson Day Celebration 67
Jerusalem (Virginia) 73
Job (biblical) 89
Jocelyn, Simeon 73–75
Johnson, Andrew 37
Johnson, Oliver 83
Johnston (free Black) 216
Johnston, Albert Sidney 102
Judson, Andrew T. 107–108
Juvenile Miscellany (periodical) 54, 110

Kansas 155, 218
Kemble, Charles 103
Kemble, Frances "Fanny" Anne 53, 103, 124, 132, 222–223, 237–238
Kendall, Amos 137–138
Kentucky 21, 47, 52, 55–56, 84, 103, 109, 132, 156, 165, 183, 201, 205, 225
Kentucky Colonization Society 47–52, 132
Kentucky Resolutions 12
Kentucky Society for the Gradual Relief of the State from Slavery 123
Key, Daniel 200
Key, Francis Scott 18, 142, 178–179, 200
Kimberly, Dennis 4
King, John P. 160
King, Rufus 106
King George *see* George, King
King William IV *see* William, King, IV
Knapp, Isaac 66
Ku Klux Klan 3

Lafayette, General 131
Lake Erie 164
Lancaster (Ohio) 32
Lane Seminary 126, 129, 139, 190–191, 212
Lawler, John 201
Lawless, Luke 179–180
Lawrence, Larkin 221–222
Lawrenceville (Pennsylvania) 37
Lee, Robert E. 36, 256
Legare, Hugh 231–232

Leggett, William 129–130, 134, 142–148
Lerner, Gerda 160
Lewis, Dixon 202
Lewis and Clark Corps of Discovery 237
The Liberator (periodical) 69, 72–73, 76, 87, 94, 104, 124, 144, 217
Liberia 19, 32
Liberty and Slavery (book) 35
Liberty Bell 163
Lincoln, Abraham 6, 37, 60, 103, 115, 207, 245, 247
Lincoln, Levi 205
Linn, John 19
Linn, Lewis F. 160
Little Round Top 38
Livermore, Arthur 24
Livingston, Edward 97
Lloyd, Edward 26
London (England) 199
Loring, Ellis Gray 83
Louisiana 16, 138, 158, 163, 167
Louisiana Territory 16, 18, 27, 49, 199
Louisville (Kentucky) 84, 156
Lovejoy, Elijah 176, 180, 212, 214–218, 229
Lundy, Benjamin 46, 64
Lyman, Theodore 151

Madison, James 198
"The Maid of Morgan's Point" *see* West, Emily
Main Street (Cincinnati) 187
Maine 26, 27, 38, 157, 225–226, 235, 245
Mangum, Willie P. 160
Marshall, John 31, 33, 84, 162–163, 251
Martineau, Harriet 66, 131–132, 139–141, 155–156, 176, 199, 238
The Martyr Age of the United States (book) 66, 139–140
Maryland 9, 26, 37, 46, 64, 81, 125, 163, 200, 210, 237, 238, 251
"Massa's in de Cold Ground" (song) 38
Mason, George 2, 4, 5
Mason-Dixon line 29, 119, 238
Massachusetts 12, 17, 26, 36, 37, 39, 55, 68, 76, 135, 155, 158, 160, 191, 203, 206, 209, 217, 219, 224, 235, 243
Massachusetts Anti-Slavery Society 216

Matilda (fugitive slave) 221–222, 224
Maumee River 164
May, the Rev. Samuel 106–108, 110
Mayer, Henry 73
McClellan, George B. 38
McDuffie, George 133–135
McIntosh, Francis L. 175–180
McLane, Louis 23
Meade, George 37
The Mediator (ship) 235
Mercer, Charles Fenton 18
Methodist 30, 213
Mexico/Mexican 31, 54, 67, 149, 175, 195
Michigan 84, 109, 198–199
Mississippi 17, 19, 51, 76, 148, 205
Mississippi River 4, 20, 22, 25, 67, 102, 125, 141, 164, 200, 236
Missouri 17, 20, 21, 23, 26–28, 48, 51, 56, 160, 175, 235
Missouri Compromise 20, 27–29, 41, 247–249
Missouri Territory 164–165
Mitchell, Charles 64, 65
The Monitor (ship) 54
Monroe, James 18
Monticello 29, 70
Morgan, Margaret 102, 210
Morris, Thomas 167
The Mother's Book (book) 84
Mull, William 176
"My Country, 'Tis of Thee" *see* "America"
"My Old Kentucky Home" (song) 38

Napoleon (Bonaparte) 16
Nashville (Tennessee) 139–140
The Nation Comes of Age (book) 70
National Assembly (of Saint-Domingue) 13
National Intelligencer (newspaper) 76–77
NEAS *see* New England Anti-Slavery Society
Nelson, Hugh 25
New England 5, 12, 87, 95, 131, 150, 163, 176, 211–213, 219, 222
New England Anti-Slavery Society 83, 86–87, 94, 106, 112, 211
New Hampshire 24, 115, 136, 143, 233, 243
New Haven (Connecticut) 73–75
New Haven Advertiser (newspaper) 74

New Jersey 18, 19, 243
New Orleans (Louisiana) 22, 33, 46, 47, 117, 145, 222, 236
New Orleans True American (newspaper) 208
New Washington (Texas) 175
New York (city) 6, 51, 56, 103, 124, 129, 130, 131, 134, 144, 225, 243
New York (state) 20, 36, 54, 65, 68, 129, 136, 146, 153, 157, 159, 160, 199–200, 209, 211, 235, 236, 243, 251
New York Evening Star (newspaper) 143
Newburyport (Maryland) 47
Newport (Rhode Island) 85
Noah (biblical) 27
Norfolk Beacon (newspaper) 79
North Carolina 17, 160, 196, 220
Northwest Ordinance *see* Ordinance of 1787
Northwest Territory 4, 27
Northwestern Massachusetts *see* Maine
Norwich Courier (newspaper) 107
Notes on the State of Virginia (book) 3, 4, 10, 44, 70, 114
The Novelty (locomotive) 53
Noyes Academy 136, 143
Nullification *see* South Carolina Ordinance of Nullification

Observer (newspaper) *see* St. Louis *Observer*
"Oh Susanna" (song) 37
Ohio 31, 37, 52, 55, 56, 84, 126, 164–165, 167, 181, 190, 198, 222, 224, 233, 235
Ohio Anti-Slavery Society 139, 182, 185–186, 188
Ohio River 4, 52, 55, 84, 156
Oklahoma 236
"Old Folks at Home" (song) 37
Ontario (Canada) 136
Ordinance of 1787 4, 59, 222
Osceola (Seminole chief) 164
Otis, Harrison Gray 64
Otis, James 218

Pastoral Letter of the General Association of Massachusetts to the Congregational Churches under Their Care (pamphlet) 12
Patton, John 221

Patton Gag 226
Pennsylvania 4, 9, 36, 37, 38, 68, 98, 102, 210, 219, 235, 236, 243
Pennsylvania [Quaker] Abolition Society 8, 10
Pennsylvania Hall 226–229
Peoria (Illinois) 245
Perrysburg (Ohio) 165
Peter (son of Sojourner Truth) 36
Peterboro (New York) 153
Phelps, Amos 160
Philadelphia (Pennsylvania) 4, 37, 38, 51, 56, 68, 121, 124, 130, 132, 136, 140, 144, 163, 191, 223, 226, 227, 237
Philadelphia Female Anti-Slavery Society see Women's Anti-Slavery Societies
The Philanthropist (newspaper) 166, 182, 185, 187, 189–190
Philleo, Calvin 130
Phillips, Wendell 153, 217, 218
Phipps, Benjamin 79, 82
Pickett, George 37
Pinckney, Charles 5
Pinckney, Henry L. 173, 174, 187, 209
Pittsburgh (Pennsylvania) 37, 175, 191
Pleasants, Robert 26
Plymouth (Massachusetts) 68
Poindexter, George 19
Point Comfort (Virginia colony) 1
Polk, James K. 159, 198, 226
Port-au-Prince (Saint-Domingue) 14
Porter, Alexander 167–168
Portugal/Portuguese 29, 31
Presbyterian 18, 139, 153, 213
Presbyterian General Assembly 191
Preston, William C. 164, 168–169, 220
Prigg, Edward 210
"Proclamation to the People of South Carolina" (speech) 97–101
Protestant 195
Providence (Rhode Island) 110
Pugh, Mr. 182

Quadroon Ball 117
Quaker Abolition Society of Pennsylvania see Pennsylvania [Quaker] Abolition Society
Quakers 8, 10, 68, 83, 191, 223
Quarrier, Captain John 84
Queen Victoria, see Victoria, Queen
Quincy, Josiah 218

Raintree Trials 53

Redding (Connecticut) see Georgetown (Connecticut)
Reese, Mrs. 82
Reformed Presbyterian Church (Philadelphia) 136
The Religion and the Pure Principles of Morality Sure Foundation on Which We Must Build (pamphlet) 77–79
Rhett, Robert Barnwell 221
Rhode Island 85, 110, 243
Richmond (Virginia) 26, 46, 73
Ripley, Eleazer W. 158
Roane, John 220
Roane, Mr. 88
Robertson, John 205, 209
Robinson, Harriett 199; see also Scott, Harriett
The Rockett (locomotive) 53
Rome/Romans 44, 91, 93
Ross, Araminta see Tubman, Harriett
Rousseau, Jean Jacques 13
Royal William, S.S. (ship) 124
Rush, Benjamin 199
Rush, Richard 199, 235
Rutledge, John 249

Sac (Indian tribe) 102–103
Sacred Music Society 129
Sage of Monticello see Jefferson, Thomas
St. Augustine (Florida) 29
St. Catharines (Canada) 136
St. Domingo see Saint-Domingue
Saint-Domingue 13, 14, 71, 197
St. John's Church (Richmond) 26
St. Louis (Missouri) 125, 175, 175, 179–181, 199, 212, 214, 221, 222, 235
St. Louis Observer (newspaper) 176, 180, 215
St. Louis Republican (newspaper) 176–177
Sak see Sac
Sam 36; see also Scott, Dred
Sanford (fugitive slave) 136
Sanford, Irene 235
Sangamon County (Illinois) 103
Santa Anna, Antonio López de 255
Santo Domingo see Saint-Domingue
Saratoga Springs (New York) 37
Sauk see Sac
Savannah (Georgia) 46
Schenectady (New York) 153
Schuykill River 130
Scotland/Scotch 177

268 Index

Scott, Dred 36, 125, 199, 235, 251
Scott, Eliza 235
Scott, Harriett 235; *see also* Robinson, Harriett
Scott, Winfield 102, 236
Second Seminole War 164
"The Secret Six" (John Brown co-conspirators) 55
Seminole Indians 164
Seqouyah (Cherokee chief) 53
Sewall, Samuel E. 83
Seward, William 36
Sherborne, John 200
Sherman, Tecumseh 37
Short, William 29, 30
Slade, William 158, 220, 223, 234, 236
Slavery (book) 161–163
"Slavery in the District of Columbia" (report) 173
Smith, Gerrit 153–155
Smith, O'Brien 16
Smith, Page 70–73
Smith, Samuel Francis 84
Smith, William 9
Smithson, James 53, 164, 199, 235
Smithsonian Institution 235
Snow, Beverly 142
Snow Riots 142
Société des Amis des Noirs *see* Society of the Friends of the Blacks
Society of the Friends of the Blacks 13, 14
South Carolina 2, 5, 7, 9, 11, 16, 19, 27, 30, 31, 33, 35, 36, 55, 56, 63, 68, 76, 92, 95–99, 101, 105–106, 124, 133–135, 137, 143, 163, 164, 168–173, 202, 206, 208, 209, 211, 220, 221, 231, 245
South Carolina Exposition and Protest of 1828 33, 61, 62, 67
South Carolina Ordinance of Nullification 95–97
South Pacific 237
Southampton County (Virginia) 73, 76, 81–83, 88
Spain/Spanish 13, 29, 31, 32
Spock, Dr. 84
Springfield (Illinois) 115
The Standard and Democrat (newspaper) 153
"Star Spangled Banner" (song) 142
Stephens, Alexander 37
Stephenson, George 53
Stevens, Robert L. 68

Stewart, James 77
Stewart, Maria 77–79, 102, 124
Stickney, Benjamin Franklin 165
Stickney, One 165
Stickney, Two 165
Stone, Michael Jenifer 9
Stowe, Harriett Beecher 37, 191
Stuart, Charles 160
Sumner, Charles 37
Supreme Court of Errors of Connecticut 120
Swift, Benjamin 220

Tait (slave agent) 136
Taliaferro, Lawrence 199
Tallmadge, James 20, 25
Tallmadge Amendment *see* Tallmadge, James
Taney, Roger 125, 163, 210, 249, 251
Tappan, Arthur 65, 66, 74, 75, 121, 137, 145, 218
Tappan, Lewis 66, 74, 121, 129–130, 137, 200, 211, 218
Tariff Act of 1828 33, 95
Taylor, John W. 20–23, 25, 51
Taylor, Zachary 102, 103
Tennessee 37, 51, 139, 140, 256
Texas 31, 54, 67, 149, 174, 175, 195, 211, 213–214, 226, 230–232, 234, 255, 256
Thirteenth Amendment 69
Thompson, George 131–132, 136, 144, 149, 151–152, 183
Thompson, Waddy 202, 208, 209
Thoreau, Henry David 194
Tocqueville, Alexis de 84–85, 103, 165–166, 238
Todd, Francis 47, 64, 65
Toledo (Ohio) 164
Toledo War 164, 198
The Tom Thumb (locomotive) 68
Trail of Tears 235
Transcript (newspaper) 144
Travis, Mr. J. 82
Treaty of New Echoata 164, 200
The Trent (ship) 237
Troy (New York) 199–200
Truth, Sojourner 36
Tubman, Harriett 37
Turner, Nat 73, 75, 79–83
Twain, Mark *see* Clemens, Samuel Langhorne
Twenty Years of an African Slaver (book) 32

Unitarianism 161
U.S. Exploring Expedition 237
Upper Peninsula (Michigan) 198–199
Utica (New York) 153, 154

Van Buren, Martin 198, 211, 226
Vanderpoel, Aaron 159, 209
Vermont 1, 37, 158, 220, 235
Vermont Telegraph (newspaper) 75
The Versailles (ship) 84
Vesey, Denmark 30, 70
Vicksburg 141, 148
Vicksburg Gamblers 140–141, 148, 162
Victoria, Queen 222, 237
The Vincennes (ship) 237
Virginia 1, 2, 4, 5, 9, 14, 18, 24, 26, 31, 33, 36, 37, 51, 59, 73, 83, 87, 89, 91–93, 98, 114, 115, 158, 205, 208, 209, 219, 220, 226
Virginia Company 1
Virginia Resolutions 62
Virginia Slave Debates 83–84, 87–91

Walker, David 43–46, 51, 77, 79
Walker's Appeal (pamphlet) 43–46, 51, 64, 70
Washington, Bushrod 18
Washington, George 18
Washington County Jail 142
Washington, D.C. 18, 36, 67, 76, 102, 103, 123, 137, 141, 177, 199, 200, 243–244
Washington Street (Boston) 151

Webb, James W. 225
Webster, Daniel 18, 55–64, 66, 67
Weld, Angelina *see* Grimké, Angelina
Weld, Theodore Dwight 128–129, 139, 161, 175, 176, 199–200, 212, 227
Welles, Gideon 36
West, Emily 175, 255
West Indies 13, 58, 131
West Point 36, 37
The Whig (newspaper) *see Cincinnati Whig* (newspaper)
Whig (party) 131
White, Alexander 9
White House 37
Whitney, Eli 12
Wilberforce (Canada) 53
Wilkes, Charles 237
William, King, IV 222
Wilson, George 30
Wilson, John 31
Wilson's Lane (Boston) 151–152
Winnebagos (Indians) 163
Wisconsin-Illinois 37, 199
Wise, Henry A. 158, 219, 220, 226
Women's Anti-Slavery Societies 194–195, 214
Wood, Joseph 165
Woolfolk, Austin 47
Worchester vs. Georgia (court case) 102

Yale College 73–75
York County (Pennsylvania) 102

www.ingramcontent.com/pod-product-compliance
Lightning Source LLC
Chambersburg PA
CBHW051212300426
44116CB00006B/545